AUTHOR
TBLBC

The Business Leaders Book Club

Series One:

Lessons Learned From The Recession

Edited By

Dr. Richard Norris and Mark Stephens

F10
The F10 Group

First Published in 2011 by F10 Engineering Ltd.
The F10 Group, Talon House, Presley Way, Crownhill,
Milton Keynes, Buckinghamshire, MK8 0ES

www.f10.co.uk
www.asktheexperts.org.uk
(0044) 08458381101

Printed and bound by CPI Group (UK) Ltd, Croydon, CR0 4YY

ISBN 978-0-9568734-0-8

Praise for 'The Business Leaders Book Club: Lessons Learned from the Recession':

"The Business Leaders Book Club offers something that most so-called business books don't: real lessons, from real executives, facing real challenges in this tumultuous age. This series is your chance to sit down with and learn from some of the sharpest practitioners in business today. Don't miss it."

Steve Farber
President, Extreme Leadership, Inc
Bestselling author of *The Radical Leap Re-Energized* and *Greater Than Yourself*

"This is a great book on how to deal with tough times in business: a series of practical case studies by entrepreneurs who have been there and come out the other side successfully"

Nicholas Bate
MD, Performance Consultancy Strategic Edge Ltd
Author of *Instant MBA* and *How to Sell Brilliantly in Good Times and Bad.*

"There is some invaluable knowledge that can be gained from others' proven experience, through reading this book."

Keith Wilby
Retired, Managing Director, B.P.G. Products Ltd

"A real treasure-trove – sixty real-life stories of how entrepreneurs have dealt with the worst recession for many years. Anyone starting or running a business will find both inspiration and information here."

Chris West
Co-author, *The Beermat Entrepreneur*

“The publishers have carefully selected authors who present some innovative and ‘recession busting’ strategies for business managers at all levels. The book also provides a great ‘dip in’ OR ‘cover-to-cover’ reference point for business leaders.”

Reggie Dickinson
Retired Director, Imperial Group and DTI Enterprise Counsellor for the East Midlands

“As an owner of a small to medium enterprise I know all too well how isolated you can feel during difficult trading periods, this is something we should all keep to hand for reference at times like those but also refer to when we are looking for some direction. The content is made more valuable because it is provided by people from various sectors who share a common theme – success comes from hard work & determination, surround yourself with good people and never be afraid to diversify and embrace change.

“In business we learn so much but never as much as when in times of recession and it is during those times that the harsh lessons can be forced upon us which are difficult to adjust to. I am sure that this book would have been welcomed by many at the start of the credit crunch however it is never too late to adapt and learn so in the future this book will help us to prepare for change and potentially increase our robustness to become as close as possible to recession proof as one can be.”

Craig Reynolds
Managing Director, Urban and Rural

“An inspirational book for new or seasoned entrepreneurs, real stories from real people solving a very real problem, the recession. Looking forward to being part of the next in the series.”

Kevin Dixie
Fuelmywebsite.com

“This book provides a very useful reference point, with useful tips and anecdotal advice that you can dip into again and again.”

Peter Butterwick
MD, Butterwicks HBS Ltd

“‘Where do I spend my time? Where do I spend my money?’ Important questions for anyone in business today. Some of the answers can be found in this book, written by recognised experts that have earned the right to speak…they know what they are talking about.”

James Knight
Author, How to Connect with and Influence People using iMA, whatcolourareyou.com

“It’s always worth listening to other peoples experiences of how to make the best of whatever opportunities exist, even during a recession. This book has some excellent firsthand accounts from experienced and successful Businessmen who have done exactly that.”

Nigel Richardson.
Joint Managing Director, EESmith group

"'*Lessons Learned from the Recession'* offers vital insights into what successful business leaders do when the business environment is dire. I look forward to future books in the series."

David Soskin
Former CEO of Cheapflights Media and Co-Founder of Howzat Media LLP

"A highly commendable initiative to tap into the wealth of global entrepreneurial knowledge, by inviting many business luminaries to reveal their thoughts, experiences and skills on how to survive in these increasingly competitive, demanding, onerous and frequently treacherous times.

"Indeed a rare, insightful, unbiased array of sound advice from the world of 'been there, done it, got the T shirt' practical business wisdom.

"Education at its unhindered best."

Stephen R Peerless.

Chairman, Norman Carr Safaris, Zambia. Also recognised business and management consultant, specialising in company turnarounds, mergers, acquisitions and acknowledged authority on the recruitment industry.

"I absolutely love The Business Leaders' series because it brings together real lessons learned from the frontlines of business. The experts featured all have 'muddy boots' in their chosen fields which means you're getting solid advice that's been tested and proven rather than just empty theory. What's more they're generous enough to share what's gone wrong as well as right, which, if you heed their advice, will enable you to massively accelerate your own business success. These books are sure to become an essential addition to any serious entrepreneur's library."

Joe Gregory

Publisher and Author, www.bookshaker.com

“The positivity and passion accentuated by the diverse contributors to this book not only makes for informative, compelling, reading, but also proves entrepreneurial spirit is alive and kicking, even in times of austerity”.

Simon Lewis,
Co-founder, Only Marketing Jobs

"Whether you are a business novice or a battle-scarred Chief Executive, this book has all the themes of good business practice running through it. We can all either learn from it or re-discover what drives a business forward in difficult times. The constant truths of ‘Stickability’, Knowing and Understanding your Market, Innovation, Change, a Positive Approach , ‘Teamship’, Leadership and Business Control are all tools which we use to keep our businesses dynamic and on an upward trajectory. It is good to see all those concepts so eloquently expressed in one place by those who have actually ‘done it’.”

Richard Ruzyllo
Managing Director, The Presentation Lab

“A great insight into the practicality and understanding of believing that you can succeed, adapt and build a stable foundation ready for the market uplift. A great reference point for anyone about to start their own business or even for established companies to show that we do not always get it right. More importantly, it provides real life examples, from entrepreneurs who have been there – worthy reading.”

Mike Wall
Group Sales Director, Jobsite

With turnover in the UK’s recruitment industry falling by more than 12 percent in the year to March 2010, the REC is well aware that the effects of the recession on recruitment businesses is likely to be felt for years to

come. Reading about how other businesses and industries have coped with the recession is very useful and the REC looks forward to future books in the Business Leaders Book Club series.

Linda Berrigan
Head of Marketing
Recruitment & Employment Confederation (REC)

"As an entrepreneur I learn so much from the challenges and successes of other business owners. This collection is very enlightening and gives a broad range of ideas for my own revenue building and growth strategies."

Kristina Witmer
Managing Director, Witmer Group

"Frontline leaders with timely examples and genuine reflection. Can a business book be more helpful?"

Alan See
Chief Marketing Officer and Vice President
Berry Network, An AT&T Company

"This is an outstanding collection of real life examples from leaders who've navigated the choppy seas of an economic downturn. The book is well written and each chapter is from a small business owner rather than an economist or some other theorist! Full of great practical application, it is worth the read."

Bill Goad
President, CMP – HR LLC
http://www.cmphr.com

Acknowledgements

This book and the series has been an idea of mine for sometime and it has only been made possible through the help, support and commitment of others.

In particular, I would like to thank Dr. Richard Norris for his belief in the project idea and his agreement to help me turn this into a reality.

Secondly, I would like to thank Ben, Kevin and Rachael in the F10 Marketing team who have all contributed significantly to the project and Jo Massie, our assistant editor, for her dedication to keeping the project moving forward.

Finally, I would like to give a massive thank you to all of the contributors for not only their chapters but for the positive support that they have given since day one.

Now that we know what we are doing the next one should be much easier!

Series One: Lessons Learned From The Recession

Contents

Foreword by Mark Stephens, Co-Editor

I am currently the joint owner/director of a business called The F10 Group. The business is based in Milton Keynes, England and we turn over around £2.5m per annum with a workforce of 25 employees. Our core business for the past ten years has been a recruitment consultancy business specialising in the Technology and Sales and Marketing arenas. We have focused in particular on several niche areas of business and have established ourselves as one of Europe's leading consultancies in the Aerospace and Satellite arena.

I joined the company in 2000, about one year into the last recession, in order to establish the Technology recruitment division. The company I had been working for prior to this, S.Com, had suffered severe losses with their contractor headcount dropping from around 2000 to less than 1000 in the space of a year. They had been operating principally in the Telco space, so the impact that government licensing had on the 3G and Telco market positioned them perfectly to take a really big hit.

I was a slow starter in business terms and spent the first eight years after leaving school flirting with University and travelling abroad, but I think that I have always had the energy, drive and confidence to try new things even before I settled into my first real job.

That first proper full-time position came in 1995, at the age of 25, in the form of a sales representative role for a National Home Improvements company, Anglian PLC.

It was noted that I had a flair for sales and after just twelve months with the company I was matching their top performers. Unsurprisingly, I was then approached by a competitor to work for them as their Sales and Marketing Manager. I relished in this new role that allowed me to utilise my creative side as well as make money from my sales capability. The most important factor which changed my focus and outlook at this time was that I started to read and learn about Marketing Strategy.

The company I worked for had no real USP, so winning business was very much down to Marketing and Sales conversion. They had good products coupled with a well-run organisation and excellent customer service. This, with the added ingredient of intelligent marketing, motivated staff and good management meant we performed very well.

I am not advocating that this is the magic ingredient required to be successful because these traditional values are being challenged like never before; predominately by the phenomenon that is the Internet, the World Wide Web and most importantly Search Engines which power the ongoing impact that the Web is having in our lives and the way we operate our businesses.

Search Engines have altered the physiological makeup of how businesses need to think in order to survive. Not too many years ago the power in industry was with the big brands with well-established names that provided the consumer with confidence. Today it is all about niche and micro niche! Search Engines and the Internet allow me to research and find exactly what I want from anywhere in the World. Reputations are easily monitored through customer opinions and online feedback; subsequently the balance of power has changed. This gives a one man band, living and working in a third World country the opportunity to compete with the major domestic brand names.

This change in behaviour is incredible and exciting. With new rules in play, there is a massive paradigm shift, increased opportunity and a new world for business entrepreneurs to play around in!

I don't know what the statistics are but I recently read that the World has seen more new millionaires in the last five years than in the previous 100. 90% of those have achieved their success by harnessing the web and adapting to the new business model. Large organisations have also thrived. Those that understood what was happening adapted their models and subsequently made it easier for the consumers to find their niche products and services.

So with all this positive change taking place and the business world promising untold opportunities for wannabe entrepreneurs, what happened for it to go wrong?

The Global Recession, that's what happened!

I don't know about you but I hate the word 'Recession' almost as much as the phrase 'Global Economic Downturn' and any other overly-abused phrase that the media have used to death in their attempts to beat us into submission over the last few years.

We switched on early at F10 to what was happening, so by the time the media got into full swing six months later, I was well and truly bored and frustrated by the daily bombardment of doom and gloom to the extent that I stopped watching the news in the morning.

My morning routine involves getting up at 5am and that gives me lots of time to think and plan my day. In 2009 I thought a lot about the impact of the 'Global Downturn' on our business, which had steadily been growing year on year. We had chosen to reinvest the majority of our profits back into the business rather than reward ourselves and in essence, we didn't want to lose what we had worked so hard to achieve.

The company was built around our own philosophy and we had created the sort of business that we ourselves wanted to work for. The cornerstones of our business are: a pleasant working environment; the best tools for the job; support and training; a career roadmap for individual progression; a generous reward structure; a solid process that helped form the basis of our identity; honesty and transparency and a supportive management style that recognises effort and achievement. Most of all we all strive to run a world-class operation.

The constant drip, drip, drip of negativity coming through the press worried me and challenged us every day to protect attitudes and remain upbeat. We banned discussions on the subject and we agreed collectively to remain positive and optimistic when speaking to candidates, clients and each other. We launched a number of initiatives that anyone who has read the book *FISH* will be able to relate to, tucked up closely to our best clients and collectively agreed to work harder and smarter to outperform the competition.

Before I start with my own chapter, I would like to share with you some of the motivations that inspired me to put this book together.

Hardships and difficulties in any faculty of life - whether it is family or business relationships - force us to evaluate and re-evaluate what we are doing.

We often get so blasé and wrapped up in what is immediately in front of us, that we forget to take the time to step back and look at the bigger picture, considering closely all the different facets that work together to create the entity within which we operate.

Like an immune system that needs a dose of illness to kick start it back into action, recessions do tend to force action upon us and act as a stimulant to enforce change. That change could be to remove elements that are ineffective, place more emphasis on those that are working or to create something new.

Through various new business ventures and subsequent new alliances formed during the past few years, we have been extremely lucky to have forged relations with some truly incredible people who have generously shared their time and thoughts with us. Obviously the most powerful lessons that we can learn in business come directly from our own experiences, but other people's experience can often help to stimulate thought and action, and this can have a positive impact. Positive thoughts put into action are entrepreneurialism in its most basic form.

Having read through all of the submissions for this book, I know that there is a good reason to be optimistic for the future.

From the inspiring chapters submitted by the self-employed, solo entrepreneur community, who demonstrate the power and influence that we can all have over our own destinies if we just have the determination and discipline required; through to the corporate influence that help to steer the bigger ships through difficult times, I am sure that there are important lessons for us all to learn from in this book.

We hope that you will be inspired by what you read and will join us on a journey to explore a range of business related subjects over the next few years through the eyes of business leaders from around the world as we produce a number of books in this series, The Business Leaders Book Club.

AUTHOR
TBLBC

Mark Stephens

Maximising Your Existing Resources

Current Position:	Business Owner at The F10 Group. Founder of Ask the Experts & the Business Leaders Book Club.
Experience:	Over 15 years in Sales & Recruitment
LinkedIn:	http://uk.linkedin.com/in/markjstephens
Twitter:	www.twitter.com/#!/ATETechnology
Facebook:	www.facebook.com/pages/Ask-The-Experts/144874512209447
Website:	www.f10.co.uk www.asktheexperts.org.uk www.free-ebookdownloads.co.uk
Contact Number:	+44 (0) 845 838 1101

Mark Stephens is Joint Group Director of The F10 Group. Mark's core areas of expertise are in Recruitment strategy, Social Media and Internet Marketing.

Mark is the editor and founder of the Social Media site, Ask The Experts and The Business Leaders Book Club.

Ask The Experts is a multi-functional hub which provides social media functionality, news, debate and expert opinion on the latest technology, internet marketing strategies and techniques.

Chapter 1: Maximising Your Existing Resources

The F10 group have remained stable throughout the last two years. We have increased turnover by 20 percent year on year and retained all key staff members, many of whom have achieved their best results ever during this period.

The purpose of this chapter is to address both the general lessons I have learned through this latest recession and those more specific to The F10 Group.

The general lessons that I have learned...

1. It is important to remain agile enough to be able to realign your business offerings quickly, but it is likely that not every facet of your business will be badly affected by the downturn.

2. Establish as early as possible which parts of your business are more recession-proof and focus your business around them. Talk to those customers most important to this strategy and propose improvements that you can offer them in order to strengthen that relationship. It is essential that you get in there before your competitors do. Our clients told us that our competitors started proposing solutions and improvements nearly six months after we did, which they found amusing, but more importantly it emphasised how far ahead we were of the competition and solidified our reputation.

3. Some customers and sectors are affected much later on by the economic downturn. For us it was the space, defence and aerospace sectors but most publicly-funded sectors did not feel the pinch straight away. High tech engineering, where projects run into the hundreds of millions and are planned to run over many years, do not respond quickly to a downturn.

4. Some areas of business are very reactionary and sensitive to the economic climate, especially where the product or service can be perceived as a luxury addition to the business.

5. Other industry sectors start to thrive during a recession and we have seen this in the areas of low-cost alternative goods and outsourcing solutions.

Recessions can create opportunities to improve services, processes and customer relations.

Our Business

1. As soon as the very first signs of the downturn started to show, we began to evaluate three things in our company. Firstly, we needed to be sure of what our core strengths were; secondly, we needed to be clear what areas of our business were most profitable (and would remain most stable in a downturn); thirdly, we needed to know who our best staff were that would help us through it. This was key to ensure that any strategy we rolled out was well researched and that we had the right people in place to action and deliver it.

2. Every business needs to evaluate their spend from time to time and look closely at what services and products are offering good value and are essential to the company's goals. We aimed to reduce our spending by up to 20 percent in some areas. We also looked into outsourcing services. There is nothing quite like a recession to get you to focus your mind on what is really essential and what is ineffective or a luxury.

3. I would say that the single most important decision that we made early on as a company, was in response to our analysis of our best performers. It wasn't so much about who they were working with to get their results, but in response to their time allocation to different tasks. It was clear that our best performers and highest paid staff were spending nearly 50 percent of their time doing administrative tasks that could be achieved more cost effectively by someone else, subsequently releasing more time to focus on activities that were more likely to result in sales and could provide our customers with a higher standard of service.

We brought in a small administration team (at a time when every other recruitment business we knew were letting theirs go) and outsourced some of the search and research functions off-shore. This had a double impact, in that it improved efficiency and it was also well received by the staff, who generally hated administration. From a sales team of 12 senior staff, five of them had their best year ever in 2009. The strategy to **maximise our best performers** was a calculated risk and it paid off.

4. Increasing, or at least maintaining, marketing activity during a downturn is essential, especially as everyone else is reducing or cutting theirs. This provides a great opportunity to extend one's business as we experience some of the green shoots of activity. Coming up with unique marketing strategies through Facebook, LinkedIn, Twitter and YouTube in conjunction with our own social media site Ask The Experts has helped maintain our brand at a time when many clients have stopped recruiting and relationships can suffer.

As our clients have started to hire again, we have been at the front of their mind. I am sure that most of our clients have watched with interest as 'Ask The Experts' has evolved into the site that it is today and some of them have even become contributors.

5. Finally, the last point that I would like to share with you, is about myself and my Co-Director Mark Flawn and the wakeup call that we had about 18 months ago through a networking group of business owners called NABO. An inspirational speaker at the event highlighted a flaw in our individual strategy which had been focused on refining the way that we work, making lots of small ongoing improvements across the business. It was what we had considered a Kaizen approach, but was what this individual referred to as 'tinkering'.

We had become so obsessed with making our business world class in every facet, that we had stopped focusing our efforts on telling people about it. In short, we needed to realign our efforts on sales and marketing activities and this was an important change in mindset that we must always be aware of, as it is a trap that many small business owners fall into.

Summary

- Recessions rarely happen overnight, so if you are agile and you can adapt quickly, you can minimise the impact
- Recessions also create opportunities to grow your business
- They offer the opportunity to re-evaluate your business focus and reduce unnecessary spend
- They affect everyone in your industry so we are all operating from the same playing field
- Responding positively and refusing to let the negativity in the media impact your office environment is essential

- It is easier to create partnerships, add value and enter joint ventures in a recession
- Client relationships can flourish during tough times
- Maximising the best resources that you already have is the smartest way to ensure that you focus on the people that will help you ride out the recession
- Add value to your clients and don't reduce your fees.

Dr. Richard Norris

How to Improve Your Business Development in a Recession (And any Other Time for That Matter)

Current Position:	Director
Qualifications:	Doctor of Veterinary Medicine, MBA
Experience:	24 years experience in Professional Services
Email:	rnorris@ypncompanies.com
LinkedIn:	www.linkedin.com/in/drrichardnorris
Twitter:	www.twitter.com/UBAwesome
Facebook:	www.facebook.com/UBAwesome
Website:	www.drrichardnorris.com www.hoofitbook.com
Links to Other Works:	http://news.in.msn.com/leadcap/columns/article.aspx?cp-documentid=4841100 http://ezinearticles.com/?4-Secrets-to-Leading-With-Excellence&id=5523645
Contact Number:	+44 (0) 1738 827813

From a competitive swimmer to a veterinarian delivering calves and doing eyelid surgery on leopards; to an army officer responsible for security and animal welfare; to a post-grad student in ophthalmology to an MBA; to unemployed to an award-winning business coach to global business development strategist; to applauded speaker, writer and author, Richard can relate to you, your team and to your organisation.

Richard is renowned for his intensity, integrity, impact and insight in self-leadership and success. Whether an interview, keynote, workshop or 1-2-1 Richard has a way to distil practical messages into engaging stories and examples that entertain, educate and elicit results.

Richard is published on-line and in print including his own book *Hoof it! 7 Key Lessons on Your Journey of Success*.

Chapter 2: How to Improve Your Business Development in a Recession (And Any Other Time For That Matter)

Recessions often elicit the knee-jerk responses of budget and people cuts across all business sectors. This is a costly mistake in many cases. The smarter organisations realise that, where possible, a recession is an opportune time to invest, NOT to cut costs. And that has been my experience during this recession.

The recession hit at a time when I was transitioning focus from owning my own coaching business to taking on an additional role as Head of Global Development for an expanding people development company whose focus was in delivering role-specific leadership and talent development. This has proven to be a potentially challenging combination for my own career development and for the development of both businesses.

Firstly, most companies and organisations react to a recession and make people redundant (and that is still on-going). I experienced that post 9/11 where I lost my new job before I had even started.

Secondly, most organisations put a hold on most or all spending related to training and development. In my new role in global development we came up against this daily with existing and would-be clients. Some existing clients wanted to reduce our engagement; some would-be clients were deferring decisions to unknown dates in the future.

At the start of the recession, I recall hearing an interview on BBC Radio 4 where an industry expert warned, "For those companies who have any people left, you need to invest in them for they will bring the resurrection of your business."

Never have truer words been spoken. And that's what our organisation was trying to do. We endeavoured to practise what we preached, thereby showing organisations 'the light' of this. Admittedly, we, like so many other small businesses, were caught off-guard by the recession.

To survive and thrive, we knew we needed to respond rather than react. In a recession most organisations seem to react - they are the ones who often struggle. The smart ones respond.

Responsive and proactive businesses, the ones we were intent on engaging with, suddenly seemed to be on the endangered list globally i.e. they were rare and seemingly hard to find.

Considering that cash flow was tight and the business development budget was also very limited, the mantra was to make every penny count. So before making any strategic decisions, it was necessary to question everything about our business to ensure our response was the right one.

Four extremely helpful questions we asked and answered were:

1. **What is the profile of our ideal client in detail and where do we find them in the highest concentration?**

Through this exercise we gained greater clarity on which clients we were intent on working with in a long-term engagement. Part of that profile focussed on those organisations who have a track record of consistently investing in their people and who are also listed in the Top 100 Companies to Work For (these lists exist in many countries).

We also identified that an affiliation with relevant industry associations would be an effective approach. Target associations had a remit to add value and provide training and development services to their members and were seeking ways to add to their own income streams. By gaining an affiliate or joint venture relationship we gained credibility. We leveraged our marketing spend through contributing content to association publications whilst they promoted our organisation to their members.

2. **How do we attract our ideal client?**

From our research of past and existing clients and from looking in our own mirror, we determined that our ideal client (not all those that we had worked with, just so you know) understood that people were NOT their most important asset – the *right people* were and are. One key finding from that research was that we all understood that knowing and promoting our values first and foremost was essential if we wanted to move from a transaction-based business to a relationship-based business.

We also adapted our business model to lower the barriers to

engagement by offering a pilot of our engagement, which had no fee if they went on to invest in an engagement of a year or more.

3. **How do we leverage our resources and our processes for greater efficiency?**

Out of this we devised two adjustments to our business development approach. The first required that we redesign the business development process so that it was more simple, effective and consistent. We made 70 percent of it virtual. No longer did we travel to see anyone and everyone around the globe. We had a screening process that filtered out those who did not fit our profile. That meant we took advantage of social media, referral networking, the Internet, webinars and the phone so that we only actually met with future clients where we knew we had more than a 50 percent chance of conversion.

The second adjustment was our focus on partnering with associations (see answer to #1).

4. **What do we need to focus on to secure long-term client relationships?**

Whilst this was easy to answer, it was more of a challenge to implement. We innately knew we had to invest in client relationships. For that we had to improve the quality of our communication. The quality of our communication would determine the quality of our relationships. We ensured that our communication, in all its forms, was open, honest, timely, clear and consistent in all directions – externally and, perhaps, more importantly, within our organisation. This kept everyone inspired, focused, committed, reassured and updated.

<u>**Summary**</u>

Recession brings change. Change is inevitable; growth is optional. To us, recession became an opportunity for growth. We invested our resources (time, money and people) in to the core activity of business development. That meant we refined the profile of our ideal client, identified some leveraged ways of locating and reaching them whilst streamlining our business development process virtually.

In addition we enhanced our core offering and developed additional low-entry offerings to attract new clients where they could try before they buy.

Throughout we have ensured that all communication, internally and externally is clear and consistent.

Simon Billsberry

Keeping it UP when the Economy Goes Down

Current Position:	CEO of Kinecticom
Qualifications:	BSc (Hons) Environmental Science
Experience:	15 years experience in Recruitment
Email:	simon.billsberry@kineticom.com
LinkedIn:	http://www.linkedin.com/pub/simon-billsberry/0/466/881
Website:	www.kineticom.com

Simon Billsberry's authenticity, intuitive business savvy, approach to adversity and heart have made Kineticom a winning company. As CEO, Simon's goal is to establish Kineticom as the first iconic global brand in the talent industry. Growing up in a British military family, Simon's energy, drive and natural business instinct shaped his identity as a risk-taker, competitor and entrepreneur.

Coming out of University, Simon landed in the people business and was fast-tracked through the ranks at S-Com, a global telecom staffing firm. After growing its client base to capture dramatic market share in the UK, Poland, Portugal, Egypt & the Netherlands, he was assigned a turn-around effort for a struggling subsidiary in the United States. US operations were quickly recovered as he led its sales and marketing operations from start-up to revenues over $20 million.

Simon then decided that his biggest career risk would be to stay under the radar and lose his spirit by becoming entrenched in comfortable politics & corporate bureaucracy. Simon and his co-founders broke off to shake up the talent industry. With a true understanding of the energy created by mutual trust, Simon and his leadership team have built a culture where employees and clients derive value from partnership.

Chapter 3: Keeping it UP when the Economy Goes Down

Kineticom is a professional services firm and has been through two recessions under its current leadership. We are the market leader in our niche and the fastest growing company in our industry in the United States.

Professional services, like many other perceived 'non-critical' business line items, come under enormous scrutiny in the economic down cycle phase we broadly term as a recession. Typically, by the time the experts and commentators have formally announced the 'R' word, we are usually deep into that phase of the cycle which has executives scrambling to take defensive 'survival' driven action, usually, but not limited to, significant and painful cuts in operating and capital expenditures.

Kineticom has not only survived two major recessions; it has thrived during them. I think of Kineticom as somewhat of a 'recession baby'. Because we were born into a recession, the lessons learned from it form part of our culture and operating philosophies. In this chapter, I will link some philosophy with practical action tips that we have deployed successfully.

1. Understand - analyse the current recession's key features

Each recession is usually characterised by the end of a prosperous economic trend and later tagged with a dramatic label. For instance, the relatively mild recession of 2001 was seen as the 'bursting of the dot.com bubble'. The most recent and severe 2008/09 recession was 'a meltdown of the global financial markets' or some variation thereof.

It is critical for upper management to translate and interpret the key features of the recession, so that the impact of it on the business can be appropriately understood and modelled.

Examples:-

a) The 2001 recession hurt technology start-ups and the venture capital community, putting many out of business.

> Action
>
> We had to increase diligence on our exposure to equity financed tech players which had previously been a very lucrative market sector.

b) The 2008/09 recession heavily impacted banks around the world. Our specialist debt financiers were sold and merged into a larger corporate bank.

Action

We had to manage this transition carefully and ensure that we had new key relationships in this 'arranged marriage'. With banks nervous and twitchy, it was vital for us to be able to manage this business critical relationship though a rushed transition.

2. Defend - cutting with care and principle

If cuts have to be made to defend and protect the business, it usually involves pain and can charge the emotions of even the most seasoned players. Due to the cumulative nature of business, the longer it takes management to make cuts, the bigger the knife necessary.

Once the quantitative component of the cut is understood, the next task is to select the line items (and often people) that will make up the cut.

This task is both quantitative and qualitative and it is the qualitative component that we have found causes the most internal tension and therefore the most impact on a company's culture. In order to make principle based decisions, we address our cuts in the following order:

1. Items that are not performing.....that need to be resolved
2. Items that are not deemed mission critical
3. Items where cost can be deferred but benefit retained
4. Muscle, but minimising revenue impact

By addressing #1 first you are reinforcing a culture of meritocracy, which is critical to thriving in good times and bad. An example of a cut in #3 was whereby Kineticom's executive team took half pay in order to avoid cutting muscle (#4).

3. Attack – get on the front foot and lead

The most effective and sensible way to navigate challenging times is to attack them with vigour. The pie has shrunk, so in order to prosper you need to be prepared to feed off the other guy's plate in order to grow stronger. This means fine tuning your organisation into a lean competitive animal and getting the focus back to the marketplace and away from the internal bruising that may have occurred.

If you have managed effectively, you should be in better shape than many of your competitors. Who knows how their businesses were geared going into this recession? Here are several things that could be features of the new competitive landscape:

1) Competitors focus on marketplace and clients may have shifted to internal issues
2) Talent that was previously unavailable may now be open to a team change
3) Customers are more open to change and are keen to see real value propositions
4) Vendors are keen to keep your business. It is important to ensure that you are getting the best value from your own supply chain just as your clients are
5) Mergers & Acquisitions: great deals are available if you have the capital & management bandwidth

Examples:-

1) In the face of tough and unpredictable economic conditions, one of our fiercest competitors executed a questionable 'defend' strategy; they retroactively cut the commission of their frontline sales people. As a result, we attacked and headhunted two of their veteran stars who had 10-15 years of experience and world class client relationships. Due to the nature of how badly they were treated, their non-compete agreements were legally void and they have been happily driving revenue for us on an even better commission plan than they have ever had. Our competitor made the mistake of looking at cuts from purely a quantitative perspective and missed the importance of the qualitative dimension (and principles) highlighted above.

   Our reputation allowed us to hit our competitor hard. The two stars could have gone to any of our competition but we were known in the industry as the best place to work as our focus is authentically on our people and hard but fair play. Our industry has an average staff turnover of over 60% per year. Kineticom's is less than 5%. We walk the talk. My point here is that you have to start now if you are to build a culture that can weather storms. If you wait for the storm to hit, you are likely to be too late.

4. <u>Smile</u> – positive communications

The good thing about a recession vs. any of the myriad of other crisis type situations is that everyone is pretty much in the same boat. The media, bars and restaurants, airport lounges and family discussions will all have the same negative and alarmist tone that comes with fear. There is no need to amplify that in the office. It becomes a source of paralysis.

Uncertainty can cause anxiety (a performance inhibitor) but it can also be a source of excitement (a performance catalyst). There have been plenty of scientific studies that show how smiling, laughing and being relaxed reduce stress hormones and performance inhibitors. It is the job of leadership to determine if the team is in a state of anxiety or excitement. Great leaders generate excitement.

It is hard to quantify the business impact of smiling and laughing but that's ok as its benefits are also immeasurable.

If management is doing everything within their power to navigate this period, then the focus should shift to the next inevitable phase of the cycle, 'the recovery'. Striking the right tone with corporate communications is critical to keeping energy positive and at the levels needed for high-performance.

That which you focus on has a tendency to grow, so focus on the positive and take the fight where it should be – in the face of your competition.

During the last recession our industry contracted 26% whilst Kineticom grew profitably by 75%.

Stefan Boyle

If you don't Change During a Recession, You're Moving Backwards

Current Position:	Managing Director of PrintRepublic
Experience:	21 years experience in Business
Email:	hello@printrepublic.co.uk
LinkedIn:	www.linkedin.com/profile/view?id=1384438&trk=tab_pro
Twitter:	www.twitter.com/Print_Republic
Facebook:	www.facebook.com/#!/stefan.boyle
Website:	www.printrepublic.co.uk/
Contact Number:	+44 (0) 845 862 5550

Stefan Boyle has worked in his family's print business for the past 18 years working his way through every department; he eventually bought the business in 2008. Since then he has diversified their offering and in 2009 started an online business, PrintRepublic.

PrintRepublic offer the full service – graphic design, web design and printing – to save businesses time and money. They don't just produce pretty designs and high quality print but also like to get involved with a business and understand what it is trying to achieve to help produce marketing collateral that achieves their goals.

It is a fully integrated service with a hands-on approach to all of the activities from building websites, creating identities and logos for businesses who are starting out or who want to create a fresh image and promote themselves to their clients and prospects. They work on cross media campaigns from conventional direct mail to e-marketing campaigns.

Stefan is married with two children and two dogs.

Chapter 4: If you don't Change During a Recession, You're Moving Backwards

My self-employed history starts in 2008 when I bought my family business. It was a printing business that had been established for about 38 years and had been very profitable and successful. We were very good at what we did and had some lovely clients, a lot of which were in the financial services industry.

We relied very much on our hard-fought reputation and we never really had to be particularly good at marketing because there was lots of business around and as we delivered great service to our clients, we naturally got some excellent referrals.

You may guess where I am going next with this. Two dreaded words...'Credit Crunch'.

I didn't really know what hit me. I had been sitting in my business, delighted that I had managed to buy the business from my parents and so I was now master of my own destiny. I had a good track record, a good client base and now all I had to do was more of the same.

I could not have been more wrong! Many of our clients in the financial services sector, who in recent years had been fantastic businesses making significant profits and growing amazingly quickly, all of a sudden stopped buying.

Actually quite a few of them stopped trading! Literally!

Businesses that were making millions of pounds and spending quite a large portion of it, benefitting my company as well as many others, just simply either didn't exist, or were put into hibernation.

Time for change

I knew I had to change both myself and my business. As the owner of a business, there is only one person who is accountable for change and for the success or failure of that business. And that person is staring back at you in the mirror!

I was stressed and frustrated.

As well as this I was lumbered with a sales team full of excuses of how quiet the economy was, how we were too expensive and any other excuse they could think of. I was working very long hours and sleeping little. I started to become a person I didn't like and I knew I had to make a change.

As many people in business would say, we were good at the job we did and the service levels experienced by our clients were first class. The major problem I had was how we communicated that to clients and very quickly I realised I had to get better at one very important skill: marketing...so I decided to learn!

Invest in Marketing

I invested in every marketing book and started to read everything remotely related to marketing that I could find both off and online. I learnt an awful lot but there was still a major stumbling block...how to put a plan together and actually implement all my ideas!

I made the decision to enrol myself on a marketing programme and very quickly I realised this was one of the best investments I had ever made. I went to every seminar for as many of the UK's leading marketing experts I could get to and started to look at my business very differently. I looked at it from the perspective of my customers!

Having really taken it upon myself to study and learn marketing ideas, trends and skills, I have noticed so many errors made by many businesses in their marketing. I should know - after all I was making almost all of them myself!

I started to implement a strategy that really changed my business. I made one really dramatic change; I fired myself from my own business! Strangely, my team were quite happy with that decision!

There is a cliché that business owners should work on their business, not in it. Trust me, it works. I was bogged down with day to day issues and couldn't see the wood for the trees. Taking myself out of the business and empowering my team changed that.

I also completely re-engineered the business and shut some of the ineffective areas of my company down. Instead I brought in external specialist skills on a project by project basis. I have automated parts of the business and partnered with companies who supply complementary services to what we do. Thus carrying out both joint venture partnerships as well as employing a number of companies to deliver some of our contracts.

My primary role in the business is to develop the strategy with a focus on the marketing. In recent years, with a small sales team of around four people, I would get more excuses than new prospects and leads. I have now focused the marketing on promoting a number of irresistible offers that generate new leads for my business literally every single day of the week.

If you look at the vast majority of websites and marketing literature for businesses in all sectors across the UK, on the whole you will see nothing but features. Dull stories about how the company has been in business for X number of years and how they 'pride themselves on customer service'! What the hell does that mean? You are hardly likely to be saying you pride yourself in terrible service!

Marketing materials that work

I always like to compare marketing literature to how you would behave when meeting someone face to face. I bet you have met sales people who just talk about themselves and show very little interest in what you are actually interested in or what problem you need solving. Why should a website, brochure, direct mail-piece or email be any different than that dullard we get lumbered with at a party who wants to talk about himself all night? It's pretty easy to see when we think how quickly we want to get away from those situations, isn't it?

Overcome fear

When prospects are interested in your business and how you can solve their problems, you must overcome their fear. People are fearful of making a mistake by choosing your business and the consequences of a bad decision on them and whatever it is they are buying.

So remove the fear, make it as easy as possible for them to see that your products and services offer significant BENEFITS, not features.
If you introduce consistent messages in your marketing that focus on the customer benefits, it's amazing the impact it can have. I have introduced this simple philosophy in my marketing and it has had a

huge impact. Whilst many business owners batten down the hatches in a recession, I have done the opposite and gone hell for leather.

Whilst the economy is in full bloom and everyone is growing, it is much harder to make serious headway and grow your business because everyone else is going for it too. If you make progress when the odds are against you, the opportunity to learn and develop is far greater and your progress will accelerate in your market.

My business is completely and utterly different now than it was before the start of the recession. We have made massive progress and although at times, it has been extremely challenging, I would not change anything.

In less than 12 months my company has attracted 700 new clients, including the world's biggest online auction site, eBay, and turnover has jumped by 40%. This is all thanks to getting better at marketing. The recession for me ensured that I had to completely remove any chance that complacency set in, both to me and my business.

I have sharpened my pencil in more ways than one. One thing I have learnt, and now continually apply the theory of to my everyday business life, is that there is always another way of doing things and nothing is forever. It is vital to implement change. This I found particularly challenging at times but I have also thrived under that pressure. I have found inner strength that I feel has helped me grow and develop my own skills which I use to try to keep on driving myself and my business forward.

Debra Zimmer
Retail Knows First

Current Position:	Founder, CEO
Qualifications:	MBA Columbia Business School BS Optics
Experience:	25 Years of experience in consumer, small business and technology marketing and entrepreneurship
LinkedIn:	http://linkedin.com/in/DebraZimmer
Twitter:	www.twitter.com/DebraZimmer
Facebook:	www.facebook.com/DebraZimmer
Website:	www.ExpertMarketingCoach.com
Links to Other Works:	www.BestFreeMarketingTips.com
Contact Number:	+1 303-834-1094

As The Expert Marketing Coach, Debra Zimmer brings 25 years of marketing experience to help you, the entrepreneur, to **attract, engage and convert your ideal customer**. She lights the path through the often cluttered, confusing and overwhelming world of internet marketing to teach you how to create your own sustainable marketing SYSTEM that **creates LEVERAGE**, **frees your TIME** and **increases your ROI**.

Debra developed this expertise as a **marketing executive at Microsoft**, where she **attracted 700,000 customers** into an online community in 18 months. She then repeated the process for another division by **attracting 250,000 members in 10 months**. From there she founded an online retail business and used her system to **grow it to six figures and put it on autopilot** for three years. She now teaches this proprietary TRIBES marketing system to private clients as well as to individuals and groups via teleclasses, home-study products, group mentoring programmes, books and through public speaking.

Chapter 5: Retail Knows First

At the time the recession hit, I owned a multi-channel home furnishings business; I was the founder and CEO. The company had started as an internet business in 2001 and in the autumn of 2005 we expanded into a bricks-n-mortar retail storefront.

At first when we opened the storefront, our sales increased quickly as people discovered us. Soon we showed only modest growth that was below our targets. We were getting great feedback from the community and everyone who walked in to the store "loved it", but no one was buying.

If at first you don't succeed try and try again

To increase sales, we brought in new product lines and tried to move older merchandise. We found that when furniture was deeply discounted, it moved. But our lease had a clause saying that we could not operate a discount outlet.

So we tried EVERYTHING; we added design services, held classes, advertised, improved store signage, held promotions and events, did direct mail pieces to new home buyers, hired better trained sales people and so on. But nothing increased sales. We developed relationships with interior designers and estate agents but to no avail. I was racking my brain and couldn't figure out for the life of me why no one was buying.

Strengthen what is NOT broken

The saving grace had been our internet store which produced a steady six figure revenue. Then in the summer of 2007, petrol prices doubled, our shipping costs skyrocketed and our margins dropped. Not a good thing. Our primary internet supplier started to slip on delivery times from six weeks to 24. Our customers became angry (and sometimes hostile) and our supplier began lying to us. I looked into expanding our internet offerings to limit our vulnerability. The problem was that the bleeding at the retail store required more of my attention.

Look for and listen to the signs

My first clue that there was a more global issue came in early 2008 when one of my sales reps congratulated me on doing so well for opening my store during the worst two years the industry had ever seen. He said they were losing accounts everywhere; that stores were shutting down.

In the meantime, Colorado was leading the nation in foreclosure rates. I thought it was concentrated to low income areas. I didn't know it was a national issue, let alone global. I wasn't alone.

The 80/20 rule is wrong!

In business school I learned to analyse my business financials in three ways: best case, worst case and most likely scenario. In the worst case, you should calculate that 80% of the things can go wrong 20% of the time. Well, they were wrong! EVERYTHING can go wrong at once!

Do your research

The only thing we hadn't tried was a different location. So that's what we did. After talking with other independent furniture stores in the proposed new location AND hearing rave reviews about how well they were doing - two out of three had just renewed their lease. We switched locations in April 2008. We moved to a smaller space in THE most upscale shopping district in the state. We lowered our rent and reduced our payroll. These changes cut over 50% off our expenses but it was already too late.

Diversify while you are strong

In May of 2008, the month we opened in our new location, our supplier for our internet products raised prices by 15%. The result? All sales CEASED! Our steady six figure sales dried up and we did not see another penny of revenue from the internet for the next six months.

Sometimes it's beyond your control

April 2008 was the first month of the recession in the US but it wasn't official for months. By August the furniture shop across the street from us said their clients had stop signing contracts. In October the stock market crashed. Customers put their plans on hold. The streets of the shopping district were empty.

By November, top architectural firms around the city were slicing their staff by 50% or more. One even laid off all his staff and moved his business into his home. There were rumours of architects standing on the street corner holding a sign and begging for work to feed their family.

Life DOES go on

I remember sitting in the store and feeling completely overwhelmed; it was like the world was crashing in around me and I was losing everything. And then the light went on and for the first time in three years I felt hope. I went home and joyfully told my husband, who was unemployed at the time, "You know, the only people who died during the great depression are the ones who killed themselves. We still have each other. We have three beautiful, healthy, wonderful kids. I've got everything I need. I don't care if we live in a tent. I have a great life."

The new store never achieved any sales worthy of note. We closed at the end of December 2008. We could not even sell our inventory at clearance prices. There just weren't any buyers in sight. Two out of the three stores we had talked with, who had claimed strong sales, closed shortly after us.

Watch the trending of the big guys

William Sonoma, owner of Pottery Barn, is one of the leading publicly traded companies in home furnishings. At the time I opened my store in August 2005, William Sonoma's stock was trading at $40 per share. At the time I closed my store in December of 2008, their stock was trading at $7.85. Had I thought to track their revenues at the time, I may have shut down sooner. Needless to say, I didn't have the deep pockets to weather the storm. Sometimes it's best to stop.

Learn how to quit

Going into business I knew that I should put a floor as to how much time and money I was willing to invest before pulling the plug. But three things happened: firstly I was emotionally attached, this was my baby; secondly I was humiliated to fail and so I hung on; thirdly I didn't know how to stop - no one had taught me how to shut down a failing business.

Watch the growth of the industry

Nine months after we closed the business, I had dinner with a friend, a successful venture capitalist, who made a comment which I will never forget. He said "the number one thing that determines how successful a business will be is the growth of the overall industry".

Have a plan B

After shutting down the store, I regrouped. I looked at what had drawn me into the home furnishings business and what I had most enjoyed. Then I designed a new business that maximised my strengths and minimised my weaknesses. I began to share my internet marketing expertise with other entrepreneurs to help them grow their business.

The architects and designers I know weren't so fortunate. Many are still unemployed, their skills not transferable beyond their industry. Those that do have jobs saw their pay checks slashed.

Develop a functional expertise that can transfer across industries. Have a skill you can fall back on.

Retail knows first

In closing, if you want to know what's happening in the economy, ask a retailer. They know three to four MONTHS ahead of the government what's happening at the consumer level. They are the pulse of the consumer. You want to know? Ask a retailer.

Tito Nath

A Positive Approach to Recession

Current Position:	Business Consultant
Qualifications:	BA (Hons) Law
Experience:	Over 25 years of experience in business consulting to the Retail, Health and Beauty Industries
Email:	tito.nath@btinternet.com
Contact Number:	+44 (0)7941511520

In a career spanning over 25 years, Tito Nath is a unique personality in the world of business consultancy having started his career as a Lawyer. His background and qualifications have enabled him to assist numerous organisations, from large, prestigious groups to small independent companies, to both prosper and grow; predominately in the hair and beauty sector. Tito has also contributed various articles for many trade magazines aimed at assisting business owners to realise their goals and objectives.

Chapter 6: A Positive Approach to Recession

Owning, managing and operating a business has become an entrepreneurial challenge. My passion is for assisting business owners identify the opportunities, exploit the windfall profits and ultimately realise their vision for the business.

A highly renowned salon I have worked with over the past two years has been able to steer its business through the battered economy and to increase turnover from £1.6 million to £2.2million. I am confident that this is just the tip of the iceberg with regards to realising the full potential of this organisation.

There are some businesses that succumb to negative conditions, while most simply develop the ability to 'adapt, survive and thrive' in the downturn. You need the right outlook and being optimistic during tough economic times is a learned business skill.

Personally, having experienced the ups and downs of the business world over the last 30 years, I think economic recession can be a good thing. Recessions can help to weed out the sub standard enterprises in otherwise overcrowded market sectors.

Companies that just don't 'get it' will be superseded by companies that do. Having the benefit of history is a wonderful thing and it tells us that recessions are temporary conditions. At some point the economy will start growing faster again. Meanwhile, consumers continue to spend and businesses continue to do business, even during recessions.

In my experience, whilst the recession poses obstacles and challenges for every business, it can also offer some areas of gain.

Firstly, you need to avoid getting caught up in the orgy of doom and gloom caused primarily by the media's obsession with the recession; they can turn a bit of negativity into a mountain of pessimism and it's easy to get sucked into that paranoia.

In view of this, it becomes understandable that some businesses succumb to knee jerk reactions and start making indiscriminate cutbacks if sales begin to slow down. The more we get absorbed by the recession, the more it becomes a reality. For example, slashing expenditure on business essentials such as marketing will inevitably result in a sharp slowdown in sales and an economic downturn will become a self fulfilling prophecy.

The first lesson to be learnt is that opportunities present themselves during a recession. I know this sounds counter-intuitive and if you are a sceptic then you only need to consider that IBM was born during the long depression (1873 -1896), Proctor and Gamble was founded during the panic of 1837 and FedEx came into being during the oil crisis of 1973...and these are but a few of the success stories. Below are just some of the key lessons I have learnt from working with high street retail businesses predominantly in the hair and beauty sector.

Be prepared to take action and don't just go with the flow of a recession. In tough times you can only grow to the degree you are prepared to embrace new ideas and new approaches. It is a key process to identify changes in psychology and behaviour in your clientele.

They may be spending less or using your business less frequently. If you are in touch with your customers, you will be aware of differences in buying habits. There are always some aspects of your revenues that are more resilient in economic downturns and you may need to focus on growing these profit centres by demonstrating how you offer **greater value** than your competitors.

Also **identify new products or services** that are complementary to your business. Even in recessions there will be innovation, development and new trends in your business sector. You need to be alert and investigate all new potential growth areas. Small diversifications may expand your appeal to a different audience, providing you with an opportunity to be a major player and to be the first to exploit these niche markets.

In a slow down, one of the first places many business cut down on is expenditure in advertising/marketing. It may be appropriate to rein in your spending on areas that are not adding value to your bottom line but **don't stop advertising!**

All businesses are reliant on their strategies and philosophies for creating clients/customers. During economic hard times, robust businesses increase their focus on both existing and new business generating activities. Bear in mind a recession can also open up access to some powerful advertising methods that would otherwise be unavailable or unaffordable to small businesses during buoyant times.

Form stronger alliances with your vendors. Work and manage your relationships with all your suppliers; in negative market conditions suppliers become even more dependent on your business which can give rise to huge opportunities to leverage better deals and favourable trading terms, as well as a stronger partnership. This will particularly become apparent if you can demonstrate you are better at weathering the market conditions than others.

There is also no harm doing your homework and dropping the name and trading terms on offer from the competition. Should you decide to switch suppliers this will help to optimise your position of strength; secure every discount or benefit you possibly can with every supplier, however small.

Rent reviews and lease negotiations in recessions can also work in your favour as a tenant. During economic boom, demand can cause rents to escalate out of control and have been known to cause the demise of many otherwise successful businesses.

Conversely during a downturn, occupiers can find it easier to argue that there has been a drop in rental values. In fear of having another empty unit as well as empty rates liability, landlords are more willing to forgo rental increases.

For example a rent review in 2004 could give rise to an increase in rental of 30% plus whilst a review in 2009 may only result in a nominal or zero increase. During this recession many tenants have successfully appealed for rental concessions and lease re-gears have offered a recessionary solution assisting occupiers to reduce rental cost.

Capitalise on the skill availability of the labour market. In economic boom recruitment can be challenging as demand for staff with experience and skills are at their highest. During this recession there has been an abundance of highly skilled individuals and this is apparent from the large number of applicants per vacancy.

There is opportunity to secure high calibre personnel at competitive salaries and generally bring down the overall cost of payroll. It may also be more cost effective to bring some roles in-house and engage new full time employees instead of using expensive contractor services in many areas from cleaning/maintenance through to public relations.

For example, using an external PR agency at the cost of £36,000 per annum could be replaced by an in-house PR and marketing manger on a salary in the region of £22,000.

Finally, remember that everything you think and dwell on will become reality whether negative or positive, so staying optimistic, focused and taking action during challenging business times will manifest itself in financial gain.

Christopher Lundie

Growing a Future-Proof Business During a Global Downturn

Current Position:	Founder and Managing Director of Covert Group
Qualifications:	HNC Distribution Management with Retail
Email:	chris@covertgroup.co.uk
LinkedIn:	http://uk.linkedin.com/pub/chris-lundie/0/991/72
Twitter:	www.twitter.com/covertchris
Website:	www.covertgroup.co.uk
Contact Number:	+44 (0) 1382 819990

Chris was born in Dundee on the East Coast of Scotland. Educated at Dundee College, Chris went on to work with WM Low Supermarkets progressing from Trolley Collector to Branch Manager. Chris continued his retail career with Safeway and John Menzies before changing direction completely in 1998 and moved into Facilities Management with the NHS in Dundee and London.

In 2001, Chris decided to set up his own Security Guarding Company, Covert, signing his first client – The Royal and Ancient Golf Club in St Andrews. Since then the company has gone from one part-time employee to almost 50 across Scotland with a turnover in excess of £3million. Chris also diversified into Contract Cleaning in 2004 and acquired his two main competitors in 2005. The latest additions to the Covert Group include a Cleaning Supplies division as well as an online Luxury Scarves business.

Chris is proud to be the President of Dundee and Angus Chamber of Commerce as well as Vice Chair of the Dundee United FC Business Club.

Chapter 7: Growing a Future-Proof Business During a Global Downturn

I set up my business, Covert Group, which provides Security Guarding and Contract Cleaning services, in 2001. The company has grown over the years organically and without debt. When the economic downturn began in 2008, we had a turnover of £2.6m and 45 employees. As a result of the recession, our main competitors started to close their local branches and centralise efforts from Glasgow and Edinburgh.

By early 2009, Covert Group had turnover of £3m with 50 employees. I suppose that I noticed the recession biting when so many of our competitors were offering services at levels at break even prices or cost plus 2%. Not a sustainable business model as most people would agree.

One of our founding principles is to never compete solely on price or to enter a bidding war. We have excellent relationships with our clients and we work with them in order to achieve a proper win-win situation. For example, some clients get better deals or packages if they chose to pre-pay or pay on invoice by BACS within seven days.

When attracting new business, we no longer offer the usual extended credit terms like 30, 60 or 90 days. Instead we accept credit card payments as well as payments by PayPal online which has really helped us achieve good financial liquidity at a time when so many others are failing. The main aim of analysing payment options and reducing credit terms was to future proof the company; it is important to keep in mind at all times this is not a lifestyle business and has a responsibility to look after all team members and customers equally.

Being pro-active is an absolute must!

We are always looking to add value to everything that we do. Long gone are the days of security personnel just sitting at a desk watching CCTV monitors and doing random foot patrols. Nine of our customers in the manufacturing sector benefit from our personnel undertaking many additional duties; our officers are the nominated first aiders, fire marshals, risk assessors and health and safety co-ordinators. All nine of these clients have realised savings of at least £20k per year each just by the value we have added to our service offering.

For us the benefits from these arrangements have included improved productivity, sickness levels down by 6% and improved personnel retention because they are receiving regular training. We have also retained 100% of all clients who we are working with in partnership as we are pretty much seen to be integral to the day to day processes of their business.

The clients have been able to 'free up' their own personnel to get on with running their own departments and allow our dedicated teams to look after the safety and care of their operations.

Towards the end of 2010 we faced two challenges that we were not prepared for: terrible weather and no postal deliveries for almost two weeks. Many of our services could not be delivered due to weather conditions, which meant we had people paid to stay at home whilst the client wasn't charged. Some of our team did voluntarily walk over 15 miles each way to get to work which does say a lot about the ethos of our company.

The mail delivery failure hindered some of our longer-standing clients' payments by cheque, which caused some minor panic during the winter months. The lessons learned were that no matter what you prepare for, there will be more challenges ahead and it is how you deal with these that will put you and your business in good shape in the future.

Talking about the future and the next 10 to 20 years, I feel it is most important that we communicate to our team when we are achieving results and when we are facing challenges. It truly amazes me how many of our people take ownership and are willing to assist. **Be transparent and honest at all times.**

Despite our turnover reducing last year by 24%, we have gradually made changes to the business and how we operate. Changes have been made one at a time and people have been included and consulted along the way about the benefits of doing so. As I write this, we have successfully converted £2.5m of new sales which had been in our pipeline.

By working so closely with our customers and our team members we have achieved the following results:

- 2011 - 65% of clients purchase both services from us (Security and Cleaning). In 2008, 20% of clients contracted us for both
- We have managed to increase our average sale by 18%
- Our number of transactions is up 47% from 210 per month in 2008 to 308 per month in 2011.

These results have been achieved by thinking smarter and working closely with all of our customers and team members.

In summary my SEVEN top tips to businesses wishing to grow and future-proof during tougher times:

1. Listen, listen and listen again to customers' changing needs and demands, don't be frightened to change what you do and how you do it.

2. Monitor and evaluate your key competitors at least twice a year.

3. Stop worrying about the impact of your decisions and get on with implementing actions!

4. Never, ever sell on price; always look to add value, features and benefits.

5. Offer alternative payment terms and get money into the business ASAP in order to safeguard cash flow.

6. Most of the changes that you are forced to make during the recession WILL strengthen the business for the future.

7. Give back to your local communities by donating time, services or resources. You and your team will feel absolutely great when you all do it. Good ethics equals good business.

Andy Gooday

How to Achieve More in Less Time

Current Position:	Author & Managing Director of Marcatus
Qualifications:	Certified NLP Coach – The Coaching Academy NLP Practitioner - ANLP The Complete Negotiator – The Gap Partnership Accredited Practitioner – FACET 5 Psychometric Tool
Experience:	15 years working in sports and fashion brand management
Email:	ag@Marcatus.co.uk
LinkedIn:	http://uk.linkedin.com/in/andygooday
Twitter:	www.twitter.com/MarcatusHq
Website:	www.MarcatusHq.com
Contact Number:	+44 (0) 207 193 1275

Andy Gooday is the Founder of MarcatusHq.com, an online software application, that makes it simple for Small Business Owners to set-up and manage their email and print marketing.

After 15 years in Corporate Brand Management Andy has wasted no time! MarcatusHq.com is the second successful business he has founded during the recession, as well as finding time to author two books: *Get Well Connected* and *Inbox Gold*.

He is passionate about business, entrepreneurship, personal development, sushi and most sports (especially snowboarding, but not cricket).

Chapter 8: How to Achieve More in Less Time

They say that businesses started during a recession go on to great things. I'm not sure who the 'they' are that originally made the statement. Having started two businesses in the last four years, I am not convinced 'they' are correct. In all probability this statistic has been twisted (like so many are) and does not take into account the businesses that have fallen by the wayside.

For all the opportunities that this recession has presented there have been an equal number of barriers. Many conversations have been opened with prospective clients simply because 'The Boss' has issued instructions to do things differently.

Conversely, many good ideas have been shelved because banks and investors have cut back on their lending to small businesses. Given the importance of the SME community in the economic recovery, perhaps the swing has been too far?

One thing is certain though: the owners and management in the businesses that are currently flying along, have exactly the same amount of time as those running failing businesses.

This topic has fascinated me for some time. What do the highly successful people do differently with their time? How can it be that two people with similar resources, skills and experience can get such wildly different results?

The two businesses I launched bring me into contact with two distinct groups of high achievers: senior management from some of the largest brands in the world and owners of some of the UK's most dynamic and success-focused SMEs.

If you are to make a success of your own business, then first you must master the effective use of your time.

These are the lessons I learned from observing the high achievers in these groups.

Planning

Many entrepreneurs suffer from what I have nicknamed 'magpie syndrome' – the uncontrollable excitement, enthusiasm and passion for the latest 'shiny thing'. Unfortunately this often comes at the expense of other important things.

I read somewhere once that the achievement of long-term success is simply the achievement of a long series of smaller successes. These are the habits I formed to ensure I constantly moved forward in the right direction.

Annually
Take a day to review where you are and to write a plan for the coming year. Ask yourself these questions:

- Where do I want the business to be in three years and thus, what are the milestones I need to achieve in the next year?
- What tools and resources do I need in the next year? (Are they realistic?)
- Have I got the right suppliers and outsourcers? (If not, change them)

Quarterly
Book out half a day with no chance of interruption. Plan in detail the objectives you need in order to achieve your annual milestones.

Fortnightly
Every other Friday take an hour or two to review the achievement of your quarterly objectives.

- How are you progressing against them?
- What needs to be done in the next fortnight?

Daily
Take 20 minutes to review your day before going home and plan tomorrow. If you plan to delegate something, then delegate it before that person has started planning their time – that way they will be more effective, which should ultimately mean that you spend less time following up on them.

Employ Technology
Very often technology can actually erode the time you have rather than make you more efficient.

Basecamp - http://basecamphq.com/

Basecamp is an online project management and collaboration tool. It means we can keep everything relating to a project in one place. It delivers messages to your email inbox and captures your replies in a 'timeline'. Not only does it make the management of projects much easier but it also cuts down on the time spent looking for a particular message or file. Its beauty is its simplicity, which is why they already have millions of users.

Kashflow – http://www.kashflow.com/

Kashflow is an online accounts software package; nothing too revolutionary about that you might think. Mostly you're right, after all it does pretty much the same functions as all its competitors. However, the success of Kashflow is not that it changes the way you do your core accounts; what it does, is change the way that you do the surrounding activities. For example, you can access your company accounts straight from your iPhone or take a photo of a receipt when you purchase something and have it entered into the books right there and then. Small things that can make a big difference.

Dropbox – http://www.dropbox.com/

I'm not sure there are many businesses these days that don't share files and documents or send them via email at some point. Dropbox is an online 'my documents' with some nifty features. In short, once registered and connected, members have a local copy on their PC which constantly syncs with the online version. Quite cleverly it allows multiple users to share, update and collaborate documents, as well as send links to non-members to download large files. Accessible from any PC via their website or via their iPhone app, it means you can always access any document you need with just a few key strokes.

Outsourcing

Outsourcing has been around for a long time, however because of recent improvements in technology like broadband and Skype, it has become much easier to outsource pretty much anything.

As well as the benefit of giving you extra time, outsourcing can provide other benefits:

- Tasks can be completed while you sleep by utilising services in other time zones (China and India are major players in the outsourcing market).
- Expertise can be obtained through an 'auction' process, meaning you will obtain a fair price. Services like Elance.com provide payment schemes that protect you from scam artists as well as ensuring you achieve the quality of work you need.

You will find plenty of different outsourcing providers on the internet. I like and use these providers:

AlldayPA - http://www.alldaypa.com/

Elance - http://www.elance.com/

One of the most important considerations when planning to outsource a task is understanding the cost of outsourcing versus the cost of your time to complete the task. One business contact of mine outsources his email management. Many people would argue that this would be impossible. However, after some careful planning and devising some rules they have a 'system' and my contact answers just a handful of emails each day while his PA handles the rest.

Self- management

Take some time to consider these questions:

What things do you do that really excite you?

Schedule time to do these regularly

What things do you really hate doing?

Could other people do these better than you (very likely if you dislike it) and would they cost less? If so then outsource.

When are you at your best?

Schedule your toughest tasks for this time; try to work in 'bursts' of 90 minutes before changing tasks

What things do you do that don't contribute to the achievement of your objectives?

Stop doing them.

What things do you need to do but are putting off?

Commit to a timescale for resolving them, diarise the deadline and focus on the critical things.

Get maximum value from meetings

After every meeting ask yourself:
How relevant was the information in this meeting?
How will this help your future work?
Ditch any meeting with unsatisfactory scores

What Next?

It has been my experience that making changes to your routine is best done a little bit at a time. So resist the temptation to change a bunch of stuff at once, you'll end up with more to do not less.

Remember, major success is nothing more than a long series of smaller successes. If you strive for one success everyday then you'll make it!

Helen Reynolds

Kicking a Downturn into an Upturn

Current Position:	Managing Director of HB RIDA
Qualifications:	HND in Business and Finance
Experience:	17 yrs in Business and Recruitment
Email:	Helen@hbrida.com
LinkedIn:	http://uk.linkedin.com/in/helenreynolds1
Twitter:	www.twitter.com/helenreynolds
Website:	www.hbrida.com
Contact Number:	+44 (0) 203 086 9677

Helen Reynolds heads up HB RIDA, a private equity vehicle which provides support to fledging and established recruitment businesses through a unique set of development define programmes which assist owners to grow and develop their own firms.

A business coach and entrepreneur, she has worked at all levels in the recruitment industry from Consultant to Director. Before setting up HB RIDA, she was acting CEO of the REC and also held the post of Executive Director of RITE, the business support arm of the REC.

Helen has provided invaluable support and guidance to fledling and established recruitment businesses and has successfully mentored well over 100 agencies, her passion for the industry and SMEs is highly recorded. A known spokesperson and commentator for the industry, Helen is a respected leader.

Helen resides on the South Coast of England and is married with two sons.

Chapter 9: Kicking a Downturn into an Upturn

Whilst most were sitting evaluating their businesses and the difficult decisions that they were going to have to make as the recession kicked off in 2008, my experiences were different.

Why?

Because I was, in fact, just starting my company HB RIDA (www.hbrida.com). The financial squeeze that was affecting the recruitment sector had consumed my every waking moment with contacts asking for advice on how they could continue trading and what they needed to do to survive.

At the beginning of 2008 the recruitment sector had around 25,000 recruitment agencies and was an industry worth over £30 billion. The recession hit several sectors quicker than others – construction for example. Naturally, this would be one of the first sectors to be affected due to the lack of lending by the banks, a freeze on new build and a whole host of development projects being put on hold.

The result? A major downturn for the labour supply market.

Having seen that it was not only SMEs but also large entities that were in difficulty, I decided to launch a business that not only provided business advice and support, but also provided a venture capital fund specifically for the recruitment sector and more importantly, specifically for SMEs. Some might say that I was crazy to launch a business during this time and to leverage my assets to create a fund. However, I have always said that all business is a risk but a calculated risk is always worth taking. You may ask why I chose to concentrate on what was probably the most vulnerable segment of the marketplace: SMEs. Well, it's SMEs that make up over 90% of the recruitment sector and they were in dire need of help.

Lift Off

On the 6th April 2009, I launched HB RIDA with my business partner James Caan. During our first quarter the levels of enquiries were more than expected and what we experienced and learnt during this time is priceless.

Regardless of whether you are a multinational or a local high street business, I truly believe that my following insights must be considered.

The recession, or indeed any quiet period of trading, is not the time to sit and reflect on what changes you need to make. You should be doing this on a monthly basis. I met with many owners during this 'dark time' who said:

"I need to make cuts and of course my first cuts are going to be on non performing staff."

What none of them had asked themselves is why they were employing non performing staff in the first place!

Lesson 1 – Who Makes You Money?

Evaluate all areas of your staffing on a monthly basis. This does not mean that you need to become Big Brother, constantly breathing down their necks to see what they are up to, but you do need to find a mechanism to track efficiency.

Something I run all our businesses by, is a pay out rate and this can be applied to any sales led business. A pay out rate is the ratio of sales generation to the costs of the employee. Costs are defined as salary, statutory contributions and other costs linked to the employee such as expenses etc. If the percentage ratio is greater than 40%, then that employee is not adding any value to your business. Less than 40% and you are making sufficient money to cover their costs and make some profit. There is no point in employing sales people who ultimately cost you money!

Lesson 2 – Know Your Staff

At HB RIDA we always perform Business Health Checks on our portfolio companies. These health checks measure many aspects of business such as operations, brand and finances. One area which never fails to surprise is around staff evaluation. Many employees never get the opportunity to truly express their thoughts on the company, their boss and their colleagues.

We produce an online questionnaire, which is completely anonymous. We ask questions such as how do they rate their relationship with their boss/colleagues? Do they feel rewarded?

How would they like to be rewarded? Nine times out of ten, regardless of how much the business owners profess that they have a very open door, we pick up on some very serious areas of complaint.

What is the biggest complaint? Well it's not feeling valued or part of a team, not being listened to and not being rewarded through non-financial means.

Know what the motivators are

Whilst people - and certainly sales people - are motivated by money, the majority of us are always motivated by something else. That something is normally as simple as saying "Thank you" or "Well Done", being taken to lunch or winning an 'Employee of the Month' award. In an era where email and social media rule, I chose to go back to basics. I remember, as a junior, being sent handwritten notes and cards by my boss. These would be short messages giving guidance and praise. I have treasured those notes to this day. They made me feel special and valued. I now send the same sort of notes to my staff and my portfolio companies. It's amazing how something so simple can make a huge difference to moral and personal motivation.

Lesson 3 – Broaden Your Outlook

You may think that during the recession all business owners should spend all their time working on and in their business. Whilst this is a business basic, it's how you do this that makes the difference.

I always spend at least one day per week networking and meeting with people. Whilst this may not bring instant results, it does enable me to promote myself, my brand, and gain me a reputation for being approachable, someone who is happy to give impartial advice and connect people who I felt would benefit from each other. This time not only serves a purpose for creating a pipeline of business opportunities, but has also gained me the reputation for being one of the best-connected people in the industry.

Creating a brand for yourself, as well as your business, is essential, especially as an SME. A word of warning though; you must keep these in balance. If you are looking to one day exit your business, those built on solely a personal brand are often discounted in value.

Becoming an insular business owner is dangerous. Every time you meet someone, your business benefits. You learn more about what's going on in the wider business world, different approaches and views to industry. Get out there and talk to people.

Lesson 4 – Haggle!

All people like to feel they have had a good deal and I am certainly one of them, but what makes a good deal? I do find that the UK is terribly 'British' when it comes to negotiating. The recession was a time when we all wanted to ensure we had got the very best deal for our money and really stretched that pound as far as we possibly could. But what many failed to do was to look at the long term.

A good deal is not only financially based. Most people discount in the traditional way, dropping in units of ten. But negotiation is not always about an initial discount. I restructured many supplier agreements including financial arrangements during the recession (yes I was 'that' person who managed to get a good financial deal during that period). I agreed to still pay people full price, but negotiated a discount on the amount of money spent with suppliers over a period of time, working on a ratchet system.

I negotiated better terms of supply, customer service and delivery over fixed periods of time, often with me as the sole consumer. Why would I do this? Well I knew at some point we would come out of the recession, we couldn't stay in it forever. When we did, I would have all the resources and suppliers around me, with many locked in to supply to me only. The result would be my competitors struggling to gain this quality of service.

I have implemented all of the above, along with many other things, in all the businesses I have invested in during the past 18 months. The effect? Well each of my businesses have doubled in size during this time. They have all doubled their staff and opened at least two new locations each. Most importantly, they have increased their bottom line.

And what of HB RIDA? Well, in total we have invested in ten businesses, a mix of online and traditional organisations. We have amassed an EBIT of some £4 million, meaning an enterprise value of over £30 million. Not bad for a business 18 months old.

And finally….

My biggest lesson learnt from the recession?

Believe in yourself. I had no doubt that I would succeed. I was aware of my own abilities, my strengths and my weaknesses. I ensured I surrounded myself with colleagues and staff with complementary skill sets. It's no good if we are all good at sales but useless at finance! I continued to learn, engage in personal development and read a lot. I learnt from others' mistakes and researched wherever I could. I started this chapter by saying business is a risk and it is, but a calculated one is worth taking. We're living proof of that!

Richard White

It Wasn't the Best Time to Launch a Magazine...

Current Position:	Joint Managing Director of Maybe Magazine
Email:	richard@maybemagazine.com
Twitter:	www.twitter.com/#!/MaybeMag
Website:	www.maybemagazine.com
Contact Number:	+44 (0) 7817 218442

A freelance sales consultant, project manager, evaluator, trainer and business consultant. A director of a social enterprise and of a consultancy business. 24 years in engineering, management and sales with BT, Xerox and Cable & Wireless.

An enthusiastic, hardworking and successful professional with much success within the public and private sectors; bidding for, winning, managing and evaluating large projects. Significant consultancy experience includes Business Process Reengineering, service operations management, IT strategy, engineering and manufacturing sector training solutions and third sector development.

Chapter 10: It Wasn't the Best Time to Launch a Magazine...

Maybe Magazine is a free, quarterly lifestyle and business magazine, distributed in Milton Keynes and North Buckinghamshire to 32,000 ABC1 readers. It sells commercial advertising space and as a Social Enterprise, attracts grants and public sector funding to help disadvantaged people learn and apply new skills in media.

Introduction to key lessons

In April 2008, after almost a year of detailed planning, we started trading. It is now somewhat of an understatement to label 2008 as a less than ideal year to launch a new business, particularly a new regional magazine in an already saturated market. Of course, as that year drew to an end, very few people in business knew how difficult things would become over the next two years.

Lesson 1

Cost reduction opportunities should, theoretically, be less in a well planned start-up. After all, if the management has spent 12 months researching the marketplace and setting up properly, as it should have done, then how much opportunity is there really?

There are two answers to this: the willingness of many suppliers to reduce their margins in order to retain their customers, and the courage and motivation that these adverse conditions give management which forces them to look long and hard at their own cost base.

In a growing company, it is often just as easy to add to bottom line profitability by saving cost as it is gaining a new customer. Just make sure you do both, all the time.

We managed to halve our costs simply because we had to and because it could be done. Each business process was analysed and suppliers negotiated with. Sales associates were moved on to a more commission-focused structure. Every contract renewal gave us the upper hand to renegotiate rates. We joined the Bartercard trading network which enabled us to sell unsold advertising space at full price (something we have rarely achieved in the cash economy) and buy many services in return, saving valuable cash.

Lesson 2

There are two advantages of launching a new business during a recession. The first is that the business (if it is viable) can only grow, even if the market it operates in is shrinking. This has a motivational effect on management and staff and protects against distracting and destructive thinking that many established players are consumed with as they try to protect themselves from the inevitable threats to their own businesses.

The second advantage is that the casualties of the recession are not just one's competitors, but their customers who begin perhaps to suffer poor customer service and even complete failure as their suppliers begin to implode. So even in a shrinking market, there are opportunities to attract the disaffected customers of one's competitors.

Lesson 3

Unique Selling Points come sharply into focus during a recession. The extra value that you claim, can be delivered to your customers, the improved ROI and above all, your uniqueness and the edge that that could bring to your customers will be examined in detail over and over again by prospects.

Their buying criteria will have hardened and may well include the need to address the failings of the current or previous supplier - failing that, as discussed above, it could well be due to the shrinking or consolidating actions of those competitors.

Our USP is as unique today as it was when we launched the business. As a Social Enterprise, we attract grant and public sector funds to train disadvantaged people (mainly unemployed) in media. We run workshops and work experience programmes in Journalism, Photography and Graphic Design and use these opportunities to build the articles for our magazine.

We are now training in excess of 150 people each year and some 70% of our magazine is created with the help and input of many disadvantaged people. During a recession, when many people are losing their jobs and seeking new opportunities to train, this remains a compelling proposition to individuals, funders and larger corporations with a genuine interest in Corporate Social Responsibility.

Summary

In Year 1 our business made a £53k loss. We moved into profit in Year 2 and we are on track to deliver good profits in Year 3. Our costs are still half what they were at start up.

We have survived and we are growing. We have lots of goodwill from all sorts of people because we are, truly, an ethical business that has made, and will continue to make, a difference to many people's confidence and prospects.

We now employ six people who we originally met through our media training programme. We push hard on both the commercial and social sides of our business and we are well placed to capture much more of the corporate CSR budget. We are also well positioned to capitalise on any growth in the economy and any tangible shift of public sector funds towards the third sector. Had we set up as a purely commercial organisation, then it is probable that we would have failed very quickly. Having uniqueness, demonstrating leadership and delivering value is surely the answer for us all.

Scott Hodson

What a Great Sport this Game of Business is...I Love it!!

Current Position:	Managing Director of the multi-award winning web company Optimum Fitness Software
Qualifications:	BSc (Hons) Human Health and Sport Science
Email:	shodson@ofsoftware.biz
LinkedIn:	http://uk.linkedin.com/in/shodson
Twitter:	www.twitter.com/OFSoftware
Facebook:	www.facebook.com/OFSoftware
Website:	www.OFSoftware.biz
Links to Other Works:	www.FitnessBusinessSuccess.com www.PerfectFitnessWebsite.com/killertechniques
Contact Number:	+44 (0) 1634 883 444

Scott Hodson is the Managing Director of a multi-award winning web company which guarantees to increase web leads, conversions and sales for ambitious businesses in the health, sport and leisure industry.

He started the company after seeing an opportunity to monopolise an industry which could benefit from innovative online technologies. Some entrepreneurs would have seen that operating in a technophobic market would make the proposition too risky....well not Scott! He saw it as a great challenge where the risks would be replaced with high rewards.

He believes that sport and enterprise are very closely resembled with discipline, a good work ethic, training, innovation and fun, all being key elements to success.

Chapter 11: What a Great Sport This Game of Business is...I Love it!

Before I explain the strategies I adopted to survive the recession, I feel I need to explain my background and how it has equipped me with the ability to take on the great challenge of building a successful business. I come from a sporting background and have been fortunate enough to play rugby union for England at University level, play senior county standard and earn over 100 national league caps.

"Play with the long game in mind whilst working the short game"
Mr James Hodson – Father and Rugby Coach from U6's to U17's

Without the innate desire to thrive on challenges and welcome the times when you are thrown out of your comfort zone and thrust into the big match scenario, I don't believe I would have been able to take The Big Recession!

I naturally find myself in leadership roles and describe my style as a 'point leader'; the guy who is at the front, leading by example and encouraging other players to put everything into winning.

So who will win the ultimate competition? My business or the downturn?

My business was the underdog...we were a novice company which was under funded, under staffed and under prepared for the big showdown.

This became my next biggest challenge...It was my Olympic Final, my Ali Vs Frasier, my United Vs City, my Ashes series and my Grand Slam decider against the French in Paris...all rolled up into one! I needed to have the performance of my life to win!

"Big game players perform in big games"
Mr. Ray Hennessey – Ex London Irish Rugby Star and my coach at University

Who is winning?

Pre-recession I was the owner of an award winning web and software business, developing innovative and robust solutions for a technophobic health and fitness industry and I relished in the challenge of running this business every day. I was very cock sure and arrogant about the way I was leading my business...

My life consisted of 60+ hours a week, going from one project to the next. Sane people from the outside looking in would call it stressful and frantic but I was surviving in a growing market, riding the good times and achieving a short term win.

To be brutally honest it wasn't sustainable and referring back to what my father taught me, I knew I had to do something about it and prepare for the long game.

Then the laws of the game changed!

The recession hit. Existing clients that used to be great payers, started to pay late (if at all). New clients wanted to pay less and were more expensive to get. Less money was coming into the industry via the public sector which affected the whole supply chain and the opportunities for good business became harder to find.

Thankfully, as a small technology business we were flexible enough to be able to react quickly to this and adopt a different game plan to stand toe to toe with a heavyweight economic downturn.

"It's the battles that we remember that help us to win the war"
Mr Jay King – Captain of Ealing Trailfinders Rugby Football Club

So whilst we dealt with the immediate risk of dodgy cash flow we had to start training the business to survive for the future.

Myself and my Technical Director, Ian Rumsey, decided we had to do three key things to increase the chances to still be standing in the twelfth round and go on to become champions of the world:

1. Surround yourself with the best people
2. Become more productive and profitable
3. Innovate

Surround yourself with the best people

Business can be a very lonely place and sometimes you are left stranded not quite knowing what decision is the right one. The business and I have always sought mentorship from more experienced business people who have been there and done that, which I think is a must for any SME.

This section of the chapter will pay homage to my willing and relentless staff. Without their hard work and technical skills my business wouldn't have survived and I wouldn't be writing this. Whilst I can provide the energy and resilience to lead the business I am nothing without my team. The whole business works because of the different skills each of my team brings to the game and without the best guys around me I couldn't be a high achiever.

But what happens when you can clearly see that you need up skilling in a certain element of your performance or the business is lacking a skill set totally?

The life blood of any business is sales and marketing and pre-recession I would have graded my business as very average in this field, but due to the reasons mentioned above we survived pre-recession...but now we needed to get very good at it and very quickly!

I am always hesitant in hiring-in renegades to add to my awesome team. The risk of bringing in an 'experienced sales manager' seemed too high to me, especially as they could easily leave and go and work for a 'Premiership Team'. I want to surround myself with people who want to be here for the right reasons, not for cash only.

The cash flow situation wouldn't allow me to hire in the calibre of candidate we would have needed to solve our sales and marketing skills so we had to learn them ourselves. This also has an additional benefit of providing me with the essential sales and marketing skills that would equip me for the future no matter what (even if we didn't survive the downturn).

I invested my time and money surrounding myself with the top business, sales and marketing experts and started to transfer their skills into my business. This provided me with an unbeatable support team and the 'back room staff' to work on the weaknesses of the business.

Together we identified that the business needed to differentiate itself and put in low cost lead generating systems to grow my sales pipeline. A defining moment in time was transforming my value proposition from a 'specialist web company for the health, sport and leisure industry' to 'an award-winning web company which guarantees to increase web leads, conversions and sales for health and fitness businesses'. This proved very successful and provided us with the sustainability we needed to continue to play the game.

This one principle of surrounding yourself with the best people in sales and marketing certainly paid off as, when we launched with the low cost lead generating system, we achieved 340 highly qualified leads in just three days, over 300% more than the whole of the previous year.

Become more productive and profitable

As the market place got harder and more ruthless we had to get leaner and meaner. We had to develop new systems and processes to be able to compete in a newer harsher environment.

The easiest (and wrong) thing to do here, would have been to carry on as normal and continue with working at a frantic pace to get through the workload just to keep the conveyor belt going; but we decided to take a little harder route. We took the decision to actively put down the tools regularly, take a step back from the pressure cauldron and look at the business in a subjective and productive manner.

The immediate hardship and sacrifice was quickly replaced by a more productive, systemised business which led to increased profits, even though turnover was reduced. An additional bi-product was improved morale, better teamwork and improved enjoyment.

We went from a 12% profit margin to a 34% profit margin in the matter of six weeks.

This sounds like an idyllic scenario and that everything was plain sailing (unintended pun here) but it wasn't. This is probably the most stressed I have ever been during my professional career which actually resulted in me quitting playing rugby, as I needed all my energy to make sure my business survived.

This goes to show that to achieve the long term goal you might have to sacrifice the short term game.

Innovate

This extends on both of the previous lessons and has provided my business with a strong foundation to build from and an opportunity for high growth.

We took the risk of investing in R&D to develop an automatic website builder. Before this innovation we would charge a small amount of money for a basic website, which had very small profit margins (and high stress rates).

To build this innovation we invested our time and money into University Interns who came into the business as the most up to date programmers and provided us with additional low cost man hours lead by my experienced crew.

This innovation has allowed us to take a small amount of money for a basic website, but this now comes into the business as a passive income stream and allows us to take on multiple orders all at the same time.

The added benefit of trying to innovate during a recession is that the government and the HE institutes will launch new schemes to encourage innovation and employment; I took this opportunity and made it work for the business.

When we hit our yearly targets for 2011 we will have enough passive income to cover 100% of the business overheads which allows us to select only high profit projects to propel the business forward.

Conclusion

In order to take on the challenge of building a successful business during a recession I would advocate to:

1. Surround yourself with an unbeatable team (staff and support team)
2. Develop new systems and processes to become more productive and profitable
3. Innovate and develop either new revenue streams or new ways of charging for services.

Rollan A. Roberts II

Mega Performance During Downturns

Current Position:	CEO, TV Host, & Corporate Strategist
Qualifications:	Masters in Business Administration Currently completing a dissertation to complete a Doctorate in Business Administration with an emphasis on Entrepreneurship & Global Business Leadership.
Experience:	11+ Years as Senior Executive
Email:	info@idream247.com
LinkedIn:	www.linkedin.com/in/rollanroberts
Facebook:	www.facebook.com/rollan
Website:	www.idream247.com
Links to Other Works:	www.amazon.com/dp/1607998459?tag=idream0a-20&camp=14573&creative=327641&linkCode=as1&creativeASIN=1607998459&adid=1112S10BY17YC3KHW3CC& www.amazon.com/dp/1602473714?tag=idream0a-20&camp=14573&creative=327641&linkCode=as1&creativeASIN=1602473714&adid=08JBA7QSRPFG4YW9JSZ2&

Rollan Roberts II is the CEO of iDream, a company that creates high growth organizations focused on doubling revenue in 12-24 months. He is a TV host, keynote speaker, and best-selling author of three internationally released books. Visit www.iDream247.com to contact Rollan!

Chapter 12: Mega Performance During Downturns

My company did not feel the effects of the economic downturn for the first year and a half. Then it hit. Business did not slowly decline, it tanked fast.

Here is the question I asked myself then and continue to ask the C-level leadership of my clients: is what you are doing at this moment the highest and best use of your time?

In commercial real estate, land is valued at its highest and best use (if it can support a high-rise mixed-use facility it appraises for more than if a petrol station goes there). Most of us have one or two major things we must get done in a day and then numerous other things that need to be handled. These major objectives may shift frequently, even daily, which is why it is critical to your success that you constantly ask yourself the above question.

Regardless of how you answer the question, your success will be equal to your ability to execute the following two principles: prioritising and leveraging. These principles will revolutionise the volume and magnitude of what you are able to accomplish in short periods of time. This method is effective in good times and particularly crucial in bad times.

1. Prioritise

There are a lot of things you can do right now, but chances are, there are only a few that make a real difference. In business, I call this the 'critical few' versus the 'trivial many'. It is core versus chore.

The critical few move the needle - the trivial many do not. The critical few are non-negotiable - the trivial many are negotiable. Most people are busy doing the trivial many to the neglect of the critical few.

For the first eighteen months of the recession, it was business as usual for my company. When much of the business (revenue) dropped off from the end of December to the first of January, the first order of business was to re-arrange priorities and separate the critical few things that were mandatory for success from the things that were nice to have and do.

Lead Generation became a high priority, whereas we had a steady stream of prospects prior. Adding value through mass-market media exposure became a higher priority as opposed to merely relying on word of mouth and past clients. Prioritising these revenue-driving activities meant we had to let some things go. We evaluated and stopped using most traditional marketing channels because they did not provide good returns on the investment. All activities in business are not equal.

One of my recent clients was struggling to turn their company around. Revenue had been declining for ten straight years and my organisation was brought in to create the first growth year the company experienced in a long time. I took the senior management into the conference room and wrote on a white board 'Critical Few' and 'Trivial Many' and underlined them. I then asked them to pull out their calendars and tell me what consumed their days. They discovered the vast majority of their time was spent on things that did not directly affect revenue.

They spent time on good things. They spent time on right things. They spent time on things that had to get done. But they did this at the expense of the few essential, core activities that drive revenue. By the time we left that conference room, the company was aligned around the critical few behaviours that set up the amazing turnaround that followed; it went from $5.6 million to north of $40 million in 22 months. That executive team was relieved and invigorated to be doing what they knew they should have been doing all along.

If you don't focus on the critical few first, you'll never get to them because the trivial many keep you so busy. The trivial many are like weeds that choke the life out of you. No matter how beautiful the garden, no matter the potential of the product or service, you will not experience the level of success and revenue you could through understanding what the critical few are for your organisation. You will be so busy with the trivial many that you don't have time for the critical few.

This is what happens in life. We get so busy doing all those extra things for work, that the most important things get neglected like family, friends and health. Prioritise the important critical few first and then add in the trivial many based on what your schedule allows. Build your life around your priorities; don't let life just happen to you.

2. Leverage

Stop trying to do everything yourself. This is the difference between self-employed people and business owners. Self-employed people tend to do everything themselves whereas business owners employ the concept of leverage. The uber-wealthy understand this concept and have employed it for generations. Instead of working themselves (building the widget, servicing the client, etc.), they hire people to work following a duplicatable system that produces a predictable result: profit.

They leverage people, not just money. And just like money compounds when leveraged, they leverage people to create money. That's why J. Paul Getty, one of the wealthiest men to ever live, said, "I'd rather have one percent of the effort of 100 men than 100% of my own." He understood the power of duplication.

It was this brilliance that Ray Kroc demonstrated. The average male can grill a better hamburger than you get at McDonald's but Ray Kroc understood the power of duplication and leverage. He knew that a consistently duplicated product and consumer experience would trump a single, massive location.

He created a duplicatable system of making hamburgers and running the business so that teenagers could do it and he built his business in every nook and cranny of the globe leveraging others to build and manage the stores. Discretion is the enemy of duplication. Most leaders only consider what works, but the best leaders consider what's duplicatable and inherently scalable. You only achieve this level of thinking when you work "on the business not in the business," as Michael Gerber would say.

We are familiar with leverage and compounding with money but most people do not understand that they are either being leveraged or doing the leveraging! Which are you? If you're focused on maximising every moment of the precious life we've been given to its highest and best use, find ways to leverage yourself. Employ leverage to your benefit by outsourcing the trivial many that are keeping you from the critical few.

We help companies do this frequently - determine what's core and outsource the chore. Anything that breaks your company's focus from its primary objective is an enemy. Leverage other people. Leverage other companies. Leverage affiliates and resellers. Leverage partnerships. Leverage independent contractors. Keep the main thing the main thing.

Avoid the primary dirty word in business - incremental. Stop chasing incremental revenue and incremental gains here and there. Instead, focus on prioritisation and leverage. You will take decisive action that will lead you through the worst downturns, coming out on the other side in better financial health than ever before.

When the recession hit our company, the only way we could survive was if we employed big levers. We lost 70% of our revenue (which represented 30% of our clients) in January 2009. The days of tweaking processes and turning dials to save some here and make some there were over.

To survive and thrive, we needed to make good use of big levers. Small businesses can make monumental gains by using big levers. The big lever is different for every company, but there is at least one for each business. The big lever for us was partnering with organisations that already had the customers we were seeking. Instead of trying to attract and win them, we partnered with a company that already had them and then added value through that relationship. This strategy, through successful execution, caused us to recoup the lost revenue, gain dozens of new clients, and actually have a record setting revenue year and 200% growth from 2008. We averted the looming catastrophe and broke through our own barriers by being aggressive, innovative and using big levers.

There are companies in every industry that have doubled their revenue in the past year. It clearly isn't the industry. It is the way most of the companies in these industries are doing business. The rules of business are changing in virtually every sector, and those that are changing the rules are winning.

Owen Ashby

Corporate Myopia

Current Position:	Sales and Marketing Consultant
Experience:	20 years experience in B2B Sales and Marketing
Email:	owen@owenashby.com owenashby@graymatteriq.co.uk
LinkedIn:	http://uk.linkedin.com/pub/owen-ashby/0/722/a12
Links to Other Works:	Ask The Experts: Owen Ashby Google: Owen Ashby
Contact Number:	+44 (0)7944 605352

Owen works with businesses to help them gain and sustain strategic competitive advantage. Over the last twenty years he has worked with organisations of all types and sizes, from Global Corporations to Start Ups.

He takes a common sense and practical approach to solving his clients' challenges and works in and within a team of talented individuals to help him execute proven processes which continue to build sustainable, competitive advantage for companies across the globe.

Chapter 13: Corporate Myopia

I work with organisations that sell to other organisations to help them gain and retain strategic, competitive advantage. Sometimes that means a complete root and branch overhaul of their strategic direction, sometimes it's about aligning their sales and marketing operations and sometimes it is about pointing out the blindingly obvious!

In fact in reality, it is mainly about pointing out the obvious.

That's not because I'm really clever and they are really stupid; far from it. It is because organisations of all sizes are complicated. They did not start out being complicated; they just ended up that way.

The problem is that people have got used to it being like that. In fact they are so used to it that for many people, how the company operates internally takes up so much of their time and so much of their effort that actually what the company does for its customers does not really figure at all.

And I believe that it has really been one of the key learning points from the recent recession. Certainly in the organisations I have dealt with over the last 24 months or so. Companies of all sizes have lost sight of why they exist.

Many of the people who work in them have lost sight of who really pays their salary because they have been tied up in the myopia that is corporate survival.

For my customers, the last five to ten years have been about developing products and services in a kind of 'arms race' and vacuum. The focus has been on matching and meeting the competitors head on.

Very few organisations ever really stopped to think or look at what it is their customer really wants or needs or how they'd like it presented and delivered to them.

In my view that is for two reasons:
1. They consider that research and validating their offering with their customer(s) will be costly and time consuming and....

2. ...they secretly do not want to know! God forbid they might learn that what they had developed, built or invested in was of no interest at all to their customers!

So instead of investing in getting to know and understand their customer, they invested more and more in advertising and marketing to promote what they already 'had on the lorry'. And then wondered why it was becoming less and less effective....yet they kept on doing it.

It is a bit like the Emperor's New Clothes or the Elephant in the Room. No one actually dared point to out that asking the customer might be a good idea, after all, they had their corporate myopia to be getting on with.

I shocked several large organisations by showing them that getting to know what their customers really wanted actually made the whole process of selling things a good deal easier.

In marketing speak I showed them how to take horizontal (generic) propositions and make them vertical (industry specific).

I reminded them that people who work in other businesses are people first and a 'corporate decision maker' second. I then demonstrated how to build two-way dialogues and peer to peer conversations rather than sales pitches and company presentations.

Those that took me up on my advice stood out from their competitors, gained credibility in their chosen markets and had some remarkable and rapid sales success.

Those that did not, are wondering where all the business has gone. They have taken another long hard look at their competitors but they still can not see it anywhere.

I wonder when the light will come on for them; perhaps next year.

Mark Wickersham

Growing Your Way out of a Recession

Current Position:	Group Chief Executive
Qualifications:	FCA (Chartered Accountant)
Experience:	20 years post university experience
Email:	mark.wickersham@avn.co.uk
LinkedIn:	http://uk.linkedin.com/pub/mark-wickersham/14/a5a/35a
Twitter:	www.twitter.com/avn_accountants
Facebook:	www.facebook.com/AVN.ChangingTheNumbers
Website:	www.avn.co.uk
Links to Other Works:	www.FreeTaxResearch.co.uk/acc www.FreePricingBook.co.uk/acc www.TaxCreditsTips.co.uk
Contact Number:	+44 (0)845 226 2371

Mark is passionate about business success and helping accountants in practice take their business from where they are now to where they want to be.

As a qualified Chartered Accountant who set up his own accountancy practice in 1996 he has worked with *hundreds* of businesses and gained a real insight into what works and what doesn't work.

Since selling his practice in 2006, his focus is very much on helping accountants become much more profitable, through better systems, better leadership, better pricing strategies and being highly proactive (especially in the area of advanced tax planning). Mark is now Group Chief Executive of AVN, an association of approximately 250 accountants. Mark and his team have helped many of those firms add tens, and sometimes hundreds, of thousands of pounds onto their bottom line profit.

Chapter 14: Growing Your Way out of a Recession

August 2007.

That was the month when Northern Rock hit the news. Swiftly followed by the sharp fall in share prices.

It marked the beginning of the financial crisis.

It was shortly followed by the near collapse of the building industry. Retail followed. And it was inevitable that it would impact on accountancy firms before too long as the economy started its plunge into the worst recession, for most people, in living memory.

My company, AVN, is an association of accountants. About 250 of the UK's leading independent accountancy firms pay our company a monthly membership fee and in return we supply them with software, tools and resources to help them improve their clients' lives.

For example, we supply those accountants with business consulting tools so that they can help their clients improve their sales, profits and processes. We also research the very latest in tax planning so that AVN accountants have access to leading edge tax solutions to make sure that their clients do not have to pay a penny more than their fair share.

By 2007 AVN was eight years old and had been very successful.

But recession could prove to be costly. Firstly, we have a very high fixed cost base, which means that a small reduction in income could turn our profitable business into a loss-making one. Secondly, we are a discretionary spend for accountants. As accountancy firms are hit by the recession and look to cut their own costs, AVN membership is one of the costs they can easily remove.

So we were vulnerable.

In January 2008 the Board of Directors went away for our bi-annual two day strategic retreat. This is something we have done for many years and something we strongly recommend to our customers and in turn to their clients. It is a great opportunity to get away from the day-to-day running of the business and reflect on strategy.

The January 2008 strategic retreat was a key moment in our future; how to tackle the looming recession. Essentially we were faced with two choices:

CHOICE 1: We could have done what most businesses do in an economic downturn...cut costs to the bare minimum and hope to ride the storm

CHOICE 2: Look at the recession as a potential opportunity, grow the business and ensure it is stronger at the end of the recession that at its start.

We opted for choice number 2.

Fast forward three years and we have grown our team from 21 to 41 people. And our turnover has grown from about £2 million to just over £5 million.

So the recession has been good for AVN and a great learning experience. The three key things we have learned over the last few years have been:

Invest in great people

I have learnt over the years that the return on investment on good people is much higher than on inexperienced and low-salaried people. When you take on a school leaver, they might be cheap, but they come with a very resource-hungry need to be hand held. Whereas someone who is used to a salary of £50,000 is paid that for a reason, i.e. they are worth it and add much more than their salary cost in benefit to the business.

Although our salary cost has risen very significantly, we have a wonderful team of people. And recruiting expensive people does not have to carry risk when you use a bit of creativity.

For example, in July 2010 when we were building our marketing team, we came across a very experienced marketing person called Luke who was working freelance at the time. Luke was very expensive...although we have since found out he is worth every penny.

We had in mind a role where he visited our customers (firms of accountants) and provided them with marketing support in their office. But rather than commit to a very big fixed salary cost we offered to pay Luke a generous daily rate for the days that we needed him. He visited over 30 of our customers over a six week period, at the end of which we had received some fantastic feedback. They were so grateful that we cared enough about our customers to provide them with a free marketing consultancy session. Even better, a third of those customers agreed to pay for Luke to continue working for them. Luke's efforts in that six week period generated enough annual revenue to cover his annual salary.

It was a 'no-brainer' decision to offer Luke a full-time position within our marketing team. In the six months since Luke has been part of our team, he has helped to sell over £100,000 of marketing consultancy work to our customers.

Here's another great example. University graduates cannot find jobs at the moment. The local University in Sheffield was looking for companies to give graduates work experience. So we arranged for the University to supply us with an English graduate called Tom and all that we had to do was pay Tom's travel expenses. Tom worked in our marketing department for about two months, using his writing talents to help create marketing material and resources; it turned out that Tom has a real talent for writing. After a couple of months of only having to pay his travel costs, we were confident in his abilities and offered him a full time position in the marketing team.

<u>Invest time and resources to make marketing the most important function within the business</u>

Up until January 2008 we were OK - at best - with marketing. Since then we have dedicated focus to marketing and now have a marketing team of six people. As well as investing in people, we have invested heavily in training and support, for example in mid-2010 we invested in becoming part of NABO.

One of the main things we have learned and implemented in the last six months is the need to create processes for systematically getting qualified sales leads and better systems for converting customers into sales. We've used processes learned through our involvement with NABO, which consist of creating valuable offerings (referred to as the golden carrot) and then using a 'lead page' (basically a single web-page solely designed to capture contact details). We offer the golden carrot for free in return for contact details. Once we have captured the contact details, we build in auto-responders and other automated ways of keeping in regular contact with those leads to add more and more value, until a trusted relationship has been developed; they are then ready to buy. The author Seth Godin refers to this as 'permission marketing'.

By the end of 2010 we had written three books; something that is much easier to do than you may expect. Those books position our business as the experts in our field and a key part of our permission-based automated sales lead generation processes. In the first three months we have generated over 1,000 qualified sales leads from the process. As well as these sales leads our brand new marketing team have generated over £100,000 of new business from helping our customers with marketing.

As I write this, we now have more prospective customers booked onto our 2011 events than at this time of year in previous years. We use events to sell our membership packages and our conversion rates are a very consistent 30% across events. So we are very confident that as a result of the focus on marketing over the last nine months, the number of new members we sign up in 2011 will be our best ever and up by about 20% from 2010.

When you come across a great idea, take massive action and make it happen, as we did with the lead generation process.

I read lots of business books. I listen to lots of audio programmes. And I go on lots of courses. I do this because someone once said, "The day you stop learning is the day you stop earning." You can never know everything; you should continually invest in your own development.

However, equally important is the action you take as a result of learning. It doesn't matter how many notes you make whilst on a training course, if you don't take action you are wasting your time. So I always commit to taking one idea from every course I attend, every book I read and every audio programme I listen to and do something with it.

You don't have to take action with every idea...you won't have time. Just focus on doing one thing. And it's the systematic taking of action after every marketing course that we have been on over the last nine months that has led to me to write three books, create three lead generation systems and generate over 1,000 sales leads.

I fully expect that within the next year our turnover will grow from just over £5 million to just over £6 million. And given that we are a business with high fixed costs but negligible variable costs (i.e. the costs to serve an extra member are small), much of the extra turnover will drop to the bottom line.

So for AVN the recession has been a great learning experience. It's a time when new opportunities present themselves and it's easier to recruit great people because of redundancies elsewhere.

Peter Sage and Anya Navidski
Towards the Stars from the Depth of a Recession

Current Position:	Principal and VP Corporate Development at Space Energy
Email:	j.bromige@spaceenergy.com
LinkedIn:	http://ae.linkedin.com/in/petersage
	http://uk.linkedin.com/in/navidski
Twitter:	www.twitter.com/spaceenergy
Facebook:	www.facebook.com/SpaceEnergy
Website:	www.spaceenergy.com

Peter Sage is a serial entrepreneur with twenty years of experience in growing fast-paced enterprises. During that time he launched, operated and brought to success over a dozen companies, six of which were large enough to qualify for the Entrepreneur Organisation membership. His strength is in identifying and creating value propositions to leverage relationships and access required resources.

Most recently Peter founded Space Energy – a new generation power utility focused on generation and transmission of clean energy and commercialisation of Space Based Solar Power.

Anya Navidski has ten years of experience in situational assessment and developing entrepreneurial solutions from strategic planning to tactical execution. Until recently, Anya was a founder and CEO of Jumpstart-up, a seed philanthropy organisation that empowers social entrepreneurs to create scalable, financially viable enterprises.

Anya is recognised by TheNextWoman.com as a Catalyst Hero of 2009. She still acts as a Chief Strategy Officer for a number of Jumpstart-up Clients and has taught at MBA and executive MBA programmes on Enterprise Development and Business Planning.

Chapter 15: Towards the Stars from the Depth of a Recession

They say raising money is hard. Well, we did not know the meaning of hard until we tried to raise money for a multi-billion dollar project to put a giant solar power station into space and beam an uninterrupted supply of clean, renewable energy down to Earth.

Why bother? Because by 2100 forecasted energy demand will massively outstrip total current reserves of coal, oil and gas. Access to energy is already creating tensions. By the year 2100, this issue will be the main source of conflict and death around the world. That is unless we tap into Space Based Solar Power.

So here we were, raising money for a project that humanity desperately needs but which many believe belongs in a book by Ian Fleming and not in the Boardroom. In our defence, when we started, the recession had not yet started.

So the story begins with Peter Sage. Peter is a serial entrepreneur with twenty years experience in growing several successful fast-paced companies; an accomplished athlete; a long-standing member of the infamous Dangerous Sports Club and a nominee for the XL Nation 'Extraordinary Lives Award'. He was a little bored and looking for the next challenge.

Stage left enters someone who Peter affectionately calls 'The Mad Scientist' with the idea of building a giant solar power station in space as a solution to the CO2 and energy supply crisis. He went on to explain that this would be energy that can be delivered safely to any point on the planet, no matter how remote. This would be energy that can fuel economic growth, transform lives and power disaster relief. Fundamental technology for this has existed for forty years. However the economics have only just made this profitable.

Did this idea have scope for growth and contribution? Check. Was this project so enormous and challenging that the thought of it gave instant goose bumps? Check. So naturally, this got Peter's attention. Fast-forward five years and Peter is the Founder and Principal of Space Energy (www.SpaceEnergy.com).

So, the cost of putting a demo satellite into space is about $300m USD.

Then add $15bn USD for the first full-size commercial satellite. Plus massive potential impact on geopolitics, disaster relief and energy sustainability of our world.

Equals - no ordinary start-up.

....Oh, and then add the worst financial meltdown since the 1930s....

A rather extraordinary set of factors and yet while raising money for Space Energy, we found ourselves falling back on the very core principle that drives all business success: Value creation.

Even in the depths of a recession there is always money out there. It is harder to get to - the bar is higher, the constraints are tighter – but it is still there. The challenge is to figure out what value you create for which investors and then how to effectively communicate that to them.

The approach we took is actually very familiar to most people. It was based on the technology adoption lifecycle – a model developed by Joe M. Bohlen, George M. Beal and Everett M. Rogers at Iowa State University. Except instead of applying that concept to product users, we applied it to investors.

At first glance Space Energy seems like an impossible project. In fact, only a handful of people in the world truly understand the technology needed to make it happen. Thankfully most of them work for us. However this created a massive hurdle when approaching potential investors.

Faced with thousands of propositions and hungry for quick a quick return, they simply do not have the time to delve into the details and witness our credibility for themselves. So we started with the 'dreamers' – people who buy into the overall vision of Space Energy and who believe someone should try to see if Space Based Solar Power is feasible.

The primary principle here is simple, timeless and yet profound. People buy people before they buy their products, ideas and concepts. In other words, if you are committed to the very centre of your being and believe with every cell that this is going to happen regardless of the good opinion of others, then that certainty, that conviction, that level of total resolve, will recruit others who also want to believe.

And so it started. Friends, family, even people we met in bars were touched by the magic of the vision to the point where they wanted to get involved and support, either passively through investment or by joining the team. Of course, leaders go there first and this was documented by a personal investment of around $4m by Peter himself and matched over time by other 'believers' who became angel investors.

This money was used to formulate the business plan, set up the corporate infrastructure and recruit an A-Class team of experts who could make this happen and fund a gruelling average of 300+ days a year on the road for the senior team, meeting with potential investors, collaborators and purchasers. This included several world governments: visits to The White House, The Pentagon, The British Parliament and high-level meetings with government officials in China and India.

However, as the global economy slid further into turmoil, we needed to adapt and so we changed our play. After all, where do you get $15B to build an orbiting power station on a scale that has never been tried before?

Keep reading.

To reach the more conservative, more traditional, investors we focused their attention on more traditional, more familiar things. We introduced a new strategy and a new way of communicating.

This transition period was exactly why Anya Navidski joined the team and why it happened at this particular time. Anya is a slightly younger, female version of Peter – a one time Russian rhythmic gymnast, a black belt, ex-Director of the Centre for Entrepreneurship at a top global business school and a founder of Jumpstart-up, a venture focused on empowering early stage, financially viable, scalable social enterprises. However, unlike Peter her entrepreneurial path was first forged through more corporate, more disciplined environments of PwC project finance, NERA Economic Consulting and venture capital.

To help close the gap between the seemingly impossible task of raising millions of dollars for a futuristic Space Project, in 2009 Peter and his business partner, Stephen Tennsel, formed a traditional Ground Based Solar Division called Space Energy Terrestrial (SET).

Diverting some (though certainly not all) resources to SET allowed the company to stay true to its vision and mission while creating a balance sheet and a track record of execution of large, more traditional, infrastructure projects. But beyond all that, it let us through the door of some of the more traditional investors, giving them a chance to get to know the company.

The strategy paid off. Our first deal was an 80MW ground based solar farm in the US that came about as a result of befriending the largest Native American Indian tribe, The Navajo. With massive social problems but enormous amounts of land, the Navajo provided an excellent opportunity for value creation at many levels. Firstly, they got a profit share and an income for the tribe over a 20-year contract period tied to the power purchase agreement.

They also got local employment for the site and a sense of satisfaction that came with them positioning themselves as custodians of the environment just like their ancestors. A real win-win. Once complete, the 80MW will allow Space Energy to draw down enough money to finalise a comprehensive system definition study and self-fund their demonstrator programme. A huge feat in itself.

However, two world governments are already in negotiation to sign the power purchase agreement following that. This would be one of the largest commercial contracts ever signed, for $167B over a 20-year period for energy delivered from space at a preliminary price of 16 cents per kWh.

With a 15% bond and a consortium of banks to leverage the bond as a line of credit, it allows a draw down facility of over $20B, enough to build the first commercial Gigawatt satellite over a seven year period. Who says the impossible cannot be done? After all, Peter's main philosophy is that if he has any idea how he can achieve the goals he sets, when he sets them – they are clearly too small! Watch this 'space' to see how the story unfolds.

To summarise the funding lessons experienced during this recession:

1. Be flexible in your approach and adapt your funding model and strategy to each source of potential investment. Analyse each approach and result and make adjustments accordingly.

2. Start with the dreamers; other people who can be captivated by the vision. With these people their wallet will follow their heart if it's 100% bought in.

3. Explore alternative ways of funding through forming win-win partnerships. Remember, there is ALWAYS a way!

4. Stay true to your vision. People buy people before they buy their products, ideas and concepts. Leaders go there first and you need to demonstrate total commitment and conviction to your product before you can expect anyone else to.

5. Value Creation: Understand the true value that you create and communicate it passionately to potential investors in terms of what it means to them. They care a lot less about what's in it for you!

Kym Williams
Business and Risk Solutions

Current Position:	Owner of Business Risk Solutions
Qualifications:	Accounting Degree CPA Program
Experience:	14 years Infrastructure, Mining and Local Government
Email:	kym@businessandrisksolutions.com.au
LinkedIn:	http://au.linkedin.com/pub/kym-williams/9/105/543
Twitter:	www.twitter.com/BusRiskSolution
Facebook:	www.facebook.com/pages/Business-and-Risk-Solutions/186639773990?ref=ts
Website:	www.businessandrisksolutions.com.au
Contact Number:	+61 (0)8 8215 0332

Kym brings extensive experience to Business and Risk Solutions through his work in private and government organisations over the last fourteen years. In particular, Kym has held senior management roles in the areas of general management, commercial leadership and people management across a range of industries. Kym's previous role was as General Manager of South Australia and Western Australia for an international engineering and environmental firm. Prior to this, Kym held senior management roles in local government, across two large metropolitan councils in Adelaide, where he managed a range of commercial and governance portfolios.

In these roles, Kym led significant change management programs to develop long term sustainability in the key areas: finance, clients, people and culture. In performing his work, Kym combines his broad experience with an in-depth understanding of the industries in which his clients operate.

Chapter 16: Business and Risk Solutions

In August 2009 we started up a consulting firm called Business and Risk Solutions (BRS).

Before this, I had worked my way up to hold senior positions in local government and in the private sector. Although this journey was rewarding, my greatest aspiration had always been to create and run my own successful business. I was also adamant that I wanted to run a business that develops outstanding people along the way.

Prior to the commencement of Business and Risk Solutions, I received a lot of well meaning advice that starting a business during challenging times was unwise and full of potential pitfalls. People would say, "stay in your safe job Kym!", "Why would you leave a global organisation during these times?" and "Keep the titles and seniority you have and avoid the risk!"

Anyone who is an entrepreneur knows that once you have identified your dream, you cannot push it aside, regardless of the challenges and potential problems.

Our business has been able to thrive on these challenges by continually defying convention. In 16 months it has grown from four to 40 people, we have set up offices across Australia and we expect to exceed revenues of AU$5 million by this time next year. I could not be prouder of our team and the manner in which we deliver to our clients. A huge part of our success can be put down to the learning of key lessons early on in our journey – lessons that continue to shape the way we do business each and every day.
These lessons are:

1. Focus, Focus, Focus

In my experience, most companies tend to try to be everything to everyone. I feel this is the single biggest reason that most never realise their full potential. Our company spent a lot of time identifying the specific industries to target and determining what services we should provide to those industries. Through this we developed our vision, which is to be the leading management advisory firm in the local government, infrastructure and mining industries. This strategy alone allowed us to eliminate the distractions, imaginary leads and general confusion that would have significantly restricted progress towards our vision. As a general rule, we avoid pursuing any project that doesn't meet our industry criteria or our designated services. This harnesses the energy of our team for what matters most.

2. World Class Culture

Another major 'game changer' for BRS was the decision to strive towards having a world class culture. There is no doubt improvements to our culture have played a huge role in our success. We've worked hard to create a constructive culture where our staff is engaged and where staff behaviour is driven by a desire to gain personal and team satisfaction rather than being driven by fear. As a result, we have become more positive and proactive, with our day-to-day behaviour more aligned with realising our vision, rather than being reactive and busy but not productive. Results for our annual and monthly culture surveys reflect the improvements and have coincided with significant improvements to our bottom-line. Studies show that engaged staff tend to be five to six times more productive than disengaged staff. For us, I feel the change has been even greater - such are the benefits of engagement for our innovation, teamwork and collaboration as a business.

3. Remove negativity and promote positivity in every aspect of your business

Like every start-up company, we have faced significant challenges in our first 16 months. Perhaps one of the biggest has been the impact of negative people. I have found that attitude is largely shaped by the people you interact with. Interact with positive, optimistic people and this will pervade your approach to work and your life in general. Since making the decision to remove a major business partner and other sources of negativity from our business, we have thrived. Our lesson is: choose your attitude, choose who and how you interact and choose your mindset. This realisation means we focus on directing our energies towards positive clients, positive people and positive intentions. It is not overstating the matter to say this has transformed us as a business.

4. The golden principle in service organisations - repeat work and referrals

We have defied conventional wisdom with our approach to creating business in difficult times. The conventional approach is to focus on finding more clients, doing more marketing and more business development. In other words, work harder to bring in new clients and leads. Our approach sounds obvious but is often overlooked. We focused more on existing clients and looked for every way to deliver outstanding value and service to them on existing work, deliverables and commitments. In doing this, we consolidated our work backlog by gaining significant amounts of repeat work from existing clients.

In fact, one client recently engaged with us for the thirteenth major piece of work in the last twelve months. We have also learned that existing clients can be the best promoters of your business. Starting out as a new company meant that gaining exposure in the market was critical. Our clients have become our 'evangelists' in our target industries, promoting our company through talking about their experience with BRS in their business networks. This has led to a significant amount of work being gained through referrals and repeat work.

5. Reward bricklaying rather than heroic efforts

During challenging times, organisations tend to reward the employees who bring in the big sale, fix mistakes (often those that should have not been made in the first place) and hold the senior roles that supposedly matter the most. In contrast, we actively reward those employees who do the 'one percenters', such as planning well, collaborating effectively, showing genuine concern for the client and working as a team by sharing the load. Being proactive to help grow the business is another critical bricklaying act, especially in a competitive marketplace such as our own. Our reinforcement of this behaviour through praise and recognition has embedded them in the daily habits of our employees.

6. World class systems

The final lesson we have learned through our journey is that you need to set your business up to succeed rather than to simply exist. A large part of this is optimising the systems and processes of the organisation. Initially, we spent considerable time designing our world-class collaboration systems. Typically, employees will spend over 40 hours a week using a company's systems and processes.

If they are intuitive to use and facilitate collaboration, this frees time up to be creative. If they are cumbersome and inefficient, the systems are a constant weight on the experience and productivity of your employees. We wanted our staff to be able to access everything they needed – anywhere, anytime. Also, our systems have been incorporated into well-known and simple products (such as Microsoft Outlook) to ensure all staff can operate them effectively with minimal training. Having accessible and intuitive systems facilitates tremendous collaboration and is a major point of difference between BRS and our competitors, allowing BRS to produce three times as many proposals as the typical consulting firm of comparable size without compromising quality.

David Leyshon

Recessions can Provide Opportunities as Well as Threats

Current Position:	Managing Director , CBS Butler
Qualifications:	BSc Combined Studies, Applied Geology and Oceanography Msc Applied Remote Sensing
Experience:	23 years in Recruitment
Email:	dleyshon@cbsbutler.com
LinkedIn:	http://uk.linkedin.com/in/davidleyshon1964
Twitter:	www.twitter.com/CBSbutler
Facebook:	www.facebook.com/home.php#!/CBSbutlerUK
Website:	www.cbsbutler.com
Contact Number:	+44 (0)1737 822000

David Leyshon is the majority shareholder and Managing Director of CBSbutler, a privately owned technical and engineering recruitment company with a turnover of over £35m. He led a management buy-out of Butler International's UK arm in 2003 and acquired CBS Appointments in 2004 - the merged companies re-branded to CBSbutler.

He is married with one son, originally hails from Wales and is an avid rugby fan.

Chapter 17: Recessions can Provide Opportunities as Well as Threats

CBSbutler is a specialist engineering and technical recruitment consultancy serving niche markets within defence, energy, pharmaceuticals, healthcare and aerospace internationally. The company provides contract/temporary staffing; permanent search and selection; managed services and testing and assessment services.

70% of the business is undertaken on preferred supplier status with FTSE 100 companies and 40% of the business is conducted overseas.

Despite the downturn, we've had consistent annual growth since I led a management buyout in 2003. In 2010, for the third consecutive year, we delivered a **50% increase** in operating profit resulting in a record trading year for the company (**£1.2 million in 2009, £1.8 million in 2010**).

So how did we do it?

Well it wasn't easy and I can't pretend that the recession didn't impact upon us heavily. The downturn obviously caused a significant reduction in demand for all recruitment services and we were no exception. This presented two major barriers – a reduction in demand for our services and the need to cut costs.

However, I have worked through recessions before and although this one was the worst in living memory, the lessons I had learned from past downturns served me well and I'd like to share some of them:

Recognise the need to make cuts - do it right and do it quick.

No-one wants to put people out of work, that's a given. But business owners have to make tough decisions for the greater good and I have learned that it is pointless delaying the inevitable. At the end of 2008, we had to take the decision to consolidate the business in light of the slowing demand and the need to rationalise the cost base.

We had always been very transparent with our financial reporting. We share our goals, plans and results through an annual 'kick off' company meeting as well as quarterly communication meetings. This was incredibly helpful in enabling our staff to understand the consequences of NOT taking action. It also meant that there were very few surprises.

- In December 2008 the Directors made a number of presentations to staff, outlining the challenges to the business and the proposed countermeasures
- In February 2009 the business had shown further deterioration and the senior management undertook an audit of all staff performance to assess the health of the business – objectively scoring each individual
- The Directors then announced that costs needed to be reduced providing detailed reasoning and that a full consultation process would be undertaken, advising certain staff that roles were at risk
- During all stages, senior management and directors made themselves readily available for one-to-one meetings and adopted a very open and honest two-way dialogue
- A single round of redundancies took place which was vital in order to minimise the impact on morale and to avoid costly retention issues.

Focus everyone left on the future – and motivate them

From there we could then concentrate on recovery and growth; what we didn't want were 'unhappy stayers' so we held meetings with all staff to set out the recovery plans and the positive impact of the actions taken. This provided a lot of reassurance. We also looked at how we were rewarding people and whether our existing reward systems would help grow the business.

Like many other sales based organisations, our people had historically been rewarded on hard numbers – i.e. a commission based on the fees that they billed. This is an approach that can lead to a purely monetary focus often at the expense of softer skills such as teamwork, managing change, problem solving and customer focus.

Consequently, we wanted to introduce a new appraisal and bonus system that combined both hard financial objectives (including sales revenues) but also key behaviours.

Namely:

- Drive for results
- Developing self and others

- Teamwork
- Problem solving and decision making
- Customer focus
- Managing change
- Planning and organising

The outcomes have led our consultants to develop far more holistic skills and competencies. We have seen step improvements in teamwork such as a **36% increase** in inter-team placements and crucially our **gross profit per employee rose by 10%.**

Add more value

Another impact of the recession was that clients really raised their expectations of service levels. In short, when recessions hit customers want more bang for their buck. Fact! Our policy was to stick to our key principles of staying close to both clients (employers) and candidates (jobseekers) and offer them extra value, not just as a way of getting through the difficult times but as a catalyst for future growth and success.

Our knowledge of our core markets has been instrumental in reassuring passive candidates (those who are not necessarily looking for a career move, but who may do so if the opportunity arises) about the jobs market and their possible next employer.

One of the major features of the recession for us was that we encountered a passive candidate community who were sitting tight because they thought a move would see them worse off. Staying close to these people and keeping in regular touch about the market and hiring organisations has meant that they have been able to move quickly when the right opportunity has arisen.

We continued working with our clients to improve their business performance through value added offerings. In a recession our client's main concerns were around retention, not recruitment, and so addressing those issues meant that again, we were able to differentiate ourselves.

We continued working with our clients to improve their business performance through value added offerings. In a recession our clients' main concerns were around retention not recruitment and so addressing those issues meant that again, we were able to differentiate ourselves.

The values added included initiatives such as staff satisfaction surveys in client organisations, resource planning and assessment centre design in conjunction with HR and Production Managers and training managers in competency based interviewing skills. All these not only helped us to differentiate ourselves from the competition but also raised levels of customer service.

As a result, we have achieved **93% customer retention** and acquired **33 new accounts** delivering an annualised **24% increase** in new business. In our customer satisfaction surveys we achieved **a 100% satisfaction rating;** of those, over **60% gave us a very satisfied rating**. Additionally **92%** of our clients rated us as more effective than our competitors.

<u>**Embrace new ideas**</u>

Like many organisations having experienced a slowdown in demand and increased competition in many of our sectors, it was vital to embrace new ways of developing business. While many recruiters have dabbled in social media tools like LinkedIn in order to source new leads, we took a different tack and established a number of invitation only niche groups which excluded any competitors.

This allowed us to not only harness the influential sector contacts but also to build an accelerated presence in new markets. By excluding other recruiters we have built a unique capability and knowledge which we can leverage for competitive advantage. Through these means we have developed revenue streams in the following new niches:

- ***Cyber security***
- ***FRES armoured vehicle***
- ***Healthcare informatics***
- ***In-flight entertainment***
- ***CBRN (Chemical, Biological, Radioactive, Nuclear)***

The new venture areas have delivered **c. £3.2million in revenue** and **c. £1.2million in gross profit** in 2010 from a standing start with significant potential for growth. In addition, there has been a substantial saving in job board advertising costs (c. £60,000+ per annum) as candidate generation for the new business has primarily been generated by new members joining the groups.

Encourage innovation

One of the most valuable lessons I have learned from past recessions is that to really encourage innovation, you have to give people the permission to experiment – and accept that experimentation can lead to mistakes – but it can also lead to that 'next big thing'. I firmly believe that innovation is one of the keys to both survival and success and that change, particularly when it is forced upon us, is an opportunity that can drive real innovation.

We hold a quarterly innovations forum which provides the opportunity for staff from each operational area to work together in creating ideas and solving problems within the business. This two hour session every three months is facilitated by the Quality Manager and the outputs are fed into management meetings.

Key examples of ideas from staff include:

- An automated skills coding facility which was developed with an external technology partner and has **saved 8% of working hours** by consultants no longer needing to manually code
- Implementation of an automated job posting system which has resulted in significant time savings
- Implementation of a new return on investment measurement system for improving the quality of advertisements, which has resulted in a **30% better return**.

Follow the money

While I would always be an advocate of sticking to what you know, we now live in a shrinking world where organisations of any size can operate in a global market place. As a result of the slowdown in demand within the domestic market, we decided to pursue increased overseas business in robust high growth countries and we increased our export business from **23% of total revenue in 2009 to around 40% in 2010**. Notable successes have included:

- The establishment of a Qatari registered company in July 2010. From a standing start this has developed **sales in excess of £5million**.
- Expansion of our aviation maintenance and overhaul recruitment division where we have developed **£7million**

in sales from countries such as Brazil, UAE, Korea, Vietnam and Hong Kong.

Evolve – and reap the rewards

I don't believe that anything we have done is rocket science but it has allowed us to not only survive the recession but also thrive at a time when a lot of our competitors struggled. I think it's about accepting that change is inevitable and reacting positively to that change rather than hoping it will all go away.

There was a terrific advertisement that Samsung ran for a new phone. It's worth a watch as it sums up perfectly what I believe:

http://www.youtube.com/watch?v=s8tWLEsLpxs

"Waiting doesn't get the pay rise," it declares. "Waiting never gets to the front, never finishes first. And then there's impatience, impatience got us faster cars, microwaves and remote controls. Patience is knowing you're bored but doing nothing about it - impatience is a virtue!"

Never a truer word.

Steve Olsher

The Recession's Big, Fat, Silver Lining

Current Position:	Founder of Bold Enterprises
Qualifications:	MBA
Experience:	More than 20 years of starting, developing, and fostering the growth of new business ventures.
Email:	steve@steveolsher.com
LinkedIn:	www.linkedin.com/in/steveolsher
Twitter:	www.twitter.com/#!/steveolsher
Facebook:	www.facebook.com/#!/profile.php?id=1322713096
Website:	www.steveolsher.com
Links to Other works:	www.amazon.com/Journey-You-Step-Step-Becoming/dp/0984479600/ref=tmm_pap_title_0
Contact Number:	+1 773-914-4001

Steve Olsher is the author of the 2010 Self-Help Book of the Year, *Journey To You: A Step-by-Step Guide to Becoming Who You Were Born to Be*, founder of The Reinvention Workshop, host of Reinvention Radio, Co-Founder and Chairman of San Francisco-based Liquor.com and President of Chicago-based real estate development firm, Bold Development. For more information, please visit www.steveolsher.com

Chapter 18: The Recession's Big, Fat, Silver Lining

2008 through 2010 were very challenging both personally and professionally. I am a lifelong entrepreneur with ventures in various industries including consulting, the internet (Liquor.com), real estate (Bold Development) and personal development (Author of *Journey To You: A Step-by-Step Guide to Becoming Who You Were Born to Be* and founder of The Reinvention Workshop). Therefore it is fair to admit that during these three years, to put it mildly, I got hammered (and no I'm not referring to overindulging on the fine products found at Liquor.com).

As they say, "sometimes you're the nail and sometimes you're the hammer." There is no doubt that, throughout this period, I was the nail...and it hurt.

Money went out. More money went out. Little money came in. The faucet that I had become accustomed to drinking from had not only gone dry but I'm convinced that someone sneaked in during the middle of the night and removed the spigot.

In late 2007, my real estate portfolio of commercial and residential properties was worth more than $50M and produced a net annual cash flow of nearly $250k. By the beginning of 2008, however, the market's shift towards the trenches was in full swing.

In the subsequent three years of pain, the value of my holdings dropped by more than 30% and many properties, which once reflected viable cash-cows overflowing with milk, were now grazing aimlessly and draining funds on a monthly basis. Internet sales and supporting ad revenue came to a screeching halt. And my six-figure personal development consulting business that used to represent my monthly bread and butter (and we're talking a nice, thick, crusty bread with homemade, whipped, pure, creamy, salty, delicious, buttery goodness) came to a virtual standstill.

What I came to learn from these tumultuous times is that with each obstacle alternate routes of travel are opened. However, in order to take advantage of the shifting marketplace and potential gains found in uncharted territory, personal and business reinvention was required...and inevitable.

Aside from the obvious, such as tightening the belt and shifting focus to that of what our customers actually need as opposed to that which we felt they wanted, we retooled our entire business. We began to shift from profit being the sole motive for our existence to that of not only making a living doing what it is that we are compelled to do, but also heeding our personal and professional responsibility for improving our community, our environment and our world.

By the end of 2010, it became clear that the Recession offered three specific opportunities that are simply not available when times are good. Historically, these recession-based keys to success have been leveraged to create more sustainable, game-changing businesses that have generational impact than have ever been created during times of prosperity.

The three recession-based keys to success are:

1. Affordable Resources

During boom times, it is a simple economic tenet of supply and demand that things are more expensive. Real estate (both for sale and for lease), infrastructure, equipment, durable goods etc. cost more and their price tags reflect the peak of the value cycle.

When times are tough, however, landlords are virtually giving away space for lease. Banks are desperate to dump REOs (properties they've taken back from owners who have not paid their mortgages) off their balance sheets. Computers, cars, office equipment, machinery etc. can be bought for pennies on the dollar as sellers need to raise cash. And financing big-ticket items and negotiating beyond the point of relative discomfort is commonplace.

In our business, we were able to lease office space for less than 50% of the landlord's asking price for the same space just two years prior, purchase computer equipment at ridiculously low prices and hire service-oriented companies at rates that would have previously been considered laughable.

2. Cheaper Labour

When times are tough, people are more accessible, both in terms of desired compensation and availability. Unemployment is obviously higher and skilled/high-end labour are often the first people let go when cutbacks hit. Because of this, folks that used to make $100k during boom times are now happy to accept $50k just to have money coming in the door. Whether or not they were actually worth $100k in the first place is a debate for another day.

In our business, we were able to negotiate fantastic deals with a number of very skilled personnel. People that, frankly, we would not have previously been able to afford were open to discussions, sold on our vision and are now onboard for the duration with the understanding that, as our business grows, their compensation will grow accordingly.

One of our current key team members, who had previously been making $125k a year, joined our crew for less than $50k. While the short-term pain to his pocketbook is apparent, the long-term potential for contributing in a meaningful way to a game-changing organisation is, in his words, "priceless."

3. Availability of Financing

Believe it or not, financing has been widely available for the right business models, teams and ideas during the recession. The banks that got us into this financial debacle are receiving huge pressure from the Feds to open their purse strings and get us out of this mess. Angel investors, venture capital funds and institutional monies are quietly being stockpiled and are ready to pour into 'the next big thing.'

While it may seem counter-intuitive, when times are tough money sits idle on the sidelines and the right opportunity can quickly land attractive financing. During boom times, money managers compete with one another for the same investment options yet, because there are so many investment opportunities, terms for the borrower are actually less desirable when more investment opportunities exist.

Therefore, when times are rough, there are fewer entrepreneurial pioneers willing to launch new businesses and put their necks on the line. Given this, and the fact that money managers only get a return on their investment when they actually write cheques, borrowers are able to negotiate more aggressive terms.

It has continually been proven that the best time to launch a new business is when everyone else is petrified to do so. This period of time, where the business can test its model, try various initiatives and build momentum, gives the business a meaningful head start when the market 'turns', given that their wheels are already in motion and they're in a solid position to take full advantage of the upswing.

In our business, we were able to open meaningful lines of credit (more than $500k for our real estate business), attract angel and institutional investors for Liquor.com ($1.25M) and carve out desirable terms that would not have been available had we been competing in an environment of multiple investment options.

Business, like life, is all about perspective. The recession holds a big, fat, silver lining that can substantially benefit your endeavour, if you choose to capitalise on and pursue the pending opportunities.

When times are good, the glass is half-full. When times are bad, your glass can overflow...Cheers to your future!

Jon Clarke

Succeed by Being Remarkable and Ignore the Doom Merchants

Current Position:	Managing Director
Experience:	17 years business experience: B2B Marketing
Email:	jon@360businessmarketing.co.uk
LinkedIn:	http://uk.linkedin.com/in/jonlclarke
Twitter:	www.twitter.com/jonlclarke
Website:	www.360businessmarketing.co.uk

Jon Clarke is Managing Director and co-owner of 360 Business Marketing Ltd, a b2b multi-channel marketing and lead generation agency. Jon has over 17 years experience within b2b sales, marketing and business strategy and has worked with a number of businesses including IBM, BEA Systems, Reed Business Information, Astra Zeneca, Ingram Micro and ACCO Brands.

Jon is also a successful entrepreneur and has owned and managed a series of start-ups and SMEs. Jon's expertise lies within building multi-channel go-to-market strategies for b2b organisations, bridging the gap between marketing & sales and delivering maximum return on investment.

Chapter 19: Succeed by Being Remarkable and Ignore the Doom Merchants

A recession is no time to bury your head in the sand. Be brave and embrace change if change is needed!

I will never forget the day that Duncan Bannatyne said:

"If the markets tell you to sell, buy. If you are advised to turn left, turn right. Ignore anyone that advises you not to set up a business during a recession."

These sound bites resonated in my head when I realised that the marketing business I was then involved with had to change. The agency was heavily focused on lead generation for b2b companies within the IT and manufacturing sectors.

Sometime in 2008, the business started to experience a steady decline in customer demand for new projects. Marketing budgets were under attack and it became rapidly clear that 'panic' was the order of the day.

After further investigation into the reasons behind the slowdown, we established that businesses were extremely worried about the financial outlook, perhaps heavily influenced by the media. Although not every customer was experiencing a direct reduction in customer demand, fear had plainly set in.

I could see that immediate action was needed to stem the tide of our business decline. But I also saw it as an opportunity to stimulate acceptance of a need for change with the agency's stakeholders.

There were two other key factors influencing my desire for change:

- Our marketing agency was often treated as a commodity service by our customers. There was little scope for adding further value, margins were squeezed, competition was fierce and up-selling opportunities were minimal.
- The world of marketing was changing. Traditional marketing techniques such as telemarketing were becoming less effective. Customers were seemingly no longer responding to outbound sales and marketing messages as before. Instead, they were increasingly

researching products and solutions online and via trusted networks.

The economic downturn only seemed to amplify this change in market dynamics. All of a sudden, phrases such as 'return on marketing investment' and 'bridging the gap between marketing and sales' became the new watchwords of marketing industry thought leaders. However, it was also apparent that many marketers and marketing agencies were far removed from sales. For too many marketers' return on investment was chiefly about the number of clicks on a web advert or the volume of email broadcasts delivered each month. There was little understanding as to what impact – if any – these actions contributed to sales.

I had already suspected that changing market dynamics should persuade my agency to change its approach and proposition. The economic climate made it essential to act swiftly and with purpose to avoid the worst possible conclusion, one no business owner ever wishes to contemplate!

My first step involved research. To help identify new trends in thinking around business and marketing strategy, market trends and customer behaviour, I began to track as many credible and relevant institutions and high profile industry leaders as I could. On my path to enlightenment, I came across Seth Godin, a truly inspirational thinker and someone that transformed my approach to the world of marketing.

If you do nothing else after reading this chapter then I urge you to buy a copy of one of his books, 'Purple Cow'. Its premise is to encourage you to create new ways to manage sales and marketing within your business *by being remarkable*. The old ways of marketing are dead. Being safe is too risky. This resonated with the position I found our business was in and helped me to muster the courage and strategy to implement a new way of thinking.

However, I resisted any temptation to radically change the entire business. The new strategy was built upon the existing telemarketing model but with an added 'multi-channel' lead generation capability. This was based upon a number of key principles identified from my research.

1. Go where the customers are; the places where they source products or solutions to problems
2. Understand their buying process and what influences them to buy a specific brand or choose one product over another
3. Recognise that everyone is different. People respond differently to sales and marketing messages delivered across various communication channels such as email, web, social media and telephone
4. Marketing must be linked to sales. Therefore measuring return on investment from marketing activity is essential.

The next stage for our business was to join forces with truly exceptional business partners. By doing so, we obtained expertise that we could never afford in-house and enabled us to keep our overheads low. This also created credibility with our customers and prospects almost overnight and, crucially, reduced the risk of failure. But the most important aspect of these relationships was to create a commercial model that enabled our business and our partners to re-sell one another's services as part of a multi-channel lead generation agency model.

It worked. The new model generated a 30% year-on-year revenue growth, whilst only increasing our headcount from nine to 15 staff. Over the next two years we generated between four and six times greater ROI for our customers and increased our net profit by 10%. It helped us to win new business with a number of major corporations and market leading brands. We managed to organically grow our customer base from just eight customers pre-recession to twenty-eight over the subsequent two years without any external investment.

Perhaps most significantly, our new approach delivered a new commercial model into our business. We migrated away from reliance upon small tactical customer campaigns that resulted in peaks and troughs of revenue and evolved towards long-term contracts that produced annuity-based revenue streams, required relatively less overhead to manage and enabled us to forge long-term commercial relationships at board level - all during the worst economic climate since records began.

We built a remarkable business, but implementing change presented a number of challenges. One of the main lessons I learned was that people often fear and resist change. Expectations and concerns with my peers and staff had to be carefully managed along the way and I often had to modify my approach. I quickly realised that, for some, change forced people out of their comfort zone. This needed careful and constant management. I focused on the positives and avoided the negative risks of not changing. Luckily, this seemed to work.

Implementing such a dramatic change across the business also required a degree of investment – at a time when support from the banks had completely evaporated. This forced our business to partner with external agencies, but also persuaded us to source an affordable marketing campaign delivery software tool that helped our business to automate many of our processes and keep our headcount low. Most importantly, it enabled us to analyse and report on exactly where the return on marketing investment was located for each campaign.

Looking back at what we have delivered in such a short time and during a major recession, we can be proud of what we have achieved. It shows that doing the right thing for the right reasons - following sound business principles and best practice can really make a difference - no matter what the economic climate. If you are committed to positive change, and pick the right strategy for your business, you will succeed.

Edward Peppitt

The Dangers of Complacency and Over-Confidence

Current Position:	Owner & CEO of GetPublished.tv
Qualifications:	BA(Hons) Member of Chartered Institute of Marketing (MCIM) Member of Institute of Directors (MIOD)
Experience:	20+ years experience in the publishing sector
Email:	ed@getpublished.tv
LinkedIn:	http://uk.linkedin.com/in/edwardpeppitt
Twitter:	www.twitter.com/edthepublisher
Website:	www.getpublished.tv
Links to Other Works:	Author of seven business and computing books published by Hodder & Stoughton
Contact Number:	+44 (0)1273 257007

Ed was Sales & Marketing Director at Letts Educational, the market-leading publisher of home study revision guides, until going freelance. He has worked as a consultant with many of the leading magazine and book publishers including Emap, Hodder, Harper Collins and Oxford University Press.

He is the author of seven books, all published by Hodder & Stoughton. He reviews book proposals and manuscripts for two of the UK's leading publishers and runs his own publishing company, Balloon View, which publishes books and home study courses for some of the world's leading personal development experts.

Ed runs regular publishing workshops for unpublished writers.

Chapter 20: The Dangers of Complacency and Over-Confidence

Between 2007 and 2009 I had established an events and publishing business that was working successfully to a very precise and reliable formula. It was a simple model, but an effective one.

I would identify a renowned expert in the field of personal development or alternative health. I would invite them to speak, using a number of London theatres with spare capacity as interesting yet cost-effective venues. We would promote the event to our own prospects, as well as to the speaker's own mailing list. The paying audience would cover all costs, including the cost of filming the event and turning it into a home study course. This would then provide us with a valuable residual income.

In 2008 we ran six events, each of which had delivered us a paying audience of between 150 and 250 people. The events were profitable in themselves; they also provided the content for a range of audio CD, DVD and home study products. We flew over Janet Switzer (the marketer behind *Chicken Soup for the Soul*) and Dr Roger Callahan (the pioneer behind *Thought Field Therapy*) from the USA. And we also hosted events for the cream of the crop from the UK, including Jack Black and Pete Cohen.

I remember the period when Northern Rock collapsed and when people first started to talk about the 'credit crunch'. Yet during this period my events appeared to be unaffected. As 2008 drew to a close, I remember friends and colleagues making a move away from live events. They were telling me how difficult they were finding it to 'get bums on seats'.

Some switched to online events – using teleseminars and webinars to present the same content but charging £10 to attend online, rather than £100 to attend a live event.

Other colleagues in the industry were pulling out of events altogether, changing tack completely. My former business partner, Jonathan Jay, persevered, although his model involved delivering regular events free of charge and this was not something I could afford to do.

But even as 2009 approached, I was not at all worried. I advertised an event about getting published in January and sold 120 tickets in three days. Things seemed just fine. I remember assuming that personal development was immune to the downturn from recession. With hindsight, I was being complacent and naïve.

The crash for us didn't arrive until June 2009. I advertised a second publishing event for the first weekend of June and invited the legendary healer, painter and leading expert in kinesiology, Dr John Diamond to come to the UK for the third weekend of the month.

My publishing event sold just 25 tickets and Dr. Diamond 35. It was a far cry from the dependable 150 ticket sales that I had relied on up until then. And I was already committed to venues that could hold 200. It came as a huge surprise to me despite all the signs having been there for months.

I saw the events through. I gave away free tickets to make both events appear better attended...but even this wasn't easy. I discovered, very quickly, that the recession was affecting not only what people were prepared to pay but also how they chose to spend their time.

The effect was dramatic. Suddenly, people were choosing not to give up a Saturday to attend an event, no matter what the calibre of the speaker. Prospects were phoning to ask when the DVDs would be available, rather than to book a ticket. In short, the audience was not there to cover our costs; for the first time our events became unprofitable and we needed to rely on the products that we created, not simply to provide ongoing income but first and foremost to cover the shortfall.

These were sobering times. I heard from others in the industry that certain speakers were still thriving. But on further investigation I found that these were the ones who ran free events. Looking at my own situation at the time, I had neither the capital nor the confidence to stage such events.

I had few back end products to sell at the events themselves, because my whole strategy depended on the event to create the products in the first place. In any case, I have never liked the model where speakers run free events and then spend them selling products and services to their audience. With hindsight, my business was set back by twelve months at least. I ran no events at all in 2010, choosing instead to rationalise and focus on the marketing of the products that we had created already. We built a solid, reliable relationship with Amazon for our books and some of our DVD courses. It cost us margin (Amazon demands 60% trade discount) but earned us some breathing space.

The recession also forced us to look at ways to develop quality products on a smaller budget. The marketplace was moving steadily towards video based training products, but to me it seemed challenging to develop high quality video materials without investing heavily in their production.

In particular, one element always seemed to make a low budget online video easy to spot: the quality of the sound. So many friends and colleagues would tell me that all I needed to do was to buy a £100 Flip camera. Yet in every video I watched, the sound was hollow, distant and tinny. Not the quality I wanted to be associated with.

It was sound though which gave us the way forward. We installed an audio sound studio in our office and we began to develop audio-based materials. Our authors and speakers would come to us, spend half a day in the studio and emerge with an edited, professional 60-minute audio product. They returned regularly and with very little effort or expense we would develop an audio course or programme that we could market jointly to our respective lists. We worked with our partners to build relationships with Audible and iTunes, which gave us other routes to market.

By the end of 2010, I feel we had turned a corner. We've started to put on events again, although this time they are more modest affairs and each one must pay its way. The sound studio is in almost constant use. We are even starting to develop some simple, video-based materials using cameras that work with our professional, wireless microphones.

So what of the lessons I have learned from the recession? I remember clearly when a diagnosis of Multiple Sclerosis prompted me to make dramatic, permanent lifestyle changes. I stopped smoking, gave up tea and coffee, altered my diet and exercised more regularly. But in reality, I was only doing things that I had been promising myself I would do for years.

The changes prompted by the recession were no different. With hindsight, I ran a business that relied on a single tactic. For as long as it worked, it was fine. But the recession exposed the flaw and prompted me to change the way we created products, forced me to work in partnership with retailers and led me to develop joint venture deals and partnerships.

All things that I should have put in place regardless of the trading conditions.

Liggy Webb

How to Support a Happy and Healthy Workplace

Current Position:	Author, Presenter & Managing Director of The Learning Architect
Qualifications:	CIPD – Thames Valley University Business Coaching Diploma B.A.S.I.E Learning & Development Modular Positive Psychology United Nations Consultant Accredited Workplace Wellness Consultant
Experience:	20 years post education experience
Email:	liggy@thelearningarchitect.com
LinkedIn:	http://uk.linkedin.com/pub/liggy-webb/5/4a7/643
Twitter:	www.twitter.com/liggyw
Website:	www.liggywebb.com www.thelearningarchitect.com
Links to Other Works:	www.amazon.co.uk – *The Happy Handbook, How Work Wonders Workplace Wellness*
Contact Number:	+44 (0) 1242 700027

Liggy Webb is widely respected as a leading expert in the field of *Modern Life Skills and Workplace Wellness*. As a presenter, consultant and author she is passionate about her work and improving the quality of people's lives. She is the founding director of The Learning Architect a consortium of niche industry experts. Liggy has developed a range of techniques and strategies to support individuals and organisations to cope more effectively and successfully with modern living and the demands and challenges of life in the twenty tens and beyond. As a consultant with the United Nations she travels extensively and has recently returned from Afghanistan which she describes as her biggest life education to date!

Chapter 21: How to Support a Healthy and Happy Workplace

There is a certain irony that in challenging and changing times when people most need the support of their organisations, it is also the time when people's investment budgets are dramatically slashed in order to save money! A false economy indeed as stress increases, mental and physical health declines and sickness absenteeism figures rocket.

During the recession, a report to the Government in the UK highlighted that the overall cost to the economy of sickness absenteeism totalled £100 billion. The number one reason was due to work-related stress.

One of the key lessons I have learnt is that an investment in the physical, psychological and environmental health of people in the workplace is essential. It is not about what some cynics deem as 'fluffy stuff' but is indeed business critical. Helping people to stay happy and healthy is fundamental to business resilience when times get tough. As someone said to me, during the recession most organisations tend to do one of three things: they will dive, survive or thrive. Despite the fact that morale is challenged, a business that recognises the importance of supporting their people will thrive.

Depression and mental health has become an increasingly topical issue with the World Health Organisations predicting that depression will be the second biggest global form of illness by 2020. Mental health charities imply that one in four people will be affected during their lifetime.

As an International Consultant with the United Nations, my work takes me to some fairly disparate destinations; from New York to Beirut to Afghanistan and yet the one commonality that exists in every workplace is stress. The most concerning issue of all, is that it is contagious. There is now scientific evidence known as 'neural mirroring' that shows we can actually catch each other's 'stress germs'. Recession, cut backs and looming redundancies provide a breeding ground for negativity and psychological discomfort.

The challenges that face us in times of recession and change, such as finding purpose, defining ourselves and managing stress, are numerous and complex. In order to address them effectively, practical and useful strategies surrounding Modern Life Skills help people significantly in the workplace to cope more positively and effectively. A holistic approach to 'Workplace Wellness' tackles physical, psychological and environmental impact.

My research has been greatly influenced by The United Nations Educational, Scientific and Cultural Organization (UNESCO) who divide life skills into subsets of categories which include the following:

- Learning 'to know' (cognitive abilities) which involve decision-making, problem-solving and critical thinking skills.
- Learning 'to be' (personal abilities) which involve skills for increasing internal control, managing feelings and managing stress.
- Learning 'to live together' (interpersonal abilities) which involve interpersonal communication skills, negotiation and refusal skills, empathy, co-operation, teamwork and advocacy skills.

There is, however, no definitive list of life skills and all of the above include the psychosocial and interpersonal skills generally considered important. The choice and emphasis on different skills will vary according to the individual and circumstances. Though the list suggests these categories are distinct from each other, many skills are used simultaneously in practice.

Ultimately, the interplay between the skills is what produces powerful behavioural outcomes. Whilst the United Nations' subset of categories for life skills lays out an excellent basis to begin with; there are, of course, other life skills that are required to address a more holistic approach to modern living that incorporates the physical, psychological and spiritual aspects of life.

Having now spent the past few years conducting research across a wide range of organisations focusing on stress and 'Workplace Wellness', I am heartened to see some very responsible actions and transformations taking place.

There are some excellent examples of organisations that actively promote healthy practices and raise awareness by providing programmes within the workplace to encourage healthier behaviours.

Organisations that help raise awareness for healthier working practices and take responsibility by supporting their people, are finding that they are being rewarded by a reduction in absenteeism, better morale, long-term loyalty and a sense of corporate community. These factors clearly contribute to a far happier, more productive and thriving workplace.

The Stats

According to the Cornell University Institute for Health and Productivity Studies in America, employers can save between $300 and $450 annually per employee as a result of reduced health expenditures from an annual wellness investment of $100 to $150 per employee.

In the UK the cost of absenteeism to the economy is £100 billion and studies by the department of health indicate that for every £1 that employers spend on wellness programme there is just over £6 return on investment in reduced absenteeism and stress related illness.

Some case study examples of organisations who have implemented wellness programmes include:

Metropolitan Police: Stress related absence levels fell from 10.2 days per annum to less than one day annually per officer.
Parcel Force Worldwide: Sickness absence was reduced by a third saving the business £55 million.
Stockport Council: 44% fewer working days lost through sickness absence equating to £1.58 million.

So what are the lessons that I have learned?

Well most certainly that responsible businesses can minimise the impact the recession has on the health of their workers by taking practical steps to address the key issues.

A happy and healthy workforce is a more productive and resilient workforce. Here are some of the valuable benefits to implementing workplace wellness initiatives which have helped organisations to:

- Reduce Absenteeism
- Alleviate stress
- Help people to cope better with change
- Promote better communication
- Reduce potential conflict
- Improve staff energy levels
- Improve mental health
- Improve physical well-being
- Retain talent and reduce staff turnover
- Improve employee engagement
- Support managers to support their teams
- Promote work/life balance
- Mitigate potential litigation
- Reduce health insurance premiums
- Reduce carbon footprint
- Save money on workplace overheads
- Become an employer of choice
- Support corporate social responsibility
- Improve efficiency and productivity.

Here is my list of practical steps that any business can take to implement workplace wellness:

- Motivational keynote speaking
- Bite-sized wellness workshops
- Lunchtime learning
- Breakfast and after work clubs
- Fit to Lead leadership programmes
- Improving food /nutrition in the workplace
- Encouraging walking meetings
- Get staff to wear pedometers
- Supply information on wellness in newsletters and on intranets
- Run wellness events for charity
- Supply wellness reading and support materials.

AUTHOR
TBLBC

Sharyn Abbott

7 Techniques to Thrive in Any Economy

Current Position:	Founder
Qualifications:	MBA Certification from San Jose State University
Experience:	20 years training entrepreneurs
Email:	Sharyn@sharynabbott.com
LinkedIn:	www.linkedin.com/pub/sharyn-abbott/0/43/929
Twitter:	www.twitter.com/#!/speakersharyn
Facebook:	www.facebook.com/profile.php?id=526879458
Website:	www.sharynabbott.com/
Links to Other Works:	www.mixingitupbook.com www.streetsmartdifference.com www.beyourownbossguide.com www.yourrighttowritenow.com www.blogifyyourbusinessnow.com

Since 1991 Sharyn has helped more than 2,500 people become successful entrepreneurs. More than 90% of them remain in business. This is an amazing success rate considering 90% of companies fail after two years and Sharyn attributes her clients' success to the educational environment and relationship-building techniques.

Sharyn has authored a number of books. Her most recent book, *Be Your Own Boss Guide,* is designed to help people match their skills and personalities with the type of business that will be the perfect business for them. She teaches highly creative courses for entrepreneurs like: "SpeakEasy", "Street Smart Sales", "Your Right to Write" and "Blogify Your Business". Sharyn is well known for her corporate sales training in the Fortune 500 arena. She has appeared on the Oprah Winfrey Show where she was featured for her innovative communications concepts.

Chapter 22: 7 Techniques to Thrive in Any Economy

Getting back to basics in business is one sure method of getting a business back on course. In the past decade businesses have been able to cruise through the motions without giving much thought to their business practices. But three years ago the cruise ship suddenly docked and the entrepreneurs of the world needed to get back to tried and true systems.

The first ill-fated tactic has to do with the perception of most business owners seeing the world through the local media's perspective. When news reporters declare there is a recession, it doesn't necessarily mean we all have to fall in line and participate. It is an opinion. No one can make anyone's business come to a grinding halt.

Even though there has been an average of 95% of new businesses fail in the first five years in the United States, I have always believed it is because they lack the systems and guidance which would have taken them to a level of sustainable success each and every one of them deserves.

Believe in your own success

When you are able to find a business in an industry which is successful, then every business in the same industry should be capable of achieving the same level of success. Often they will be capable of even better results through their ingenuity. Many times entrepreneurs forget to capitalise on their previous successes, whether that is to utilise systems, resources or contacts from previous positive achievements. Since it has worked for them in the past, it will more than likely work again.

When I worked in the corporate sales arena I kept a sales journal. I kept my success stories in the front of the journal but what proved more useful in times when I faced difficulties were the challenges I had dealt with. I wrote them from the back towards the centre of the journal. What is peculiar is the challenges we faced with clients in the 80s are nearly the same thirty years later with minor variations due to technology.

What else influences a person's ability to be successful? It has been proven that the people we associate with will dictate our own level of success. When you surround yourself by driven, success-oriented individuals, your chances of succeeding increase drastically.

Another determining factor is our very own belief systems. When we believe we are capable of success, it is more likely to become so. It is one of the components to becoming successful and possibly the most important aspects overall.

Develop your skills

We are given very few methods to learn how to implement purposeful time management and organisational skills. Yet these two business skills are more vital to thrive in business than nearly any other techniques.

When a business is in start-up mode or lacking enough clients or cash, it is necessary to spend no less than 50% of the time marketing, selling and reinforcing referral relationships.

In 1995 I created a Power Partner concept for my business clients. I challenged them to meet four new Power Partners (strategic alliances) every single week until they had no less than 50% of the business required to keep them in the black the Power Partners had referred to them consistently for a three month period. During our dot.com bomb era my clients were able to increase their revenue between 500% and 1200% within two years because of this practice.

This was at exactly the same time that 25% of all of the businesses failed in the Bay Area. Yet, the entrepreneurs who followed this one tactic, experienced success beyond any level they ever had done in the past.

Outsource under $100

One of the major challenges entrepreneurs experience is having the discipline to accomplish all the same tasks that companies who might have ten times the number employees as they do. I have often had the conversation with my clients about outsourcing anything they could pay less than $100 an hour for. In reality, if you can hire it out and dedicate the time for more sales and marketing you'll generate more than $100 an hour. The time you gain will more than make up for the expense of hiring out the service. It is especially more rewarding when you don't enjoy the business task you are outsourcing.

I am particularly good with numbers and always did my own bookkeeping but found the longer I was in business the longer I would put off the task of keeping my books up to date. Then one day after meeting a bookkeeper I asked her what she would charge to take over the task. It was only $200 a month. I made sure to use the time to do more marketing. In the long term I not only increased my business drastically but I became more efficient and started having more fun with clients as well.

Taking time management courses and efficiency programmes every year can be the best strategies to increase your profitability you can ever apply. For one thing, during the course you will remove yourself from the daily activity of the business and be able to take a step back. Sometimes viewing your business from the outside looking in will allow you more clarity. You will be able to see more than would be possible when you're involved in the day-to-day operations.

Keep in Touch

I mentioned Power Partners and the ability to build business through referrals. Establishing and maintaining relationships is more critical in today's business climate than ever before. The day of the "this is what I do, do you want some of it?" sales routine is long gone, as it should be.

Up until the time my database was over 6,000 contacts, I would call all those whose names started with an A or a B in January; C or D in February and so on. By the end of the year I had called everyone in the database. Some were clients, others Power Partners while others were resources that would update me on activities or business changes in the community.

It was amazing how much information everyone would tell me. It was well worth the effort to find out what they knew and to reconnect. They knew more of what was going on in the community than any newspaper.

One of my favourite techniques for creating new business is to develop Joint Ventures. With the advent of Social Media, I have been able to get radio interviews, authors to interview to create collateral material to build a membership site and hold teleseminars as well as webinars. I take the time to get to know the contacts on Facebook and LinkedIn and when I discover how we might help to each other, I'll suggest creating a programme. Almost everyone is receptive. It is one of the fastest methods of expanding my client base and gives exposure to a wide audience I never would have been able to reach without their help.

I always remember to ask for referrals and I always get them. In fact, more than 50% of all my business has come through referrals since 1993. It's rewarding when you can develop a level of business where half of it comes from those you've already done business with. It makes getting through each month much less stressful as well.

If it isn't working, change it

For years I refused to set goals. I was sure the only purpose in writing down goals was to know what I wasn't achieving. Then one day I looked at the end results of how many people I needed to talk with to get a new client and the idea of goals finally sank in.

When I was in corporate sales, I typically added two to three new clients a month. I would approach no less than 20 each week. Having a 10% close ratio is a great ratio for any business, but I never achieved any better than half a percent. Then when I started my business consulting organisation in 1991, my ratio was five percent

I began to keep track of how to make my ratio decrease and discovered if I called between 9am and 11am or 1pm and 3pm, I was able to talk with more people live. Less than 50% of those I left messages with actually returned my calls, so it was important to talk with people on the first call. I also realised it was easier to talk with those who were used to participating in organisations such as chambers of commerce, trade associations and service groups as they were generally more receptive to being part of another group. Within a year my average ratio was one in eight dials yielded a new client.

I knew I had to call 30 people every week to make my desired outcome. All I needed to do was stay focused. But what made it so much easier was to rely on the solid relationships I had created over the years to make sure I always had at least 50% of my business referred to me.

Overall, the basics of business boils down to doing whatever it takes to get the results you are looking for. At times it takes more hours, at other times it requires stopping and regrouping.

If it's not working, change it. When it is working, always look to see what you can do to make it better.

AUTHOR
TBLBC

Neil Giarratana

Go Immediately to Plan B

Current Position:	Retired CEO and author of *CEO Priorities*
Qualifications:	Harvard Business School MBA
Experience:	32 years as chief executive of companies operating in Europe/worldwide or the United States/Southern Hemisphere
Email:	giarratanan@yahoo.com
LinkedIn:	www.linkedin.com/pub/neil-giarratana/12/673/7ba
Website:	www.ceoprioritiesbook.com
Contact Number:	+1 847 321 0153

Neil Giarratana spent 32 years as a CEO in diverse industries, including cosmetics, toys, luxury leather goods and durable good manufacturing. As the senior executive, he managed companies both in Europe (he is fluent in German and French) and the United States. He holds a BA in international relations from Stanford University and an MBA from the Harvard Business School. Although 'retired', he is currently involved in writing his second book (core subject: sales management) as well as consulting to several CEOs and their companies located on the West Coast of the United States.

Chapter 23: Go Immediately to Plan B

Having been a CEO for almost 32 years, I have always found economic downturn periods to be the greatest test of my abilities.

The uncertainty of the future and the knowledge that one's fate is not totally in one's hands certainly exerted a definitive and sobering influence on my thinking about how to guide my company forward and through such troubled times.

In a recession, it is my firm belief that the key signals a CEO needs to continuously send within and outside his company are: power of conviction; the courage to face up to realistic and distasteful planning; the need for goal-focused leadership and caring for one's people and their concerns. Without this approach, failure can be just a quarter or two away.

We all know recessions are not normally the stuff of grand tales and heroic efforts. Pain, worry, concern, hurt, frustration and disappointment – for everyone concerned – are more than often than not the rule of the day.

The key issue is not only a matter of knowing or surmising that a recession or down period is imminent. Rather, the questions I have often had to answer involved my judgement as to when the recession would hit its zenith and for how long and how intense the resulting damage for the company might be.

A very untidy equation, particularly when one considers the following factors:

- Every company is normally set up for aggressive growth but now the company faces the need for a realistic plan revision, involving per force, both cost and sales revenue/margin reductions.
- Standing in the way of that initial realistic preparation are several human emotions, among them hope and ego. Hope that the 'problem' will be short-lived, supported by the critical assumption (non-delusionary) that if a market share battle breaks out the company will win it. Ego because management will tend to rationalise the possible effects: it thinks it has its arms completely around the

planning phases as well as the necessary, required steps to ensure that the company remains financially strong during the 'crisis'. As a result, the 'takedowns' against the original budget are often very moderate.

- An even more serious impediment to serious and effective budget adjustments is management level job or position loss concerns. These concerns often represent the real drivers of a short-term and short-sighted 'soft' planning approach and thus to any serious and necessary reduction in planned or anticipated results.

This creates the following short-term, mental result: hunker down, be hopeful and positive, maintain operational integrity in all parts of the company and promise that when things get better, income and bonus payments will again be at the top of the company's priority list.

Wrong emotional attitude

In my opinion, the first official revised budget, 'Plan A', represents almost always the more dangerous one. The reason is simple: management is using velvet gloves or rose-tinted glasses to handle the analysis and judgement of the critical assumptions and critical success factors that need to be included in any solid plan. No Chicken Little in this company.

Result: An often conscious negation of increasingly clear macro economic and markets indicators and their potential to do considerably more damage to operational results than the plan 'envisions'.

The correct strategic approach

Through personal experience, here is what I prefer to do:

• In its financial and operational planning, my management should not assume that the already so-called 'stringent' steps contained in Plan A will do the job. Management may want to sell that thinking to everybody, but in reality, it is often only deluding itself.

• Make the critical assumption that Plan A will not be enough and that therefore it will at some time be necessary to reduce further a number of the key benchmark goals contained in Plan A.

Result: the necessity for the almost always necessary but much more distasteful Plan B.

If management were, right from the start, to combine both Plan A and the more seriously hurtful second stage reduction (the tough Plan B), it would then create an Initial Plan which would be much more realistic and which would more likely match the market and operational situation the company will in fact face. Taking the tough and usually unpleasant step in the first instance is, in my opinion, the more effective one in such situations.

Example:
For ten years, I was the CEO of a company producing automatic garage door openers for new construction and retrofit. A major part of our business was directed toward new single family dwellings, a market which from 2006 experienced a unit building volume decline of over 75% in the course of three years. While we were not able to avoid several years of losses, we were able to substantially cushion their effect by using the reserves we had built up in the previous good years.

But more importantly we were able, by going to the Plan B step almost from the start of the Recession, to minimise our losses by almost 55% compared to what they would have been if we had started off with Plan A and then at some later point in time moved to Plan B. This immediate and tougher procedure meant millions of dollars in operational 'savings' (loss avoidance) to the company over the period in question.

Note to file: There is nothing worse than having to develop at some later point in time, an additional plan containing additional reductions instead of being able to operate right from the beginning with a realistic 'worst' case scenario and then enjoying a moderate to perhaps good chance to beat the forecasted results contained therein. Up-tick surprises are better and more motivating to everyone concerned, including the stakeholders (!) than constant down-tick revisions.

Dangers and caveats
While the Combo-plan may be the more prudent and professional approach to maintaining the company's position and relative health, there are in my experience, a number of potentially negative/de-

motivating effects that definitely need to be both considered and resolved:

-- It will necessitate the company taking the bigger - and thus more distasteful - planning step instead of opting for the easier road using a succession of smaller but ever more painful ones, each of which could mean potentially more destructive discussions and perhaps acrimony.

-- A reduced plan may seriously affect the timing and volume of the capital investment necessary for long-term growth; it will often seriously affect personnel and motivation because of the need for the downsizing of the organisation.

-- It will require an enlightened management and HR function to devote extra priority time and effort to keeping its remaining best talent happy and performing at high levels of efficiency and focus.

-- It will require some potentially very hard discussions among management because not every member of the team will see the same dangers in the same way.

-- It will require the company to do some very serious cost-containment thinking and perhaps also require a re-positioning of the company without the advantage of organic growth in the market.

-- It will require management to play fair with its people and not to choose personal aggrandisement at the same time it is asking for major sacrifice and patience from its employees.

-- It will require the company - and the responsible individuals in management - to consciously put aside hope and ego. And to stop rationalising every danger or negative development.

Resolving these issues in an enlightened and motivating fashion is the real test of a top executive's professional skill, diplomacy, and yes, courage. Without them, a CEO can potentially exacerbate an already serious situation to the extent that the company itself may be endangered.

Dr. Ed Derbyshire

Keeping the Key Team on Board During the Hard Times

Current Position:	Managing Director
Qualifications:	MBA, DBA
Experience:	30+ years experience in high-tech companies including two green field start-ups plus mergers and acquisitions and company integration
Email:	ed_derbyshire@yahoo.com
LinkedIn:	www.linkedin.com/in/edderbyshire
Links to Other Works:	British Library – *An exploration of the importance of trust in the post-acquisition integration context in high-technology industry*
Contact Number:	+44 (0) 2392 626300

Ed Derbyshire has over 30 years experience in technical, technical management, management and director level roles, and is currently a Managing Director. He is experienced in mergers and acquisitions with in-depth knowledge of integration practice including identification and retention of key staff.

Having a strong entrepreneurial drive, he has set up two green-field start-ups. A professional lecturer in business studies, he brings the academic and practice worlds together to develop and inspire individuals. He is strongly motivated to improve both his own performance and those he is involved with.

Chapter 24: Keeping the Key Team on Board During Hard Times

Recession brings with it times of hardship. As responsible managers we have to consider what steps we have to take in order to protect and grow our businesses. In particular, we need to retain our key team members at these times.

Why? Well, these key team members make a critical contribution to the business. And it's not always the obvious ones either. Without the key staff, our businesses will decline, as much of the intrinsic intellectual property leaves with them. An example of this is related below.

One company we ran due diligence on with a view to acquiring its operations, designed and built high tech amplifiers. These amplifiers were at the cutting edge of power handling and mechanical design at the time. Early on we identified the lead design engineers as critical to the acquisition – lose them and we thought we'd lose the value of the deal. However, as we invested time in working directly with the workforce (as opposed to just the senior management behind closed doors) it emerged that there were other 'key workers' that had initially escaped our notice.

One such example was one of the machinists who was responsible for machining a key part of the amplifier. Although the piece value of the part was only measured to be a few hundred pounds, the contribution to the amplifier was enormous. Not only would a missed or incorrect dimension cause the product to malfunction but we also discovered that the machinist had developed an unrecorded (non-process captured) method of improving the machining. The effect was to further improve the product's performance and consistency. This had occurred without the knowledge of the senior management and even the engineering manager!

Had a cursory effort at identifying key team members at senior meetings sufficed, we would have missed this gem and possibly had a poorer performing device as an outcome. Even worse would have been the inability of the engineering team to identify where the poorer device performance originated from.

There are several lessons we can learn from this story:-

Carefully review and identify all key staff
This can only be achieved through engagement with the team and takes time and energy. A review of the team listing is not sufficient.

Once identified, take active measures to retain these staff
This calls for a number of approaches. The usual and easy avenue of incentivising through increased pay or bonus is not necessarily the way to go. Maslow's hierarchy of needs identifies monetary reward as much lower on the average person's real needs. We should consider recognising achievement and maintaining or building respect whilst allowing these staff to have fulfilling and creative roles wherever possible.

Build trust with your key team members
Trust between staff and management is critical in successful retention. Trust can be built through openness, communication, reliability and integrity. This calls for a deliberate policy by the senior management in all four of these aspects of trust. For example, we can address the desire for recognition through public commendation at team meetings. We should also be careful that we 'walk the talk', that is, we deliver on our promises and follow through on our actions and statements.

Conducting business in as transparent a manner as possible is also important for our team. If they feel they are getting an accurate (not too rosy or too pessimistic) view, this engenders trust. We should also not lose sight that trust runs between managers and staff and staff and managers. It is not enough to carry out these trust-building actions to encourage the team to trust us as managers; we can only succeed in this if we ourselves place our trust in the team. It doesn't take long for staff to sense a lack of trust in them on their manager's part!

To conclude, I can relate a story I heard regarding retention of team members. A company, hard hit by the recession, was unable to continue operations of a subsidiary division. The only apparent way forward was to divest the division without delay. This was duly carried out but not before another party indicated an interest in the team members to be divested. Much discussion ensued and the team was subsequently taken over by the other party.

However, the point of this story is that all the key team members were retained by the new company even though the takeover was actioned toward the very end of the notice of redundancy period. It is interesting to note that these team members were fully briefed from the initial decision to put the division 'at risk' through to the notice period and as the interested party emerged, negotiations commenced and were finally concluded. Trust levels were maintained during this difficult period through openness, reliability, communication and integrity, such that all key team members transferred to the new company.

Clearly an investment in the understanding of who the key members of staff are in your organisation and the taking of steps to ensure their retention is a worthwhile use of management time in order to safeguard and grow the business under the harshest of conditions. As we all know recessions can offer opportunities – without our key staff members we are less able to take advantage of them.

Roger Whittaker

Blind Faith and Creative Instinct

Current Position:	Factotum of The Stani Gallery
Qualifications:	Fellow of Institute of Management
Experience:	30 years in Management Consultancy
Email:	art@thestanigallery.co.uk
LinkedIn:	http://uk.linkedin.com/in/1rogerwhittaker
Twitter:	www.twitter.com/rogerinthepink
Facebook:	www.facebook.com/thestanigallery
Website:	www.thestanigallery.co.uk
Contact Number:	+44 (0)845 504 9696

Roger is Factotum of The Stani Gallery – an art gallery in Milton Keynes - and a Director of Pink Connect – a Telecoms, IT and Energy services company. He has worked for national and global companies; been employed with a client, contractor, consultant and public authority; managed a variety of functional and operational teams and worked as a builder, retailer, engineer, marketer and designer in the construction, oil and water industries.

Chapter 25: Blind Faith and Creative Instinct

We opened an art gallery when other retail businesses were closing down on the high street. A local estate agent said it would never work; we had never run a gallery before nor lived in the town where it was located and even our friends were cautious with their encouragement.

We were driven by a number of things. Primarily our desire was to own a gallery, to exhibit my wife and other artists' work and our belief in ourselves to run a business. We also recognised that we needed to either fulfil the dream and turn it into reality or let it go.

Some nine months later and we have trebled the number of artists displaying their work, established a customer base of several hundreds, from both near and far and been profitable from day one.

Were we lucky?

If you mean we were just in the right place (shops closing?), at the right time (recession?) with the right product (impulse purchase?) then no. But if you mean we were prepared to take the opportunity when it presented itself, then yes.

This, above all else, is the key to success both at a strategic level – should we open a gallery at all – and tactical level – what art should we have in it? The phrase 'you create your own luck' being particularly relevant.

Because, if you do not take measured risks, keep trying new things and trust your instinct and judgement to stimulate your market, then you become solely reliant on customers finding you and knowing what they want in the first place. And guess what? They always have a choice of supplier or provider and most of the time they only have a rough idea of what they want and therefore need help to decide what is best for them.

So what has worked for us in our retail business?

For a start, we change over half the art on display bimonthly to suit a different theme; we deliberately have low priced/high volume items as well as the converse. We introduce new artists regularly and have extended the product range from not just paintings and prints but to include scarves and metal figures. As long as the work is unique and distinctive, local and original and of course of the right quality, then it fulfils our criteria for our art and the philosophy of our art gallery....in short our USP!

More than that though, our intention is to always stimulate the customer with interesting and novel artwork. This makes us a great place to pop in to have a look around and, when the time is right, to buy a special present or gift. This is also helped by us changing the window display daily.

Just attracting local customers and passers by though is not enough. We have experimented with leaflet deliveries at targeted households in nearby areas, advertised and obtained editorial coverage in various local newspapers, displayed our art in local pubs and restaurants to promote ourselves jointly, attended art & craft shows and supported local charities in fundraising events. In short, we look for opportunities to promote ourselves often in collaboration with other businesses with similar needs in order to build brand awareness and establish ourselves in the community...and not necessarily for instant sales.

Then of course, there is building an online presence with your website, blog, through business directories and event listings to ensure you always have something to say, others are happy to say it for you and you are not far from people's minds.

And the learning points?
It is very hard work and you need more hours in the day than you ever have! You also need a wide range of skills covering all aspects of business, both front and back of house, if you are to be successful. This means you either need money to buy in what you cannot do yourself or get a partner to invest the time. In our case my wife looks after art selection, sales and artist co-ordination while I cover marketing accounts and infrastructure because you really cannot run any business to its full potential unless you focus on all the key aspects. Even with our complementary starting skills, we have still had to learn more...about finances, VAT, Tax, operating a till, stock control, websites, SEO etc...as you always need to know something about everything and we do not have unlimited funds!

As well as time though, you do need to re-invest carefully in your business in learning through marketing, customer behaviour and trialling new products and services. This naturally then leads to being prepared for when things do not to work out as expected. For example, we have found some leaflet campaigns to not work at all, our preview evenings to not be so well attended, art we really liked which hasn't sold and even days when hardly anyone came in to the gallery for no obvious reason we could think of.

And then there is the normal business start up dilemma, what do you actually compare your progress to?

There are no last year or week sales figures available, no customer numbers and feedback, no knowledge of best or worst sellers, acceptable price or trigger points, seasonal or weekly trends. There are in fact no benchmarks and you are in the dark most of the time and have to create the light as you go!

It's not just about YOU

What really began several years ago as a hobby activity for my wife has now been turned into a commercial enterprise that fulfils the needs of those that buy the art as well as the artists who produce it. The business is therefore no longer, if it ever was, just about us.

And the best bit of all is when you truly realise that!!

We take no pleasure from proving the doubters wrong, but tremendous pride in justifying the trust and belief of those that have and continue to support us. The blind have truly led the blind in our case and we have invented the way forward together at every step on our journey with little more than blind faith and creative instinct.

Kendra Lee

Lessons from a Tough Economy

Current Position:	President, KLA Group
Qualifications:	BA in International Business & Business Administration MS in Accounting
Experience:	Earlier career with Sybase and IBM Founded KLA Group in 1995 Client list includes Fortune 100 companies around the world as well as small to mid-size IT providers.
Email:	info@klagroup.com
LinkedIn:	www.linkedin.com/in/kendralee
Twitter:	www.twitter.com/KendraLeeKLA
Facebook:	www.facebook.com/KLAGroup
Website:	www.klagroup.com
Links to Other Works:	www.klagroup.com/resources/articles.cfm
Contact Number:	+1 303.741.6636

Kendra Lee knows how to shorten the time to revenue in innovative ways. Author of the award winning book, *Selling Against the Goal* and president of the KLA Group, Ms. Lee is a top seller, prospecting and lead generation expert, and sales advisor. Her client list includes Fortune 100 companies as well as small - mid-size IT providers.

Under Ms. Lee's direction, her organisation has assisted sellers in increasing referrals more than 328% in just seven weeks, penetrating SMB markets in just six weeks, driving new client acquisition more than 31% year over year and moving from solution to consultative selling in only nine months. Specialising in the IT industry, KLA Group works with manufacturers, distributors, and solution providers to break in and exceed revenue objectives in the small and medium business market.

Chapter 26: Lessons from a Tough Economy

From our perspective, the recession arrived long before it was officially 'here'. In fact, about 12 months before the declining economy became a major news topic, we had noticed that a lot of our big projects – and especially our enterprise clients – were becoming a lot fewer and farther between.

In that way, we were pretty lucky. We didn't wait for an official announcement or a front page headline to take action because we already knew that the ground was shifting beneath us.

Most of our clients couldn't afford big training programmes and development projects anymore, especially when declining travel budgets were factored in. They had more need for consulting and training than ever before, but they had to do it in a way that was much more cost-effective. And so, the question that came to us was the same one that occurred to a lot of other businesses later: what do we do now?

We couldn't really turn to our competitors for inspiration, since many of them were clinging to ideas that hadn't been working for a while, hoping that the market for expensive speakers and training companies would eventually return. We couldn't see that happening, especially as the economic picture started to look more and more bleak.

After thinking things through and doing some forecasting, we knew we needed to take our business in a completely new direction. But unlike some other companies who started scrambling around for new revenue streams wherever they could find them, we looked at things from a client's perspective. What were they really screaming out for and how could we be the ones to give it to them?

That question led us to change our whole business model, taking it from one centred on a handful of large clients to a new version that focused on helping a broader range of organisations on a personal level. The result was a clear win-win – our customers got exactly what they needed in a way that was far more affordable to them, while we were able to diversify our income a little bit and come out of the experience smarter and stronger.

As a result of this change, I can honestly say that KLA Group is doing better than ever before. Our sales and revenue are up across the board, something that is virtually unheard of in our field right now. What's more, we're doing it by serving a wider variety of clients.

Prior to the recession, 90% of our business came from Fortune 500 clients. These were great accounts to have but they were also the most vulnerable to an economic shift. Now, we get only 51% of our business from them, and the rest is made up of small and mid-sized businesses. Having a diverse client base has made us more flexible and resilient.

By responding to a change in the economy with the attitude of putting our clients' needs first, we were also able to come up with a handful of ideas that wouldn't have been there otherwise.

For example, we weren't selling anything on our website in the past, but it now contributes more than a fifth of our revenue. That didn't have much to do with technology. Rather, we let our customers tell us what types of programmes they needed and then made sure we had the solutions that fit the bill.

That's probably good advice whether you're in a recession or not.

If I had to put my finger on one single lesson that a choppy economy has taught us, however, I think it would be this: Trust yourself and your own instincts. Don't be afraid to change.

Deep down, we realised pretty early on that it was going to take some major changes to keep our company growing and evolving. It would have been very easy to sit back and tell ourselves that things would turn around in no time and that our customers would come back to doing and wanting the types of training programmes they had always used in the past.

At the same time, we just knew deep down that wasn't going to be the case. If we had waited and simply hoped for business to get better, where would we be today?

KLA Group today is a company that works with clients across the board – from Fortune 500's to smaller organisations that are just getting started. We aren't completely dependent on direct client projects anymore because we earn money from on-line training programmes as well. These outcomes have only been possible because we adopted the mindset of our customers, rather than trying to force old ideas that weren't working to stay in place.

To succeed in our field, and most others, takes the willingness to do the right thing at the right time. I think leaders tend to recognise challenges and opportunities more often than they think but hesitation holds them back from making important decisions. As the recession shows, however, the best time to make a move is the moment you need to, so have some faith in your own abilities, keep in touch with your customers' needs and then make the right call for your company.

Debbie Payne
The Box with no Walls

Current Position:	President, DP Leadership Associates. Partner, Deberna International
Qualifications:	Master of Arts degree in Leadership and Training Management and Organisational Behaviour Certificates
Experience:	25+ years experience in allied health, adult education, leadership and organizational development, internal and external consulting
Email:	debbie@dpleadership.com
LinkedIn:	www.linkedin.com/in/debbiepayne
Twitter:	www.twitter.com/#!/debbiepayne
Facebook:	www.twitter.com/#!/leaderwisdom
Website:	www.dpleadership.com www.deberna.com
Links to Other Works:	Tri-namics Book www.deberna.com/id2.html LeaderSpace Book www.blurb.com/books/1908182
Contact Number:	+1 604 209 5069

Debbie Payne's MA, RODP, CDA years of experience as an adult educator, facilitator, manager, leadership consultant and organisational development and learning specialist provide context for her to link leaders in all aspects of their lives. She creates system wide frameworks, develops teams, coaches clients, explores dialogue, and creates and delivers custom leadership development courses, programmes and workshops. Debbie has written over 25 curriculum publications and articles and is the author of several books. She is President of DP Leadership Associates (founded 2001), Partner of Deberna International (founded 2004) and works with her clients in British Columbia, across Canada, and internationally.

Chapter 27: The Box with no Walls

Typical for many folks laid off after six months of job-hunting, I decided to launch full-time into my own consulting business. It was February 2008, a nice month in my mind. I had the best financial year of my life that year and have had two successful years since with 2011 also looking very strong.

People I spoke with told me I was crazy, that it takes years to build a consulting practice; that I should be prepared to starve for the first five years. I was also told that it was a poor time to start as we were in a recession, that no one needed consultants and that I should seriously look at finding some kind of job, even if it was not in my field. This was a box I did not want to play in, one that I simply decided was not for me.

I believe my success came mostly from knocking down the walls of the box. I expected to have success and I presented as a well-established consultant with an outstanding skill set. I marched into networking events, workshops, seminars, conferences or wherever I could find people gathered. I gave away ideas, I gave people my book, I consulted for free, I set strong, yet realistic fees that successful consultants would charge; most of all I was confident.

When people asked me,
"How is business, are you busy?"
"Absolutely," I would say, "business is great."

I hung out with the most successful consultants I could find. Within a month I had several excellent clients.

It took me over two years before I found myself in a business development phase. Surprise! Not having experienced this due to my early success was such a good lesson. I am still learning this lesson and finding ways to tear down more walls of the box, thinking and seeking ways to work with different kinds of clients.

What has helped me most is to look for clients that other consultants are not working with, to explore unusual funding partnerships and sources, to collaborate with other consultants and do joint proposals, to celebrate and to bring my incredible network into the conversations early on.

I refer colleagues that can help my clients, ask other consultants if I can shadow them or if they would like to shadow me, reach out globally into new fields, sectors, industries and countries as well as to work within my own community and see what kind of clients I can actually walk to. I volunteer my time in places where I can meet new people that might find my work interesting. I also stretch myself as well by taking on work that I have never done before; it helps me learn and makes me a more flexible consultant.

My work focuses on people development, in particular leadership development. These skills are not hard, technical, core skills that businesses require. They are often called 'soft skills'.

These are much more difficult to master, learn and teach and are fundamentally necessary for successful leaders and organisations to cultivate. How we work and learn together matters. It matters as much as what we do.

Often when times are tough or a recession hits, we stop thinking or focusing on 'the how' and instead try to reduce employee costs, downsize while still getting 'the what' done. In doing this, we are focusing on the short-term 'what' rather than 'the how' and this short-sightedness leads us to a downward spiral. Organisations without growth and development are like ghost towns. I look to work with organisations that understand people investment and who want a vibrant, creative, value-driven workforce that can help them recover from a recession.

So, the walls of the box disappear when I can be successful with clients in helping them see through the walls, even helping them shift the box to a new place or to design a new box. I love to hear the term 'no-box thinking' rather than inside or outside the box. This helps me free up my own mind, to help me think from the viewpoint of my client's customer and to see their organisation not only from 30,000 feet but two inches away.

My passion is fuelled by seeing opportunities where others see problems; I ask, listen, ask, listen, listen and listen. I try my best every day to model the leadership I advocate: to give away my time; to contribute to leadership thought; to develop others in any way I can and to listen to what is said or not. This brilliant partnership has provided me with an insight into consulting that knows no walls.

Jonathan Jay

Beat the Recession (and Your Competition) with Marketing

Current Position:	Chairman & Founder: Nationwide Alliance of Business Owners (NABO)
Experience:	Entrepreneur, Business Growth and Marketing Expert
Email:	info@nabo.biz
Website:	www.nabo.biz
Contact Number:	+44 (0)208 788 9064

Jonathan Jay is a multi-millionaire entrepreneur and marketing maverick obsessed with helping business owners to reach their potential.

He's the Chairman of the Nationwide Alliance of Business Owners (www.nabo.biz); the founder and Managing Director of SuccessTrack; the founder of The Coaching Academy UK; the author of four books (*Sack Your Boss*, *The Marketing Secrets of a Multi-Millionaire Entrepreneur*, *Marketing Secrets for Small Business Owners* and *Unsung Business Heroes*); the star of TV's 'Now I'm The Boss'; a magazine publisher ('The Achievement Report' and award-winning 'Personal Success'); a popular and in-demand speaker; as well as being the UK's highest-paid business consultant.

Chapter 28: Beat the Recession (and Your Competition) with Marketing

I set up a company offering business owners training in marketing at the start of the recession. About the time when pundits were predicting training and marketing budgets would be slashed across the board and naturally enough, there were those who thought I'd be closing my company's doors within a few months. After all, who would want to pay thousands of pounds to learn to market better when money was so tight?

But something I learned long before this recession was to only pay attention to what prospective clients wanted and simply block out the rest.

Ten years ago, I used my last £145 to set up The Coaching Academy (UK). The prevailing view then was that only Americans could teach coaching and a UK coach training organisation would never take off. But I knew from my prospective clients they really wanted to learn coaching in this country and they didn't want to do it via an American correspondence course.

During the eight years I owned The Coaching Academy we trained thousands and thousands of coaches and became the leading coach training organisation in Europe. It was so successful that I was able to sell it to a private equity company for millions.

Therefore at the start of this recession I didn't pay very much attention to the forecasts of doom and gloom. I knew that savvy and successful business owners are always looking for ways to improve their results, recession or not. I also knew that the best way they can do that is by improving their marketing skills.

How did I know that?

I listened to what business owners told me. I attended networking meetings. I paid thousands and thousands of pounds to travel around the world to attend seminars with highly successful people.

I believed then, as I do now, that a recession is simply a time when all business owners need to become even more strategic in their thinking and spending.

But you don't need a recession to make you think and spend in a smarter way. And you don't need to wait for a recession until you learn lessons from your mistakes. We make mistakes and miss opportunities and they are always painful and memorable, regardless of whether the economy's in a boom or bust period.

I made plenty of mistakes, missed many opportunities and learnt many lessons during the early years of my previous business.

I employed a large sales team for a long time and paid them a fortune in salaries and bonuses to make cold calls. I set targets; I cajoled, enthused, reprimanded and probably screamed but the results were never what I expected. Then I realised if I used marketing more effectively, I probably only really needed one of them – just to answer calls (because if I did my marketing successfully, people would come to us, we wouldn't have to chase them). After sacking all but one of my salespeople, profits quadrupled and peace reigned in the office.

Probably the biggest mistake I made was trying to do everything myself, believing I needed to be involved in every aspect of the business, no matter how trivial. I worked horrendously long hours and yet still didn't achieve the results I wanted. It was only when I realised my time should be spent solely on marketing the business and that I needed to delegate everything else that profits increased.

It took a while but I also learnt that when something isn't working, ignoring the problem won't make it disappear. It will just get worse and worse. You must take action, no matter how painful you think it's going to be.

Today, if something (a direct mail or email campaign, a newsletter, a seminar or a freelance contract) isn't returning a profit and is actually costing the business, I immediately stop it, whatever it is.

Of course, you can only realise you're making a mistake by measuring your results. And of all the things I've ever learnt about running a profitable business this is key - measure everything.
I learnt plenty of lessons during the 'boom time' of the 1990s and the recession of the past few years...and I have been sharing that information with UK business owners since setting up SuccessTrack and the business association I founded, the Nationwide Alliance of

Business Owners (NABO). So far, 39,000 of them have learnt what really does and doesn't work. My team of experts and I give business owners practical, proven systems that they can use the moment they leave. If they use the systems, they get results.

Take John Haslam for instance. Like me and many other entrepreneurs, he also made the mistake of trying to do everything himself. When he first joined NABO in November 2009, he was running two businesses - Jeves Magazine and Leaflet Distribution and a home cleaning franchise, Molly Maid. He worked 18 hours a day, six days a week and collapsed on Sundays. Worse, he had almost no cash flow because he was too preoccupied with networking, delivering his product and taking phone calls to send out and chase up invoices.

He had no time left to follow up the leads he received from networking events or to use the marketing techniques he'd found to be successful in the past.

"I was chasing my tail because I wasn't getting the bills out fast enough," admits John. He committed to making three major changes immediately: to systemise and outsource his business procedures; to get an administrative assistant and to move out of his home office into a rented office.

"I stopped getting any direct phone calls and that saved me about 16 hours a week. I employed someone to take care of all the paperwork for both businesses - all the billing, the admin - and that freed up another 10 to 12 hours a week of my time."

No longer exhausted, he could begin working *on* the business instead of *in* it.

He's been able to halve the number of hours he works and last year he doubled his profits for the first time in 10 years. Now, John spends all of his time focusing on building his business.

"You look and think that it's impossible to double your business in this current climate and yet I did it," says John. "It's all about having the tools to make things happen and having the time to think about my business – I now spend all my days doing marketing. That's all I do."

He's not the only one to revitalise and benefit from improving his marketing - Stefan Boyle, the owner of an online print company, Print Republic, is another. In less than 12 months, his company has attracted 700 new clients, including the world's biggest online auction site, eBay, and its turnover has jumped by 40%. All thanks to getting better at marketing.

Two years ago, Stefan took over his family's printing business. For 40 years, the company had operated as a traditional printing company but Boyle realised it was time to change.

"Margins had eroded over the past few years. The printing business was just getting very hard. It was becoming a pricing game. And I didn't want to play it."

He knew that to achieve the success he envisioned he needed expert marketing help.

"Any marketing we had ever done, be it newspaper, magazine, advertising to direct mail or email, had always bombed. If I sent out a 10,000 mailing, I was always massively disappointed. I got to the stage where I didn't do it anymore; I just didn't advertise because I never got a return on investment. I didn't really know what I was doing wrong."

That changed once he signed up for NABO's Business Development Programme: he discovered not only what he was doing wrong but more importantly, how to make his marketing successful.

"I realised we were making the mistakes that other companies in my industry and almost every industry were making: we were talking about ourselves. Every piece of marketing I had done before had really talked about how good we were, and how customers or prospects should use our services, but we didn't quantify it. We didn't talk about it from a customer's or prospect's perspective. NABO made me change my approach.

"NABO taught me how to start with an offer that is tempting and draws people in. Once you do that, you've got a relationship and then you can build that relationship and offer more products and services to them."

John and Stefan are just two of the many thousands of UK business owners who have learnt that marketing effectively can give a company the edge it needs to prosper – regardless of the state of the economy.

So, in conclusion:

Listen to what your clients and prospects really want and give it to them. Ignore doom and gloom merchants. Use marketing effectively and sales will follow. Learn from your mistakes. Stop doing what isn't working - immediately. Measure everything. Take every opportunity to get better at marketing. Systemise your business. Don't try to do everything yourself – focus on profit-making activities and delegate or outsource the rest.

Daniel Priestley
Make your Name Known

Current Position:	Managing Director/Founder of Triumphant Events, Author of *K ey Person of Influence*
Email:	info@triumphantevents.co.uk
LinkedIn:	www.uk.linkedin.com/in/danielpriestley
Twitter:	www.twitter.com/DanielPriestley
Website:	www.triumphantevents.co.uk/
Contact Number:	+44 (0) 844 477 1618

Daniel Priestley is a successful entrepreneur, international speaker and best-selling author. Daniel started out as an entrepreneur at 21 years old and has since built several successful businesses in the UK, Australia and Singapore.

He is the founder and Director of the International Event Marketing and Management Company, Triumphant Events.

Triumphant Events promotes training courses and events featuring many prominent speakers, authors, entrepreneurs and thought leaders from around the world. On average over 20,000 people book into a Triumphant Event each year.

Daniel is actively involved in fund-raising for several NGOs and Charities (PeaceOneDay.org, The Hunger Project and The Pachamam Alliance).

Chapter 29: Make your Name Known

People are always looking for the secret to wealth and success and it's often staring them in the face.

Never have I heard of someone who says "I discovered some secret to making money and within a few months I got rich." Normally I hear people say "I discovered I had a passion for something, I kept at it and finally I 'popped'."

The 'overnight success' often takes five to seven years.

So how do you take your passion and your last five to seven years of experience and leverage it? How do we get you to 'pop'? The trick is not more hard work; the trick is that you must 'make a name for yourself'.

Consider all the people you know who make great money, who live exciting lives, who have influence and success in abundance. I can guarantee you that they are well known in their field – they have made a name for themselves.

People who have established their name, attract more opportunity, earn a premium on their time and don't spend countless hours chasing new business. Once you make a name for yourself you become a magnet for money and you free up your time and energy from the chasing game.

So which comes first, the chicken or the egg? Must you first become successful and thus make a name for yourself or do you do the things required to make a name for yourself and then become successful?

Is it even possible to deliberately become a 'key person' in your industry or is this something that happens through years of hard work alone?

Clearly you must be good at what you do. However, years of hard work often don't pay off. Many people spend so much time doing the work and far too little time building a reputation.

Building a reputation requires some skills that most people don't invest enough time in. If you do things that impact your reputation in a positive way, you will attract more opportunities and therefore make a name for yourself.

I had created a multi-million dollar events company in Australia before I came to the UK but I hadn't made a name for myself. Since arriving in the UK, the five things I have focused on are:

1. **Pitch:** Learn how to pitch yourself really well so if you get into a conversation with someone you are able to engage their imagination, be memorable, credible, clear and believable. It takes practice but it's a MUST. There will come a day that you have a chance meeting with a big heavy hitter and in that moment you'd better have clarity about what you are up to.
2. **Publish:** Write down your key ideas, create articles, blogs and even a book about what you do. With few exceptions, it's nearly impossible to make a name for yourself if you aren't publishing your ideas somewhere. Writing your ideas down allows you to deeply explore some of the knowledge you may take for granted and then spread your ideas to your market with ease.
3. **Productise:** Make 2011 the year that you break the shackles of trading only time-for-money. Not everything you do of value requires you to be in the room, your sales pitch could be put onto CD or made into a download. Your orientation session could become a workbook. Buy back your time by turning some of what you do into a product. Often the difference between a regular income and a great deal of wealth is having the right product.
4. **Profile:** Raise your profile online and in the media. Make sure you dominate the front page of Google when someone searches for you. The great advantage of social media is that it connects you with your peers and your clients as well as lifting your rankings in Google. Connect with all the right people in LinkedIn. Get featured in a press article and post it online. Make some YouTube videos. If Google can't find you in 2011, you are in serious trouble.
5. **Partnerships:** You don't have enough time in the day to do everything yourself. If you put your time into creating a

brilliant product, partner with someone who has wide reaching distribution. If you have a great brand, partner with someone who has highly functional products. Network, connect and partner with the key people in your industry.

When I put these five steps in place I found that I was able to attract a lot more opportunity. I was asked to speak at events. I was asked to join top teams. I often had to charge a premium for my time. People with a great reputation can often turn down work if it doesn't inspire them, so you will have more fun in your industry as well.

Never has there been a better time in history to make a name for yourself. New technology and the widespread sharing of resources make it easier than ever to do all five of the steps listed above.

Not until recently has it been possible to easily write a book and have it available for sale world wide at the click of a mouse. Only in very recent times could you create articles or videos and share them with the world with ease. It's a new phenomenon to be able to make and sell products globally without spending fortunes on the process. It would be mad not to be making the most of these new trends.

I have found that these steps will also release you from your current geography. Your published articles and your products can easily end up impacting people all over the world.

A self-employed consultant in London is mostly limited to the one city. The same consultant with a book and a product could be offering their services globally.

No need to look for some special secret to wealth. The secret is:

You are already standing on a mountain of value but you need to let the world know about it. After you've made a name for yourself by completing these steps, expect to see more opportunity, more fun, more inbound enquiries and even a lot more money.

If you put more focus into building your reputation, enhancing your brand and making a name for yourself in your industry, you will discover a whole new world of opportunity is waiting for you.

AUTHOR
TBLBC

Chris Smith

How to Smile Through a Recession

Current Position:	Entrepreneur, general doer and dogsbody!
Qualifications:	BA (Hons)
Experience:	Nearly 20 years in business – Recruitment, Tech and Web
Email:	chris@paginglist.com
LinkedIn:	http://uk.linkedin.com/in/chrissmithyourpeoplemarket
Twitter:	www.twitter.com/#!/ThatChrisSmith www.twitter.com/#!/UsePaginglist www.twitter.com/#!/YPMarket
Website:	www.yourpeoplemarket.com www.paginglist.com

Chris Smith was joint founder and owner of ecrmpeople, a technical staffing business that grew into the world leading solution provider to the IT Asset Management and Service Management Software Market. Started in a spare room, at the point of exit the business was turning over £12M GBP and had over 120 contractors on assignment worldwide as well as making executive level appointments into the leading software vendors in its markets.

Currently Chris is investing and involved in a number of start ups. These include www.yourpeoplemarket.com, a revolutionary online recruitment marketplace and www.paginglist.com which enables people to call and SMS their social networks and contacts without ever revealing their number and enables people to maintain absolute control of their connection.

He is also very proud dad of two and any spare time he has he spends covered in poster paint and papier maché.

Chapter 30: How to Smile Through a Recession

I founded ecrmpeople in 2000 on the cusp of a recession before selling the business in 2007, more or less just before the credit crunch really bit.

Ecrmpeople is a recruitment and staffing business that lead the world in the delivery of technical resources into the markets of Asset Management and Service Management software. Our client base included some of the world's largest blue chips through to bleeding edge software consultancies.

I left ecrmpeople in 2009 at the end of a post-acquisition 'lock in' period and am now involved in two new projects: yourpeoplemarket.com (again in the recruitment space) and paginglist.com (a business that bridges the privacy gap in social media). Unquestionably the application of the below is as relevant to both these start ups as it was to ecrmpeople.

Recognition and Acceptance

The first thing to do with a recession is to recognise you are about to go into one - ideally before it happens and before your competitors do! All too often businesses will refuse to even mention the word 'recession' let alone make the required changes within their business to survive and thrive through it.

In its simplest terms, the sooner you recognise you are in a recession the sooner you will do something about it.

To put it bluntly your business is a 'barometer' for the markets you are involved in and you need to be proactive in looking for changes from what your perceived operational norm is.

Key indicators for us were:

- Extended decision cycles
- Relationship leverage
- Margin and price pressure
- Extended and delayed payments

As soon as you as you accept and 'normalise' the recession into your business, the sooner you will do something about it. By this, I mean cut the bullshit and sit down with all your key team members and tell them how <u>you</u> see things:

a) It's going to get harder and more effort is required from everyone's teams to hold position and grow
b) All customers need to be put through a strict health check (old and new). There is no point in writing or chasing business which you won't get paid for. Be ready to take the emotion out of a decision
c) Develop a more energised and can-do mentality. Though we are facing down hard times (externally) what remains under our control is the mindset you attack it with. Though it's vital to recognise and accept the recession is happening, leave the doom and gloom at the door. It will kill the creativity you need to fight it and to outperform your competitors
d) Lead from the front and keep the office doors open. Communication is at all times king but never more so in a recession - it is VITAL that the senior management team practise what they preach. For example, if you introduce new performance metrics in any shape or form, then the team leaders need to be the first to embrace them and deliver against them
e) Give and breed the commitment that you will do everything to survive and grow, to get people through it and come out the other end an even more robust and aggressive business.

<u>Cut the fat NOT the muscle</u>

When you need to reduce a cost base to keep things alive you cannot afford to be shy in wielding the knife.

Now is the time that you need to truly understand that you are getting the utmost bang for your buck and, though it can be difficult at times, developing some objective 'laws' by which you make financial decisions can be key to your survival.

At ecrmpeople we developed three simple laws across the core of our business: SALES, PEOPLE and CUSTOMERS.

1) SALES – If what you are doing does not move you towards your next sale, then why are you doing it? Cut it and focus on what will deliver.

2) PEOPLE – If the team member you are dealing with is not ready to give 100%, then why are they here? Time and money are best spent on people who are up for the fight.
3) CUSTOMERS – Are they properly financed? What exposure does working with them represent? Be ready to cement relationships or ready to walk away in a positive manner.

In its simplest terms check everything you spend your money on, to the extent of not just considering its cost but its impact on your bottom line.

A recession is probably not the time for getting a snazzy new logo but that doesn't mean a sales competition should be cut too!

Be the best place to be

During a recession, one way 99% of people try to keep things ticking is by reducing commission and reviewing staff packages. Let your competitors be the ones to do this.

The quickest way to lose your best performers is to change the way they are rewarded as the market becomes tougher. If your commission plans are right and they work during the good times, then stand by them as they will certainly be good enough to get you through the tough times.

Quite simply if you think hacking back the payments you make to the people who perform will help you get through a recession, then you're wrong. The issue is not the amount you pay to the performers.

If anything you should look to review the packages of people who are not making commissions, not those who are. If someone is supposed to be making a living from sales commission and they are not making any, then what more of a flag do you need to know that it's not happening for them?

Importantly, now is the time to make your office the most fun and energetic place that it can be. Doing so means that before long you will have some of your competitors best people looking at your company with envious eyes, making all the more simple to attract the best talent into your business – most of whom will bring a raft of fresh experience and contacts.

Creating an environment where people want to be and can thrive does not cost much – in fact 90% of it is down to the way you treat your staff. Even if all you do is remember the basics of smiling and making time to laugh, you will already be doing more than some of your competitors.

Today ecrmpeople continue to grow and its revenues recently topped GBP£15M in what have been incredibly tight trading conditions. It is undoubtedly testament to the cultural footprint that the adherence to the above has instilled into the infrastructure, processes and, above everything else, THE PEOPLE in the business that this has been achieved.

Finally, recessions are perceived as terrifying, business-eating monsters that cannot be stopped and crush everything in their path. This is not the case...just be ready for it, be quick to take action and be fearless in your passion to survive and grow.

However, one final word of advice...don't tell your competitors.

Zeeshan Rahat Kureshi

Recession: Misery or Opportunity?

Current Position:	CEO & COO
Experience:	Masters of Science in Information Systems MBA
Email:	zeeshan@celebritydialogue.com
LinkedIn:	www.linkedin.com/profile/view?id=22316103&locale=en_US&trk=tab_pro
Twitter:	www.twitter.com/celebritydialog
Facebook:	www.facebook.com/home.php#!/pages/Celebrity-Dialogue/319239817171
Website:	www.celebritydialogue.com

After completing his MBA in Banking and Finance, Zeeshan Rahat Kureshi did his Masters in Information Systems (MSIS) at University of Texas at Arlington (UTA). He had the honour of winning the Graduate Level Paper and Presentation Contest at the annual National Collegiate Conference (2003), making him the first ever UTA student to win the honour at this national level event. Zeeshan was the Vice President of AITP Student Chapter at UTA. He was also included in the Dean's List for Graduate Programmes.

Apart from being the CEO and Chief Editor of CelebrityDialogue.com, where he has interviewed hundreds of international personalities, Zeeshan is the Chief Operating Officer of a Telecommunications and Internet company, ConnecTel. He has prior experience in Advertising and BPO industries. Zeeshan initiated CelebrityDialogue.com in February 2010 to bring to focus lives and stories of wonderful people from around the world in the form of interviews. Since then, numerous interviews of amazing personalities have been featured on the web magazine and the project has received tremendous appreciation. Zeeshan's vision is to make CelebrityDialogue.com the biggest repository of quality interviews in the world.

Chapter 31: Recession - Misery or Opportunity?

The lessons that I wish to share from this latest recession are best told through my personal story of what happened to me during the last three years.

I still remember those days back in September 2008 when the current financial crisis was just beginning to emerge. International news headlines were fraught with disastrous news flashes such as: 'Fannie Mae and Freddie Mac seized by the government'; 'Bank of America buys Merrill Lynch'; 'Lehman Brothers files for bankruptcy' and 'Bush Administration announces a bail-out plan'. It was as if the world had come to an end.

Amid all this chaos there was this feeling lurking somewhere in my heart that somehow I would not be affected by this recession. I knew the phrase 'hope is the key to life' and was hoping to remain unscathed by the terrible events that were unfolding around the world.

"I am far away from the US and my country is not even financially connected that tightly with them," I thought. Still, I knew there was not much that I could do had my fears turned into reality.

Murphy's Law states 'Anything that can go wrong will go wrong'. And so the inevitable happened.

I was working with my brother in his out-of-home advertising business at that time. The business came to an almost abrupt stand-still, partly because of the recession and partly due to some internal industry issues.

I was already working as a management consultant on a part-time capacity for an IT company. Our industry and company hit the end of the road suddenly and I was offered full-time employment in the IT Company.

It was a difficult decision for me. How could I leave my company where I had worked for so many years? How could I stop working with my brother who had been good support for so long? How could I leave the industry where I had gained so much experience?

The ground reality was that despite everything, I had to think about my family: my wife and child. Difficult decisions in life, sometimes, must be taken before it's too late. So after carefully analysing the present situation and future prospects, I took the plunge.

I switched my role to Chief Operating Officer at ConnecTel. The company provided internet, telephony, data and IT services. I did not have much idea about the intricacies of this sector but I was willing to learn. I had to learn fast and I had to be good at decision making. The company was already making heavy losses and I felt I was about to face, probably, the biggest challenge of my life.

There were a few critical problems in the new company. First, the personnel (from department heads to lower staff) were not punctual at all. Why? Because the CEO was never really in the office due to his engagement with other projects.

In short – this company was being neglected. Hence I introduced a proper attendance system and enforced strict timings. Initially there was opposition but slowly things calmed down and improvement was obvious.

Secondly, in most cases standard operating procedures were either not practised at all or they were not written. I started documenting the SOPs and built them from scratch wherever they were missing.

Thirdly, a proper chain of command was missing in most cases and people did not know to whom they should report. I made an organogram and communicated the reporting structure to everyone.

We decided to expand our network by deploying more fibre optic cable and by entering into some new markets. Primarily, this decision was made keeping in mind the needs of corporate clients who, despite recession, needed reliable and fast internet services that were not really available otherwise. 'Fibre Optic' was the buzz word around the town and we decided to capitalise.

I am pleased to state that since I joined this company, our revenue has grown more than 100 percent and we have started to make profit. Our clientele is ever-increasing and we are still hiring.

In no way can I take all the credit for this success, but behind every success story there is a team. I am thankful to my team for its support.

Another wonderful thing happened to me during this recession. I started my own web magazine, CelebrityDialogue.com, with the aim to make it the biggest repository of quality interviews on the Internet.

During this journey, I communicated with so many wonderful people around the world and shed light over their achievements and accomplishments on CelebrityDialogue.com. Sharing the stories, habits and successes of highly talented, international individuals provided me, and the visitors of my magazine, an insight into their brilliant minds.

I was able to build strategic alliances with people thousands of miles away and have fulfilled my lifelong dream of having a business I can call my own.

Had the recession not arrived, I might never have been able to muster up the courage to initiate this project. Hence, there are a few invaluable lessons that I learned from this recession:

1. No matter what happens, never give up
2. People end up knowing what their true potential is during harsh times
3. Recession is not always bad for everybody
4. Recession can make you do things that you never thought you could do
5. Recession can bring strangers together to develop synergies
6. Friendships and relationships are tested during bad economic conditions
7. Recession can give you time to rectify and strengthen internal procedures.
8. And most importantly: there is always light at the end of the tunnel!

The Business Leaders Book Club
Series One: Lessons Learned From The Recession

AUTHOR
TBLBC

Paul Dunn

Between Your Ears!!

Current Position:	Chairman of Buy 1 Get 1
Experience:	Created awesome businesses. Speaks around the world sharing how to do it with others.
	paul@b1g1.com
Email:	http://sg.linkedin.com/in/paulsdunn
LinkedIn:	www.twitter.com/pauldunn
Twitter:	www.b1g1.com
Website:	The Firm of the Future:
Links to	www.books.google.com/books?vid=YkDvAAAA
Other Works:	MAAJ
	Write language:
	www.books.google.com/books?vid=wnykAAAA
	CAAJ
Contact Number:	+65 6898 2446

Paul works with businesses to help them gain and sustain strategic competitive advantage. Over the last twenty years he has worked with organisations of all types and sizes from Global Corporations to Start Ups. He's known worldwide as the 'Wizard of Wow'. He's passionate about unleashing the power of giving. He adds that special 'buzz' to businesses, transforming enterprises from within. His ideas are rarely 'conventional' yet they become totally sustainable, creating competitive advantage for companies across the globe.

Chapter 32: Between Your Ears!!

In 1981 when I first started speaking, a mentor of mine said, "Always remember, Paul that the economy is between your ears."

And as he said it, he pointed to my brain. The way we think determines everything.

And now, 30 years later, not a day has gone by (yes, that's a lot of days) when it doesn't show itself to be true.

It was true when I was creating great businesses after being one of the first 10 people at Hewlett Packard in Australia. It was true when I was travelling the world showing others how to create great businesses. And it's true now in my role as Chairman of Buy1GIVE1 (which most of the world now know as B1G1).

Yet nowhere was that lesson hammered home more than in the 'GFC' or whatever name you put on it.

But of course, it's more complex than that....or is it really?

I love what US President Obama said in his Inauguration speech delivered right at the height of the economic 'turn-down'.

"Our workers are no less productive than when this crisis began. Our minds are no less inventive. Our capacity remains undiminished."

It's true isn't it? But you might argue that people's capacity to buy changed and so that was the problem.

Well, it might be true that the people you were working with (your customers and your then current clients) capacity to buy changed. But elsewhere 'stuff' was happening; sales — great sales — were being made.

Take just one example, the iPhone. It sold faster during the GFC than at any time before. Why?...Because it became a *must have* for a whole swag of people. People who didn't necessarily want nor need an iPhone but people who wanted to 'belong' to what Apple stood for.

Just read that last sentence again, 'People who didn't necessarily want nor need an iPhone, but people who wanted to 'belong' to what Apple stood for.'

That, for me, was one of THE most important lessons. As *Start with WHY* author, Simon Sinek, so wonderfully points out, "People don't buy what you do; they buy what you stand for." Or in iteration, "People don't buy what you do; they buy what you believe in."

Now I imagine you're nodding. Most people do when they hear it for the first time. "Oh yes," they say, "that's **SO** true."

So if you are nodding, then this becomes the most important question — what is it you believe in? What is it you stand for?

After all if people buy what you believe in you'd better tell them, right? You'd better let them see it, hear it, feel it, touch it. As Simon Sinek pointed out in a recent conversation — "Your why MUST be front and centre."

Your why is what gets you up inspired every morning. And when you really get it, it becomes powerful and compelling enough to make you choke or even shed tears.

But for many, the WHY is waffle, rambling or worse still, a kind of 'generic' feel-good. They simply don't cut it. (By the way, to REALLY get to your why, pretend you're a child and just keeping asking 'why' to every attempt at getting your why until you get one that brings a lump in your throat).

Which leads us to a second major lesson from the GFC: the way in which we communicate now has to be different. And I believe there are four key things that are so much more important than they ever were — the GFC has simply magnified the need for them. Here they are:

TRUST
AUTHENTICITY
CERTAINTY
BREVITY/SIMPLIFY

Look at each word and then you'll realise that they're all related. Again these were ALWAYS important but now they're even more so. And that's because one big thing that happened in the GFC was that our trust in all our institutions, politicians and companies totally plummeted.

It was a watershed. And it leads, I believe, to the biggest lesson of all: for far too long, our society had become one of taking. And the universe, in what my friend Dr. John Demartini points out is 'always being in perfect balance', reacted.

Hence the reason we're now seeing the rise and rise of what trendwatching.com refers to as 'Generation G' where the 'G' stands not for 'Greed' but for 'Generosity'.

It's a huge movement. And it's a Generation that, unlike the Generation X, Y and Z, does not depend on the year of your birth — Generation G spreads itself across all age groups.

Generation G gives back. Generation G volunteers (in huge numbers). Generation G has a sense of purpose. As authors John Gerzema and Michael D'Antonio point out in their 2010 book, SpendSHIFT, people are searching not so much for value but for values.

And that dovetails beautifully into where we began these 'lessons from the recession'. Knowing your why is clearly related to knowing your purpose.

And instead of that purpose being taking, the lesson is to make it a purpose of contribution. That's the biggest lesson of all — one that is, of course, timeless. But one that the recession reminded us we'd forgotten.

And for us in B1G1 it was a huge lesson. But in an unexpected way.

B1G1 started pre-GFC (in 2007) with one simple goal; to create a world full of giving.

Why? Because that's the way to create a happier world.

Our theory and practice has been that the way to do that is NOT by having massive or even small one-off events, nor is it through ad-hoc giving. It is done by making giving a habit. You do it by making sure that every transaction gives back in some measureable, defined way. You buy a coffee and a child gets access to water; you buy a book and a tree gets planted; you buy (or sell) a TV and a person who's cataract blind gets the gift of sight.

Some people call that transaction-based giving. In B1G1 we call it 'Embedded Generosity'.

And to make it work, you truly focus (or niche). The GFC taught us that.

But in 2007 when we started, the time was very definitely different. We could, in effect, suggest we were all things to all people.

But, bearing in mind those four communication principles above, we learnt that FOCUS was essential. From being all things to all people we moved to dominate one niche (and that is SO important - just OWN a niche). For us the niche became business and exclusively SMEs.

When we did that niche-ing we began to discover some fascinating things. For example, we found that of the $390 BILLION given to US-based charities, only four per cent of that was coming from business.

And we realised we couldn't wait for business to come to us; we had to go to them.

And so we began a series of live Seminars. Seminars that captivated those who came and catapulted B1G1's growth; so much so that by the end of 2010 we were able to announce that 1,000,000 people had been given access to water through B1G1 - a staggering number.

That simply would not have happened had we not been focused or niched. Because we were niched, we were able to communicate with:

TRUST
AUTHENTICITY

CERTAINTY
BREVITY/SIMPLIFY

We were able to say that B1G1 exists because businesses have the power to change our lives. That became our powerful WHY. That became, for an increasing number of businesses, their mantra too — they simply wanted to belong.

And we've seen amazing things. Even businesses that have been going for years are actually embracing and more importantly EMBEDDING the giving. And in one now fairly famous case, even changing the business name to reflect it (against my advice by the way!)

The business was (for nine years) 'Integrated Office Solutions' in Melbourne, Australia. They're a great business too. B1G1 impacted their team; they got an even greater sense of purpose. And so now, they're 'Make a Difference Office Supplies'. See what they're doing here at www.14reasons.com.au.

And so B1G1 is now able to make even bigger impacts. Just in the latter part of 2010, we were featured in Fast Company, on Springwise.com, on Trendwatching.com, on Mashable.com (that was thrilling for us) and, believe it or not, even in Forbes Magazine.

That was such a huge surprise. We were looking at the stats (as of course we do every day) and we noticed this amazing peak in people joining from Russia, from Kurdistan and even from Korea.

So we started digging. And there we were in Forbes Magazine…in Russia (and in Russian!)

Masami Sato, B1G1's founder, loves to tell us that there's a gift in everything … if only we look closely enough. And perhaps the gift in this is as simple as knowing that the economy really is between our ears.

Derrick Hayes
Your Mind is Recession Proof

Current Position:	CEO of W.O.E. Enterprises – Chief Encouragement Officer
Qualifications:	BA – Business Administration from College of Business at Tennessee State University.
Experience:	Encouraging Entrepreneurs since 1992
Email:	info@derrickhayes.com oneword@bellsouth.net
LinkedIn:	www.linkedin.com/pub/derrick-hayes/3/710/516
Twitter:	www.twitter.com/Encouragement4u
Facebook:	www.facebook.com/getawoe
YouTube:	www.YouTube.com/Encouragement4u
Website:	www.DerrickHayes.com www.MotivationToYourMobile.com
Contact Number:	+1 706-615-1662

Derrick Hayes is the Creator of Derricknyms, Author of One Word Is All It Takes and Developer of the Motivation To Your Mobile Android Application. Derrick is an alumnus of Tennessee State University is available for small and large meetings, church events, academic speaking engagements and workshops.

Please visit Derrick's website at www.DerrickHayes.com to book him for a speaking engagement or media event or send an email to info@DerrickHayes.com.

Chapter 33: Your Mind is Recession Proof

In June of 2008 I walked away from my job as a Juvenile Corrections Officer. I had carefully planned my exit as it was a dream to leave on my own terms and on the table I had over $20,000 in contract opportunities.

Business and life are parallel. The things I went through in 2003 prepared me for the recession of 2008. I was separated from my wife and eventually divorced. The family strain was also felt when I was not with my children full time. Feeling like I had lost it all, I knew I had to change my thinking to change my direction.

The first signs of the 2008 recession were when phone calls were not getting returned and contracts not getting signed. The $20,000 I had counted on to help me survive was down to zero. I thought about what I did in 2003 when all the chips were down. The main things I learned then were to be mentally tough and never give up.

In order to increase revenue in tough times I knew I needed to get exposure. I started searching the internet for ways to get my name in the game. After hunting for information I came across resources like Help A Reporter Out (HARO) and Reporter Connection. I signed up for as many free PR newsletters that I could.

My initial goal was to get one interview. I realised over time that there were many different ways to gain access to the media. I now knew it was realistic to go from unknown to known with the resources that were available to me.

I started to contact reporters and took notes on what they responded to and did not respond to. From scratch I learned how to get blogged, quoted, interviewed and how to find contributing author opportunities.

One of the most exciting things I discovered during the recession was the power in marketing your products and services in gift bags. People thought I was crazy when I said if you give it away they will eventually pay. I designed a flyer that meeting planners could print out and place into the bags. This was a win-win where I gave a discount and the conference or event promoted me to their audience. The valuable lesson I learned was that organisations are more willing to do business with you when they have the opportunity to get to know you.

The two things that the recession shared with me that I will always practise in my business are:

- Be Yourself. Live life the way you want to and not the way that others think you should. In all of us is a gift and our purpose is to tap into that greatness.

- Give it away. Let the universe sample the greatness inside of you.

Here is what I learned from other business owners during the recession:

1. Everyone was not affected by the recession the same. When I first heard 'recession' I assumed that everyone lost everything. You have to start from where you are and make the most of each opportunity.

2. You have to look in the mirror and be accountable. You can't blame anyone else for your failure. Find out what works for you and make it work.

3. Work hard and produce quality work. When you put in the time the results will show. Ideas that you put into place today may not bear fruit for 12 to 18 months from now.

4. Pace yourself to be able to produce more. Once you learn how to do it right, put what you do into a system so that you can measure what you do and always strive to get the best results.

The way I implemented changes in my business was to write down the things I did everyday that made me successful. These concepts I turned into a social media system that helped increase my chances of getting booked for an interview by 50%.

The tips I would give to anyone entering and exiting a recession are through the word ENCOURAGE. These strategies will help you succeed in business and life.

Educate: Learn more about your industry.
Nurture: Get a mentor to guide you.
Challenge: See how much better you can become.
Offer: Put ideas together and see opportunities.
Uplift: Inspire others in good and bad times.
Rise: Even when you fall, get back up.
Adjust: Another way can open the best way.
Grow: Mature and turn your mess into a message.
Expect: Thinking positive will knock negativity out.

If you ENCOURAGE your dream, success will be on your team.

Results from Change

Back in September 2008 I was looking for ways to cost effectively market my business. I was on Twitter one day and my prayer was answered. I don't even remember what I was searching for when I came across HARO. I have had tremendous success in a short amount of time. I have been blogged, interviewed on radio and become a contributing author in nine books.

I have been promoted for free in gift bags at over 100 events internationally including the U.S., Canada, U.K. and Sweden. Some of the major organisations include Boy Scouts of America, Big Brothers Big Sisters, Girls, Inc., Canadian Council Aboriginal Business and Energy Up.

One of the Business Relationships formed by giving back was with Energy Up. Energy Up is an organisation inspired by the work of Voltage that gives back to inner city youth. Voltage is a celebrity trainer with Katie Couric as a client. When I provided Derricknyms for graduates in the Energy Up program, I also included one for Katie. A personalised Derricknym that I designed is on the wall in her Hampton home. Every few months representatives from Energy Up now order Derricknyms from me.

I took what I learned from the recession and turned the knowledge into three eBooks.

1. Social Media Strategies To Position Yourself as an Expert.
2. Put It In The Bag: Guide for Entrepreneurs to Market in Gifts Bags FOR FREE at meetings, conferences, and events all over the world.
3. Raising Money In A Recession.

I have been featured in stories on major websites such as DiversityInc.com, CNNMoney.com and MSNBC.com

The strategies I learned during the recession have helped me become a contributing author in nine books.

The recession not only forced me to think I can, but to think differently. You will never know what you can do until you try. When I had to I learned how to. When you open your mind you will realise that nothing can stop you, not even a recession.

Your Mind Is Recession Proof.

Currently I teach and educate others on how to find cost effective ways to market their business. On average I'm blogged or quoted in various publications up to 14 times a month. In January 2010 I started writing quotes and gave birth to the DAILY Derricknym.

After realising that there were five billion mobile phone users worldwide I developed the 'Motivation to Your Mobile', an Android Application, to give people a positive way to start their day.

AUTHOR
TBLBC

Martha Urquhart

The Climate on the Inside Overcomes the Climate on the Outside

Current Position:	Curriculum developer Writer Facilitator, trainer Consultant, coach
Qualifications:	Currently enrolled in the Master's in Adult Education program at the University of Alberta, Canada Bachelor's in Education degree from the University of Victoria, Canada Certificate in Adult and Continuing Education.
Email:	lemonaidelife@gmail.com
LinkedIn:	http://ca.linkedin.com/pub/martha-urquhart/20/946/21

Martha Urquhart strives constantly to move forward, to expand her comfort zone and to reach her potential. Her extensive experience in the adult literacy and English as a second language fields has given her the ability to help businesses to adopt literacy-friendly practices in order to be accessible to more people.

She is able to inspire others to develop their own potential and she has the ability to illustrate through modelling, coaching and instruction, the steps involved in doing so.

She invites you to visit her on LinkedIn or to email her, lemonaidelife@gmail.com.

Chapter 34: The Climate on the Inside Overcomes the Climate on the Outside

At the time of this latest recession, I had been working for a non-profit educational organisation. Recessions are good for educational organisations; it's the bull markets that they have to guard themselves against.

Instead, knowing that most of the small family-run businesses within my community in northern Canada remained in operation throughout the recession, I approached the one that I knew would be able to provide advice on how to stay afloat throughout the various economic throes.

Slave Lake, Alberta, Canada, serves a vast geographical region because, even though it only has a population of slightly more than 7,000 people (according to the 2009 census), it is the largest centre for 275 kilometres in any direction. The major industries in the region are oil, gas and forestry, with the forestry industry being hit the hardest in this most recent recession.

Joyce Robinson has seen her business, The Business Factory, grow dramatically over the past 19 years. In the beginning, she partnered with another individual to offer bookkeeping and secretarial services to the region. Then in 2002, Joyce bought her partner out and became a limited corporation. At the same time, she and her husband took over a local printing business amalgamating that service into their offerings. Joyce ran the business services while her husband, Doug, ran the printing business. Both aspects of the business were conducted in separate locations.

In 2005, they purchased and moved into one building, right on main street. By this time, the town had a population of over 6,000 people. Shortly after moving, they incorporated promotional items into their profile.

By 2007, the town's population reached an all-time high of over 7,000 residents. The Business Factory was booming. Since adding the promotional items in 2005, Joyce's annual revenue had increased by 25% each year. As a result, from 2005-2009, the staff increased from three to nine. Then the recession hit.

Effects of the Recession

Throughout 2009, Joyce did not see one drop in the sale of promotional items. Instead, this one aspect of the business that she had thought would decline the quickest stayed constant throughout the year, remaining consistent with the previous year's sales.

The only effect that Joyce could see that the recession had on her business was that, for the first time in its history, there were up to six businesses that were delinquent on their printing orders. They did not pay for their order, did not bother to pick up their order or chose to forfeit on their order. These were companies that either went bankrupt or simply chose not to start the business at that time. Since these orders were from small companies, the financial effect on her business was minimal.

Since September 2010, printing orders have been flooding the business, increasing the sales in that department by 15% to 25% per month. Because of the latest dramatic increase in revenue in just a few months, Joyce is feeling the need to create yet another position, increasing her team to ten.

Successful Management Habits

Joyce believes that the secret to any successful business is having dedicated core staff. Over one third of her team have committed themselves to their work, considering their positions as 'careers' and not simply jobs. Through the development of specific habits, Joyce has built a positive working environment. Her team feel they have a vested interest in the business and the enjoyment and dedication that her team have towards their work is felt by the customers. Joyce's management habits include:

- Trusting in the core staff, assigning them specific roles and key positions so that Joyce does not have to manage those areas of the business.

- Asking for their advice when interviewing new team members and discussing qualifications and personalities of essential employees. Since the office layout is open, it is critical that new employees fit within the established group. Any conflict creates tension that can be felt by all.

- Seeking the advice of her core staff when Joyce needs to make decisions about taking on new projects. She consults with them on what new services should be added, who would have the time and skills to take on any new projects and how best to complete a project.

Competing Against the 'Big Ones'

The greatest competition that Joyce faces in today's global world comes from the online companies who can offer prices so low that she cannot compete, regardless of what corners she cut. She knows her prices are higher than many of her competitors; however, she refuses to sacrifice quality for price.

Joyce was worried when a popular chain 'box store', also offering business services, first moved into the small town. However, she has found that their presence has not affected her business in any way. She welcomes the competition as, once a customer has ordered with a large-scale operation, they often return due to the quality of service that Joyce can offer with her personalised business touch, which includes services as simple as:

- Keeping an extra printing order on the shelf for regular clients in case they require an order immediately or in case they misjudged the quantity they required when placing the initial order.

- Giving random discounts to clients as a thank-you or throwing in some extra promotional items into an order.

Joyce understands how quickly people will stop accessing a business if that business stops promoting its services and products. Being that her business offers advice and products to other businesses on how to promote themselves, she takes her own advice:

- Promote, promote and promote some more

- Consistent advertising on the local radio

- Her business grows by word of mouth more than any other type of advertising. Her customers appreciate the quality of product they receive, as well as the personalised service and recommend her business to others in their field.

Joyce has produced semi-annual flyers in the past but found that the only increase in sales came from her regular clients. Very seldom would a flyer distribution bring in new clients. She finds that there is no need for her to raise further awareness through flyers or printed advertisements as her business has more than enough to keep her busy.

Community Involvement

Since Joyce operates her business and lives within a small, isolated, rural, northern town, she understands the importance of being involved in her community. She offers any non-profit organisation in town ten percent off all their printing orders. She is often asked to donate the posters for fundraising events. And she sees a constant stream of individuals and groups dropping in to ask for donations for some worthy cause.

One lesson that Joyce knows she has to learn is to say "no." She finds this hard to accomplish because there are so many organisations that are worthy and in need of local sponsorship. One solution she believes will help is to set a donation budget and specifically choose which organisations she is willing to support through her business.

Mottos to Do Business By

Joyce has a few simple mottos that she has crafted over the many years of operating her business:

- Learn as you go
- Live and Learn
- Try not to make the same mistake a second time.

These mottos were illustrated when Joyce implemented a policy and procedures manual 15 years after starting her business. The increase in staff, and her experiences with some staff that took advantage of her flexibility and willingness to accommodate, required the need to have policies and procedures outlined clearly. Even with a policy and procedures manual, Joyce believes that businesses have to allow flexibility for staff to accommodate family needs and childcare concerns. In this way, and through other methods, her team feel appreciated, which is perhaps the most important trait a business could adopt.

William C Brown

Cost Cutting is Not Enough

Current Position:	VP Manufacturing and Operations
Experience:	BS in Engineering, MBA, 30+ years of experience in 3 international companies, 6 years in foreign countries, Six Sigma Blackbelt, Certified Quality Manager, APICS training
Email:	wmcbrown@yahoo.com
LinkedIn:	www.linkedin.com/in/williamcbrown
Website:	www.wmcbrown.com
Contact Number:	+1 949.243.6666

Bill Brown is currently the VP of Manufacturing and Operations for Ossur Americas.

He is a manufacturing and operations professional with over 30 years experience improving organisation performance, with extensive experience in quality, lean manufacturing and plant and operations management. He has managed organisations of 700 people, P&L of $150M and spent six years working internationally.

In his career Bill has started and managed organisations and functions in four countries, has downsized and closed plants, transferred products around the world, and developed high-performing organisations that reach world-class levels of performance. He is trained as a Six-Sigma black belt, is a Certified Quality Manager, has an MBA and is now pursuing higher education in Supply Chain excellence.

His passions are organisational excellence and world-class manufacturing.

Chapter 35: Cost Cutting is Not Enough

The most common reaction when facing an economic hardship is to 'tighten the belt' to rein in spending. While I agree that it is important to have strong cost control, I suggest that a two-pronged approach is even better, specifically one which maximises benefits while minimising cost.

In doing so, we drive higher VALUE. As is always the case, a beneficial outcome is achieved when the marginal return is greater than the marginal cost associated with any action, so clearly an improved economic position is achieved when benefits are driven to higher levels, while simultaneously reducing cost. So, the logical question is how to do this?

Our company is recognised for its innovative Prosthetics products and is also the third largest player in the global bracing and supports market; we offer a comprehensive line of custom-made and off-the-shelf products for ankle, foot, neck, spine and arm. These quality products support joints and other body parts for both therapeutic and preventative purposes and combine some of the most effective technologies available today.

We operate internationally with six of our 14 sites in North America. Recent market dynamics (recession and competition) have put a lot of pressure on our sales prices, which subsequently put pressure on our profit margins.

In response to the subsequent need to improve cost, about 12 months ago we chose to aggressively step up our efforts to implement Lean Manufacturing principles. While the concept was originally pioneered in Toyota more than 60 years ago, many companies still have not yet fully adopted this methodology and in fact, at that time we were just on the front end of our own implementation.

Additionally, many people think that this concept applies strictly to manufacturing operations; this, however, is simply not true. The application of Lean Manufacturing concepts in business processes is Lean 'Thinking' and works equally well regardless of the industry, company, business or business process. Lean Manufacturing and Lean Thinking are about eliminating the waste that prevents delivering the desired product or service to the customer in the most efficient manner.

We have found that Lean Manufacturing applied to manufacturing processes coupled with Lean Thinking applied to our daily operations and business processes, had a profound effect on cost and the performance of our business processes.

The results after less than two years of Lean application are quite exciting. In 2010 alone we have:

- reduced our operating cost in one facility by almost 10% (with productivity up 40% in targeted areas)
- improved throughput by 40% in our most demanding product
- safety has improved by 40% across all the sites
- quality trends are all improving.

On top of this, this Lean focus helped to support achieving the highest delivery performance in the history of the company - up 8% to near perfect in the course of 2010.

Let's look at some of the lessons learned that can be universally applied:

1. Put the customer first

Lean puts the customer in the centre of every business decision because ultimately the customer is always impacted by changes in how we conduct our business and after all, customers do have choices. Essentially we need to develop a personal connection with our customers; we are finding that if our employees learn to regard their customers (whether internal or external) as a family member or even as 'boss', they are more apt to provide the kind of service that will truly delight the customer.

In our particular case, we have our site directors reaching out to make a personal connection with their biggest customers to establish a one-to-one relationship, to get to know them, their pressure points and how they define our success – a vast improvement over the previous internal focus. As we all know, once we understand the rules of any game (in this case the customer sets these rules) we can win. We also know that it is far more cost effective to keep existing customers than to acquire new ones and we feel this personalisation is a key tactic. With this improved understanding of the role of the customer at every level of our business, we are playing to win.

2. Engage and empower your employees

We commonly hear that employees are our greatest assets – but do we treat them as such? Are they respected for the knowledge that they possess in the function that they perform?

In reality, no one knows their job better than they do, so we need to acknowledge them as experts and involve them in identifying improvement opportunities with their part of the process or transaction. Lean regards the employees as 'expert' and the approach of 'go to Gemba' means we need to go to where the work is done and involve these local experts in improving their environment, their results and their productivity. This drives immense value with virtually no cost.

Further to this, a study of the practices in the 'Best Places to Work' venue complements this approach and can serve as a guide to inspire extraordinary effort from our employees.

Setting employee engagement as an objective and finding ways to measure it will drive value with virtually no cost; especially since some of the biggest gains come from just increasing this awareness along with some supervisory style improvements.

3. Communicate your Vision and Mission

What is your purpose? Why does your organisation exist? What roles does it have in the larger company? What is required to be a huge success? Do all employees know the answers to these questions?

Understanding this and having the leaders lead by example will drive alignment of intent, attitude and related behaviours. You will no longer have an 'army of one' but instead a whole workforce aligned to achieve your goals. In Lean, there are formal processes for driving alignment throughout the entire organisation, but the simplest way to accomplish this is through consistent communications.

4. Have big goals

Once you are effectively communicating and have some alignment in purpose, make sure your goals are significant, make a difference and energise the employees to offer their best effort. Our goal is to achieve world-class levels of performance in a very short period of time. To do this, everyone needs to buy into these ambitions and to truly be empowered to do their best work. Jim Collins in *Good to Great* calls these 'BHAGS' (big, hairy, audacious goals), while Stephen Covey calls them 'WIGS' (wildly important goals).

Regardless of their name, having ambitious goals can galvanise the workforce to accomplish nearly impossible feats. Remember JFK's 'put a man on the moon' challenge?

5. Have the right performance measures and make them visible

In Lean, we call this 'visual factory'. I recently had a very interesting experience that put me on the 'benefits' side of this thinking. Over a short period of time, I had the opportunity to be a patient at two different hospitals - each one commonly recognised as good but each markedly different in their attitudes toward their customer (in this case, me).

I later noticed that the better of the two had their Purpose and their Goals statements prominently displayed, had posters that showed their focus on the patient (their 'customer'), used surveys to measure patient satisfaction and asked for and reacted to customer feedback. You can imagine the difference this approach made in patient handling. If you had a choice, which would you prefer?

In one case, I felt important, in the other not so; small things can make the difference between 'good' and 'superior'. Observing this difference first-hand as a customer has further convinced me of the power associated with the diligent application of the above points. Why not measure your performance against the goals of 'superior' performance? This could make a profound difference in your business.

6. Ask "why" and challenge the process

I learned long ago that effective leadership is about challenging the status quo. We need to consciously look for improvement opportunities and believe that by making small improvements on a regular basis, we will at some point achieve excellence.

This is the spirit of 'Kaizen' in Lean Manufacturing. My boss once said it very well:

"OK is not OK."

If we are not continually improving, we are falling behind. As leaders we need to set the direction and be pace-setters for change. Lee Iacocca once said, "Lead, follow, or get out of the way". In recessionary times, it is more important than ever to truly 'lead' because 'following' is generally not a winning strategy in the competitive, recessionary world of today.

Lessons learned in this recession are the same lessons that will lead to a state of excellence after the recession. Frugality is important but so is efficiency. Making the best use of resources, respecting and involving employees, putting the customer first, setting big goals, consistent communication and deploying visible measures lead to waste elimination and a culture of continuous improvement, thus driving increased value. Further emphasis on cost control is synergistic and leads to even greater success.

The company that I am currently associated with understands this very well and this is why 'Efficiency' is now a Key Focus Area for us.

As the VP of Manufacturing and Operations for North America, I know that we can be wildly successful in accomplishing all of our ambitious goals by applying these Lean Thinking concepts to everything we do; we are rapidly establishing a mindset of unlimited thinking and can-do attitudes in our employees that will lead to world-class performance even in a difficult market.

Wendy Shand

Marketing Harder Helped our 'Toddler' Company out of Nappies and Grow 97% in the Recession

Current Position:	Founder, www.totstotravel.co.uk
Experience:	6 years running a fast growth business with 97%+ growth rate during the recession
Email:	enquiries@totstotravel.co.uk
LinkedIn:	http://uk.linkedin.com/pub/wendy-shand/6/177/3b5
Twitter:	www.twitter.com/#!/Totstotravelmum
Facebook:	www.facebook.com/home.php#!/group.php?gid=113344788710490
Website:	www.totstotravel.co.uk www.holidayhomerentalsite.com
Contact Number:	+44 (0) 845 26 941 26

Multi-award winning Tots to Travel www.totstotravel.co.uk) gives parents with small children and babies peace of mind and a stress-free family holiday experience – from start to finish. Frustrated by the lack of safe, family-friendly holiday accommodation, Wendy Shand, mum of three, set up this unique holiday lettings agency giving families exactly what they want from their holiday.

Wendy is an author, a role model and mentor for women in business and has a growing media presence as an expert on family travel and the holiday lettings industry. She is regularly called upon to comment on small business issues and is a pioneer in using the internet to achieve a better work/life balance.

Chapter 36: Marketing Harder Helped our 'Toddler' Company out of Nappies and Grow 97% in the Recession

Our holiday lettings company, Tots To Travel, was barely out of nappies when the recession hit and, like all new 'parents', my husband Rob and I had no idea what to expect.

When the last recession happened, the two of us had been at university and so hadn't really been affected by it.

This time around, we were the owners of a fledgling travel firm and were understandably concerned by the damage a recession might wreak on a company like ours. We'd invested so much money, time and energy in it and had just begun to reap the rewards – we'd won awards and were building a great customer base. We had so much to lose.

In the early months of the recession, we had plenty of sleepless nights and nail-biting days. When the world was being struck by something so profound, we wondered how we could possibly escape unscathed.

It certainly didn't help that everything in the news was so very depressing.

Things got worse: over the next 12 months, a few of the largest travel companies went to the wall. Some of the medium-sized and well-known holiday companies followed. It happened almost without warning with the result that hundreds and hundreds of passengers were left stranded overseas, unable to get home.

The press carried stories about customers being concerned about the safety of their holidays. People started to ask us, "Well what would happen if you went down?"

There was a prevailing sense of doom within the travel sector and it was impossible not to be affected by it.

As the threat of job cuts spread, we feared that people would be less inclined to spend on big ticket items like holidays, just in case they were next in line for redundancy.

By November 2009, we were really worried. In the travel sector, November/December is not a good time anyway - traditionally cash flow is at its lowest level. Even outside a recession, you can spend the weeks before Christmas biting your nails, fretting whether January will bring the rich pickings you desperately need.

But the situation in November 2009 seemed even more worrying. 'This could be really, really bad,' I thought.

It was then that I realised we had to do whatever it took to survive. We needed a different approach. At that point, survival was my primary concern. I didn't imagine for a moment that we would come out with 97% growth rate we've achieved.

The first change I made was to stop listening to the news because the stories were too depressing. There was a very real danger that if we did continue to listen to all the gloomy stories and forecasts, we would begin to believe that's how things were. If we began to believe it, then our fears would be apparent to our team (we employ more than 20 overseas marketing agents who source family-friendly holiday properties for us). It was crucial that Rob and I were very positive and strong so that our team would believe it would all be okay. I think that's been a critical factor in our success.

Another was my decision to find a mentor, someone who'd 'been there, done that, got the T-shirt' and who could show <u>us</u> how to do it. Later that month, I attended a marketing seminar. I was so inspired by what I heard that I attended a two-day seminar about two months later and then signed up for a 12-month Business Development Programme. I had found my mentor!

By then, I was convinced that effective marketing would make a crucial difference to our business. Although Rob and I had used PR and marketing since setting up Tots To Travel, my mentor encouraged us to do far more and he showed us how to do it more effectively. He helped us to start thinking bigger. Forget "surviving the recession," he told us, "and start focusing on thriving." That meant out-marketing everyone else.

So, while many companies slashed their marketing budget and stopped any PR-related activities, we did the opposite. Last year we actually spent more on marketing than we had ever done before because we had so many strategies to implement.

One such strategy was placing advertising inserts in targeted publications. I started on a small scale (placing 10,000 inserts for about £1,000) in a magazine that catered to one of our niche markets, families with twins or multiple births. That campaign brought 300 new leads in eight weeks – that meant we added 300 people to our database and we could start to build a relationship with them.

Another was to write a book. My mentor told me quite early on that we needed to write a book. It is a huge positioning tool; it builds your credibility and sets you up as the only expert in your field. He gave us the strategy and demystified it. He made it seem possible and achievable. And indeed I realised how easy it would be to do, with a little bit of application.

I could have fiddled around doing some of the other marketing stuff, but actually the biggest element of it was to actually write the book. So that's what I did and within a month, I'd written the book: *Empty Weeks? How To Get More Bookings & Make Money From Your Holiday Home.*

We've used it as a marketing and promotional tool ever since: we offer it to people within our niche market in return for their contact details. Once we have those details, we can start to build a relationship with them.

And there's a big PR element to it too. For example, *The Daily Telegraph* committed a freelance journalist to write an article about me, the book and about the holiday lettings market.

Demand has been high – in just one 24-hour period, for example, I mailed over 200 copies of the book. It has brought us hundreds of new highly-targeted customers in less than 12 months.

Through the Business Development Programme, we learnt many more marketing techniques including advertising, web-based marketing, publicity and sales. We learnt the importance of automating as many business processes as possible

All of the marketing efforts would have come to nothing however, if we hadn't also learned another crucial lesson from the recession - that to succeed, particularly at a time like this, you must be inordinately customer-focused. You can't assume you know what your customers want – you have to ask them. I've learnt to really listen to what our customers tell us and then respond. I think in the past we probably did too much talking and not enough listening.

I now know how crucial it is to build relationships with prospects and understand their pains and needs before coming up with solutions. It's such a mistake to jump in and try to 'sell' the first time you make contact with your prospects – it's the equivalent of proposing marriage on a first date.

Two years ago, we were apprehensive about the negative impact the recession would have on our very young company. Now I see that the recession has been a positive catalyst for the business. It forced us to change; to seek out better, more effective ways of marketing our business and for that, we're grateful. Goals that seemed a long way off a few years ago are now a great deal closer.

To summarise, the lessons we learnt during the recession are:

- Don't listen to gloomy economic forecasts. They'll have a negative impact on your thinking. What's more, your fears and doubts will become apparent to your team members.
- Be totally customer-focused. Take the time to build relationships with your prospects before asking for a sale. Don't assume you know what your prospects and customers want - ask them.
- Find a mentor, somebody who has a proven track record and who can provide you with practical guidance. Listen to the advice they provide and take immediate action.
- Expand your belief about what is possible. Dare to think big.
- Don't cut back on your advertising and PR activities during an economic downturn. Instead, increase your marketing.
- Measure everything you do.

AUTHOR
TBLBC

Jeff Gitterman

Financial Advisors and the Recession

Current Position:	Founder and CEO – Gitterman & Associates Wealth Management, LLC and Beyond Success Consulting
Qualifications:	AAMS, LUTCF, Registered Principal and Securities Licences, Coursework in Graduate Masters Program in Conscious Evolution
Email:	jeff@BeyondSuccessConsulting.com
LinkedIn:	www.linkedin.com/pub/jeff-gitterman/7/119/58
Website:	www.BeyondSuccessConsulting.com www.gawmllc.com
Links to Other Works:	www.amazon.com *Beyond Success: Redefining the Meaning of Prosperity*
Contact Number:	+1 848-248-4864

Jeff Gitterman is an award winning financial advisor and the founder and CEO of Gitterman & Associates Wealth Management, LLC. www.gawmllc.com. He is also the co-founder of Beyond Success, a consulting firm that brings more holistic values to the world of business and finance. His first book, *Beyond Success: Redefining the Meaning of Prosperity,* was recently published by AMACOM.

Over the past several years, Jeff has been featured in *Money Magazine*, *CNN*, *Financial Advisor*, *AM New York*, *Affluent Magazine*, *New Jersey Business Journal* and News 12 *New Jersey,* among others. In 2004, he was honoured by *Fortune Small Business Magazine* as *One of Our Nation's Best Bosses.* Jeff also serves as chairman of the advisory board to the Autism Centre of New Jersey Medical School, an organisation that raises significant monies each year for autism research and support services.

Chapter 37: Financial Advisors and the Recession

In the wake of the recession, people are finding financial advisors, especially good ones who have really deep relationships with their clients, more necessary than ever. Many advisors are greatly weighed down by their own internal panic about what happened and therefore have very little capacity to deal with their clients' fears and concerns.

This crisis has called on all of us to re-evaluate our lives. I think it's starting to become clearer to all of us that the endless accumulation of material wealth is not a sustainable way to live. We need to refocus our values and beliefs on things that are ultimately much more satisfying and attainable. We need to focus on what we can do and give to the world rather than what we can just take from it.

My own understanding of the power of giving came about many years ago, when I was just starting out as a financial advisor. One of the initial appointments that I'd have with any new perspective client is what we call in the industry a 'fact-finding session'. The idea is that you are there simply to get information and gather data like their date of birth, place of work, the kind of house they lived in, income, assets and so on.

One day, I was getting out of my car and about to walk into a prospect's house to try and sell a term life policy. I was way behind on my bills and my mind was going on and on about how much I needed the sale. Desperation poured out of me as I caught my reflection in the car window. I stopped, looked hard at that reflection and said to myself: "Who would want to buy anything from you? Look at how desperate you look!"

I decided in that moment that I needed to drop my desperate, needy attitude and walk into this prospect's house with the confidence of someone who didn't want anything. I took one last look at my reflection and saw that I had taken on an air of serenity and that's when I began to realise that I really didn't need anything; that deep down there was nothing for me to get. I dropped my need to make a sale. I became still and quiet.

I soon began to approach more of my clients this way, putting all my attention on them, without any desire or expectation for myself personally. And to my amazement, my meetings really started to transform and my success as a financial advisor grew exponentially.

Although it sounds like a bit of a cliché, I was able to see firsthand as I was going through my own crisis around wealth and success that the more I gave to others the more I received in return. In turn, I quickly began accomplishing more in the world and my income grew substantially.

It's going to be very difficult for advisors who do not have the complete trust of their clients to continue to make smart decisions and many have and will continue to lose business. My number one piece of advice to advisors is this: under any and all circumstances, be honest. It's critical that we maintain a very open and honest relationship with our clients, as the worst thing any of us could do would be to mislead them right now.

I believe that now is the time for extra special service. We need to be calling our clients before they call us. We need to be out there in front. We need to show our clients that we're confident in the direction we're moving. Any lack of confidence in our own ability to navigate the current investment climate is going to make it really difficult for them to follow us.

Too many of us spend our lives waiting to get something from the world so that we can show up as the person we always knew we could be. Deep in our hearts we think there's something missing. But when we flip that mindset, we can discover that by becoming a giver rather than a taker, we can become agents for change in the world. In the end, it was only through giving to others that I was able to find the kind of happiness that I was really looking for.

Keith Kennedy

Doing More With Less

Current Position:	VP Sales and Marketing
Experience:	21 years experience in sales with a more than a decade in sales leadership.
Email:	kkennedy@phdx.com
LinkedIn:	www.linkedin.com/pub/keith-kennedy/8/241/6b9
Website:	www.phdx.com
Links to Other Works:	www.orthoworld.com/site/index.php/publications/bonezone www.orthoworld.com/knowent/orthoknow/2010/orthoknow1010.pdf
Contact Number:	+1 505-764-2894

Keith Kennedy brings to PhDx over 18 years of experience in sales, marketing and management. For nine years he worked for a Fortune 500 pharmaceutical company where he was responsible for building a sales team during two major sales force expansions in the Southwestern United States. Through his direction and leadership, Mr. Kennedy's sales team consistently outperformed national and regional averages. Throughout his healthcare career, he was responsible for sales and marketing in nine different disease states.

Mr. Kennedy also worked for a major Independent Review Board where he served on the Executive Leadership Team. His position encompassed all sales and marketing functions, product development and creation of organisational infrastructure. During his IRB career, Mr. Kennedy's clients included most major pharmaceutical companies, medical device companies and hundreds of individual physician and hospital sites. Throughout his career, Mr. Kennedy has been awarded national and regional awards and has served on multiple state and national committees and boards.

Chapter 38: Doing More With Less

The recent recession is undoubtedly the worst that most of us will experience in our professional careers. The US economy has shrunk over 4%, more than at any other time in history; corporate profits have been reduced and companies that do have money are stockpiling cash instead of spending. Needless to say, companies that survive this recession must be smart and do more with less.

Background

I am Vice President of Sales and Marketing for PhDx Systems Inc. We provide software and professional services to the medical device industry that allow them to track surgeon and patient reported outcomes on their respective implantable medical devices. We specialise in the orthopaedic, spine and cardiovascular markets.

Over 90% of medical devices are approved via an FDA 510(k) in which new products are approved on the merits of previously approved products without conducting clinical trials. Once new products are approved, some companies conduct studies to follow the outcomes of their product to substantiate marketing claims, improve managed care status and increase awareness of their device with surgeons.

In other words, the product and service that we sell is not a ‘have to have’ service but rather a ‘nice to have’ service. Just as in consumer spending, discretionary spending is the first area to experience a reduction in a tough economy. When money is tight, companies tend to pull back on these services as well. Here is how the economy affected various aspects of our business and what we did to adjust.

Competition

The good news is that in this economy, there is attrition within competition. In our industry, we have noticed that the companies that focused solely on offering the lowest price and were counting on high volumes to drive revenues are disappearing. Companies that offered poor service are also going away. Many of the new, start-up companies that relied on venture capital funding have also left the market as funding sources became more difficult. Less competition is always beneficial.

As competition experiences a drop in business, we have kept our eyes open for the opportunity to form partnerships or mergers. The valuation of many companies has decreased dramatically.

We have also found that in this economy, companies who previously would not consider a partnership are much more willing to work with another industry partner, especially if there is synergy between services. These partnerships have increased our exposure to customers that were not previously our clients.

Company Focus

In a down economy, it is critical for a company to evaluate their business segment. Are there new products or services that can be added to fill a void left by a competitor that has vacated the market? Are there services or products that your company offers that offer little value and should be removed from your product line? Have your customers buying decisions changed?

The latter was an issue impacting our business. One example is the hospital market which in the past had made up a small portion of our business. In the tight economy we noticed a large increase in the number of hospitals in need of our services. We are finding that they are very interested in capturing data that will equip them to market their institution in the increasingly competitive healthcare environment. Hospitals are also utilising data to improve their reimbursement rates from managed care companies. These recent changes in the hospital market have caused us to shift our tactics and product offerings to this market.

Customers

Our industry has been hit by the economy less than most other sectors. Depending on the analyst and market segment used, the medical device industry has experienced three to five percent annual growth in the last two years which is much less than the double digit annual growth many companies were accustomed to over the last decade.

Most analysts expect seven to nine percent annual growth over the next few years and the industry will most likely surpass the $300B annual mark in 2011. The expected increase in growth is based on the fact that many patients delayed orthopaedic implant surgery due to loss of insurance tied to a job loss. This growth will be at risk due to increasing pricing pressure as a result of healthcare reform and an increasingly difficult regulatory approval process for new medical devices.

They may be spending less and deferring expenditures, however, they still have work to do. As with the economy, our customers have in some cases downsized and those remaining employees are overworked and looking for a vendor that can offer additional services to fill the void of the employees they have lost.

Our company was able to maintain revenues (no decline or growth) in spite of a 10% reduction of staff and less spending by our customers. We were securing new clients during the recession which normally would have had a nice impact on revenue, however, we saw attrition in our former customer base due to companies closing their doors or lack of venture capital funding to cover new projects.

Though many customers still have business to conduct, they are expecting to receive our services, in many cases, for less than they may have spent in the past. In many cases, our customers are receiving prices from our competitors that may be extremely low. In cases such as this, it is important to maintain the value of your service. As the saying goes, 'the bitterness of poor service will remain long after the sweetness of a low price is forgotten'.

During the recession we have maintained the value and price of our services and have seen customers come back to us after first choosing a lower priced alternative.

Employees

Unfortunately, a casualty of the recession has been mass layoffs. Our company is no different and we were forced to do a small workforce reduction. You would certainly cut your cost of living and evaluate unnecessary expenses at home when income declines; companies operate under the same rules.

As damaging as a layoff is to those that lose their job, it is also a risky situation for the employer, because of the employees that still remain and steps must be employed to protect morale. In a good economy, a layoff can dramatically impact morale of those still employed as they lose co-workers that are friends and begin to question the viability of the company that employs them.

A side effect of this economy is that layoffs have become so common that the remaining employees might question the situation less than in the past. Here are a few steps that we took to maintain morale:

- Cut expenses – Nothing sends a worse signal to your remaining employees than laying people off when you continue to spend money on frivolous items. We put new equipment purchases, employee lunches and dinners and extra marketing items on hold.
- Make all the cuts at once – Certainly it is hard to predict the future, but it is important to let your employees know that reductions in workforce, furloughs and/or pay freezes will not become the new normal but rather these steps are a onetime effort to control expenses. We made this tough decision and announced a small layoff, pay freeze and mandatory furlough all at once.
- Take advantage of slow periods – While this method is not always possible, many companies experience cyclical periods where business dramatically drops. The minor layoff we did was not quite enough to bring expenses in line with income. Our next option was to enact a mandatory furlough during our slowest week of the year, between Christmas and New Years day. Most of our customers' businesses were closed during this time so the impact to business was minimal. We were able to notify employees four months prior, which allowed them enough time to accrue the necessary vacation time so that they could take time off with pay if they desired. Surprisingly, this method worked so well that we had employees asking if we could do the same week-long furlough the following year.
- Increased communication – We have increased the frequency of employee communications via email and face to face meetings. We felt that it was important to continually update our employees on the financial status of the company and also ensure they were constantly updated on our customer base as changes occurred.
- Have fun – Yes the recession was bad, but a positive attitude is infectious and employees still want to have fun. The employees that you have remaining are most likely working harder to compensate for the work that was previously performed by those that were laid off. We

have been able to hold a few small events that cost the company very little but have made a big difference in morale. These events are planned by a volunteer committee and include routine company potlucks, cookouts and an occasional breakfast. We have even taken advantage of a government programme that reimburses employees for commuting to work by bike or bus.

Marketing/Prospecting

In the recession, we employed less expensive ways to prospect and market to potential customers. A tendency in a down economy is to pull back on ALL marketing efforts which will have a further negative impact on your business. If customers can't find you, they can't spend money. Instead of spending money on large scale marketing we have scaled back to more targeted projects.

For example, attending a trade show is much less expensive than exhibiting at one; now we only exhibit at three yearly trade shows. The money we are saving on exhibiting fees has been used to attend more shows than in the past, which still allows us to meet with prospects. We have also used trade shows as a central place to hold many customer meetings, thus reducing our travel budget to meet with each individual customer.

It may also be a good time to consider spending money on a refresh of your marketing materials or website. Keep in mind, as the economy goes, so goes the marketing business which has been heavily impacted by the recession. Many top firms are willing to work for less and will give your project more attention, quicker turnaround time and typically the work will be done by more experienced staff than would normally happen in a busy economy.

In summary, the recession, which many say is now behind us, has left scars, but like any challenge it has also taught us much. We are more focused on our business and meeting our customers' needs. It also taught us the value of employees and forced us to evaluate how we treat and show value to our employees in ways other than the standard yearly pay rise.

The best analogy is one similar to when you are faced with a move of your family from one home to a smaller home: it forces you to evaluate the worth of every possession. The economy has had this same effect on our business; we have become very effective at evaluating everything we do. Before every project or acquisition we now ask ourselves, will this project improve the well-being of our employees, customers and ultimately our bottom line? The answer in many cases has caused us to do more with less.

Nick Smith

The Middle East Property Roller-Coaster

Current Position:	Owner 21C Property and Business Advice. Freelance Journalist
Qualifications:	Masters Urban Design; Bachelors Town Planning; Fellow Chartered Institute Building
Email:	nicksmith21c@gmail.com
LinkedIn:	http://om.linkedin.com/in/nicksmith4
Twitter:	www,twitter.com/nicksmith21c
Contact Number:	(00968) 95209934

Nick Smith is a real estate and business professional, with development experience in the UK, Middle East and the USA. A town planner and urban designer by qualification, Nick's professional interests are the creation of value by design and service, and the making of special places in our towns and cities. Nick currently runs his own consultancy, and is also a freelance writer. He enjoys current world affairs, sport, music and entertaining. Nick is married with three children.

Chapter 39: The Middle East Property Roller-Coaster

'Build them and they will come' – the much quoted mantra of the early 21st century in Dubai and then other parts of the Middle East.

All went well for a few years, buyers put their money down, some construction started and properties were 'flipped' by speculators, often several times, making them easy profits. Construction was delayed then due to poor planning and site supervision and lack of critical experience of project managers. Some iconic buildings, the Burj Arab, the Mall of the Emirates ski slope and latterly the Burj Khalifa, were finished, in a blaze of fireworks.

But critically, the massive oversupply of residential properties and office space still blights the Dubai market. And some banks took haircuts and are now overly cautious. Real demand for property was never properly considered; there was a big vision, the implementation of which was financially underwritten by government incomes. After the events of late 2008, the property speculators disappeared, leaving no-one to buy. Genuine end users were scarce. Some speculators and buyers couldn't fulfil their contractual obligations and absconded, to avoid jail.

My story was as a Brit in Oman, the cultured quiet neighbour of glitzy Dubai, some four hour drive to the south-east. In early 2006 I joined 'The Wave, Muscat' as CEO, a start-up development project which was planning 4000 residential properties, three hotels, shops and offices, a Greg Norman golf course and 60 hectares of reclamation, creating a 300 berth marina.

"Push ahead, go, go, go," said the board.

We did and offering real freehold to our residential customers, sold to those in the queues. Little market research was done, or was needed then, as purchasers were banging on our sales office door in vast numbers. Construction contracts were let in phases – not over-committing our build spend and therefore preserving cash.

We collected money from our purchasers in phased payments in line with build progress, unusual for developers but critical for us. Our borrowings were minimal. Our financial model was primarily driven by return on capital. By mid 2008 we had sold over 800 properties, grossing some $500m. I wanted to make this development truly world class.

First completions were in October 2008 and now there are over 600. A few purchasers have defaulted but this has been manageable. And cash has been preserved, with build slowing to reflect reduced market demand. Yes, the scheme will take longer to complete than originally demanded by the shareholders. But it is secure, and recently won 'Best Development in Arabia' by Bloomberg. Quality systems and customer service, leading the way in the Middle East region, meant we kept most customers with us. Recession or not, these aspects are both critically important.

For me, I lasted nearly four years, a CEO sixty, twenty-four, seven. The business was sound but I should have managed the board better. The members were a mixture of nationalities, taken from government and business, largely of Arabic origin. I should have spent more quality time with them individually, to understand their 'buttons' and to prepare them for all eventualities. Recession is unusual and unwelcome and to think of it as a springboard is difficult without previous experience of the improving cycle, which generally comes after. Culturally, failure in the Middle East is not acceptable and we couldn't sell in late 2008 and all of 2009. The board bade me goodbye.

Understanding market dynamics and determining where the demand for property purchases will come from now is the key; a simple business pre-requisite, but one not in-line with that often repeated Dubai mantra. Whereas before the recession we spent maybe 5% of our time on this, it should now occupy 75%.

Creating a flexible product, and then evolving it and value engineering each aspect, follows on from this demand driver.

1. In short, the need now is to make the business fundamentally a sales operation – the simple order taking of 2006-8 has gone forever.

2. New skills, structures and remuneration packages are needed.

3. Organisations must be flexible enough to respond quickly; understand markets in depth; use cash wisely; and get the best

personnel reasonably possible. 'Making do' will not cut the mustard.

4. It is easy to get caught up in the vision and 'can-do' philosophy of the leaders of the Middle East. Being part of such a society is stimulating and rewarding, but the basics of sound business – know your market, price your product, make it well, use your cash wisely and find the best people – are always critical.

I now advise a number of property and business clients in the Middle East and elsewhere, assisting them to grasp opportunities and overcome challenges.

Rhondalynn Korolak

Do you have what it takes to Survive in ANY Economy?

Current Position:	MD of Imagineering Unlimited, Best-selling author of *On The Shoulders of Giants and Financial Foreplay*
Qualifications:	Taxation attorney; Chartered Accountant; Clinical Hypnotherapist; Master of NLP
Experience:	17 years senior management experience
Email:	info@imagineeringunlimited.com
LinkedIn:	http://au.linkedin.com/in/imagineering
Twitter:	www.twitter.com/rhondalynn
Facebook:	www.facebook.com/pages/Rhondalynn-Korolak/95846158050
Website:	www.imagineeringunlimited.com www.imagineeringprofit.com
Links to Other Works:	www.financialforeplaybook.com www.yourguidetogreatness.com

A 16-year veteran of marketing and finance, Rhondalynn Korolak, holds degrees and professional designations in both law and chartered accounting and is a certified Master Practitioner of NLP, Thought Field Therapist and Clinical Hypnotherapist. Her CV features an impressive list of accomplishments in senior executive positions with Price Waterhouse Coopers, Max Factor, Covergirl, Village Cinemas Australia and Coles Group Ltd.

She is the author of *On the Shoulders of Giants*, *Financial Foreplay* and *Imagineering Your Destiny* and has been featured in national business publications in Australia and North America. She specialises in business acceleration through financial insights. She is a featured contributor for CNN, Yahoo, Sunday Life, Fast Thinking, Dynamic Business, Australian Retailer, Cosmopolitan, Working Woman, 3AW, MYOB etc. Rhondalynn was independently ranked as one of the Top 100 Business Coaches in the World in 2008.

Chapter 40: Do you have what it takes to Survive in ANY Economy?

In 1949, thirteen men (out of a highly skilled team of sixteen) died battling a relatively small blaze that turned deadly in Mann Gulch, Montana. Upon investigating the circumstances of why thirteen of the 'smoke jumpers' died while only three lived, Norman Maclean wrote a book entitled *Young Men and Fire*, which is the true story account of that fateful expedition of the 'smoke jumpers' – fire fighters who parachute into the back country to fight fires.

Maclean found some startling and interesting facts. Mann Gulch is surrounded by steep canyon walls with the northern slope at a 75% incline. When the wind turned suddenly on the smoke jumpers, they found themselves in a race with the fire up those steep, treacherous walls. Unexpectedly, the fire also started to spread much faster than anticipated.

One of the amazing and notable things that Maclean discovered was that the thirteen who died had continued to carry their tools – heavy poleaxes, saws, shovels and heavy back packs – while attempting to out-run the fire up those steep walls. In other words, the thirteen who perished had run as far as they could with all their equipment, even though that equipment was worse than useless in a race with the fire.

Their inability to drop their heavy tools and packs ultimately prevented them from being able to outrun the raging fire. Now you must understand, to these seasoned fire fighters, their tools were much more than just simple objects – they represented who they were, why they were there and what they were trained to do. They were educated to fight fires, not outrun them. Dropping their tools would have essentially meant abandoning their knowledge, beliefs, training and experience.

Now this might not seem like a hard choice to make to you, but because these specialised fire fighters hadn't been trained for such an unpredictable, deadly moment, they had no alternative models or maps for behaviour to guide them. What this true story highlights is that in moments of uncertainty and imminent danger, clinging to the old 'right' way might seem like a good, safe idea... but more often than not, it may actually prove deadly.

The three survivors of the blaze were forced to think outside the box and develop alternative methods of escaping the fire. Once they figured out they were no longer 'fighting the fire' but were instead trying 'to outrun it', they realised they had to drop all of their useless equipment.

One survivor used an innovative technique called the 'escape fire' where he took a match and lit a ring around himself so that the fire would 'jump' over him. When he tried to suggest it to the other men, they ignored him and continued running up the steep slope because the 'escape fire' technique had not been part of their extensive training and preparation. Their inability to drop the tools and equipment that weren't working and seek new methods to escape is what ultimately led to them being engulfed by flames and smoke.

So some of you may be sitting there, reading this and thinking "but what does this have to do with you and your business?"

Well nothing and yet... perhaps, EVERYTHING.

The global financial crisis of 2009 ripped through the financial markets and negatively impacted businesses (both large and small) around the world. In many ways it behaved exactly like the fire that engulfed Mann Gulch 60 years ago – it was fast, unpredictable, almost impossible to outrun and changed the way that most of us will choose to invest and run our businesses forever. And, as I'm sure most of you would agree, many businesses are still reeling and recovering from it.

The biggest lesson that I personally learned as the aftermath that unfolded was this: change is inevitable – your ability to deal with and handle uncertainty is directly proportionate to the results that you will enjoy, personally and professionally.

During the crisis, I was forced to take a good hard look at my business and the way that we had been operating. I asked myself, **"What are the poleaxes, shovels and backpacks we're running with and how might they be holding us back?"**

At the time, I had been running a very successful coaching business working face to face with clients at around $2000/month. However the small business market had been hit hard and I realised that we needed to change the way that we worked in order to survive and address the needs of our customers. I completely transformed the model we work under by developing innovative coaching products and online services that could be delivered online to business owners around the world for a fraction of the price. These services are highly unique, relevant, cost-effective and targeted to the specific needs of each business owner. We are literally changing the way that business owners learn, measure results and improve their own performance.

Perhaps if it had not been for the global financial crisis, I would not have been forced to re-examine the business and innovate. In many ways, it has provided us all with an ultimatum - change and evolve, or die.

What existing beliefs and models of behaviour do you need to drop today in order for you to survive and prosper in these uncertain economic times? What training, attitudes, decisions or experience need to be abandoned in favour of a new, innovative approach?

It has often been said that 'the thinking that got you to here, won't get you to there'. Never has the simplicity and wisdom of this statement been more poignant, than it is today. Those of you who adopt and learn the critical skills, tools and mind-set necessary to survive and thrive in any economy, will be the winners in all of this.

But, this has always been true. Survivors and successful people triumph because they are flexible and willing to do whatever it takes to get the results they desire. New or changing circumstances always necessitate a new perspective or approach; the alternative, 'doing the same thing over and over again and expecting a different result' is the definition of insanity and can only lead to suffering, disappointment, pain and even death.

AUTHOR
TBLBC

Maria Matarelli

The Importance of Improvements and Personal Development

Current Position:	Project Management Consultant, Coach and Trainer
Qualifications:	Certified Professional Coach (CPC) Project Management Professional (PMP) 6 Sigma Green Belt (SSGB) Certified Scrum Professional (CSP)
Experience:	10 years experience in Consulting, Project Management and Professional Development
LinkedIn:	www.linkedin.com/in/mariamatarelli
Twitter:	www.twitter.com/mariamatarelli
Facebook:	www.facebook.com/mariamatarelli
Website:	www.bevilledge.com/maria
Links to Other Works:	www.mariamatarelli.blogspot.com www.selfgrowth.com/experts/maria_matarelli www.scrumalliance.org/articles/178-from-meager-beginnings-to-masterful-ends

Maria Matarelli is a Certified Professional Coach with more than 10 years experience in project management, business consulting and training. She is also a personal mentor and coach to individuals looking to gain new skills and change perspectives. Maria is the President & Founder of the Illinois Regional Agile Users Group (IRAUG) and offers her time in support of other Not for Profit groups. Maria has a real passion for helping her clients identify their goals in order to achieve them.

Chapter 41: The Importance of Improvements and Personal Development

Setting the Stage

I've always believed that the best way to weather times of famine is to save in times of prosperity. That's why I began taking steps to protect my career long before I was forced to by company downsizing and other impacts from the economy.

Planning When Times Were Good

One of the best things I did to increase my future marketability was to take advantage of my company's training reimbursement program. At the beginning of every year, I carefully planned which courses I should take to maximise my opportunities for professional development.

When the economy began to decline, one of the first things my company cut was the training reimbursement program. Because I had already allocated and used my reimbursement for the year, I was not affected by these cuts and was able to avoid any loss of benefits (at least at first).

Another habit I carefully cultivated during the good times was to establish a solid professional network. Because I had been proactively networking with people in my industry throughout my career, when harder times came along, these same peers and colleagues forwarded job opportunities to me.

By keeping in close contact with my network through social media and professional websites, I was able to do more than just react I could keep up with the ebb and flow of the market, which gave me tremendous insight into looming threats as well as any potential opportunities.

Showcasing My Value

During a recession, companies don't stop needing services; they just need different services. As these changes came, I looked at where my own strengths matched these new needs. For example, when companies began looking for ways to streamline operations to keep their competitive edge, I highlighted my expertise at increasing efficiencies, streamlining practices and reducing waste.

Similarly, as companies became more aware they needed stronger teams, I updated my career profiles to showcase the skill-sets that delivered this value. When I identified gaps in my skills, I planned out how to fill them. I took on additional responsibility at work, began leading training (both for fellow consultants and for clients) and worked on special projects. This improved my own resume while adding value to my employer and clients.

Reassessing My Direction

Eventually, cutting benefits wasn't enough to keep my company afloat. As positions were eliminated, many of my colleagues joined the ranks of the unemployed.

I credit my additional training, solid network and commitment to continuous improvement for affording me interviews and job offers, even during difficult times. Another factor in my favour was that I was willing to consider relocating or travelling. Making myself more available for travel, even by just a percentage, expanded my options.

Defying the 'Impossible'

The new role that I took on during the cutbacks was limited but I felt fortunate to still be gainfully employed. That didn't mean I had to settle for the status quo though. While advancement, bonuses and raises were all described as 'impossible', I managed to attain all three.

Though my position had been described as fixed, with no room for advancement, by asking questions and providing quality work above and beyond my job description, I found an exception to that rule and was able to move to a more challenging role. Similarly, though we had been warned that raises would be capped at 5%, by stretching my skills and showcasing my accomplishments, I was able to exceed that.

When we were informed that we would lose our bonuses as part of the massive reduction in benefits, I approached management and fought for my compensation. Because I was able to document my performance, value and client rapport, I was able to keep my bonus. I learned that what might seem impossible can be overcome with hard work and a willingness to ask.

The Need for Change

All the planning and proactive networking in the world, however, didn't make me immune to the realities of a recession. Eventually, we all received a 20% pay cut. I got a paper promotion, which aside from a new 'prestigious title', ultimately meant that I had twice the responsibility at 20% less pay.

Even though I was able to negotiate a tiny raise after three months, I was essentially doing more work for much less compensation, with the ever present feeling of impending doom that more cuts were on the way. This was accompanied by a timely notification from my apartment complex that they were raising my rent by 40% to get everyone up to 'market rates'. Though I managed to negotiate the rent increase to something slightly more palatable, blows were coming from all directions.

Taking a Risk with a Higher Possibility of Reward

After a while, it just didn't make sense to stay in my current situation. I began interviewing for other jobs but wasn't overly excited about any of them. I soon realised that I didn't want to be an employee or long-term consultant for just one company. I was confident in my abilities and wanted to take more risk, with the possibility of more reward.

After thinking it over, I left my job and partnered with the owner of a company. I brought ingenuity and ideas for market expansion to the table. I found new clients for the company and developed new revenue streams. I re-invested the revenue I generated back into the company and became a partner. I worked day and night to ensure success. It was nothing short of hard work and sweat equity.

I led departments, secured new clients, performed training, consulting and coaching and began a job that I love; a job with freedom and flexibility. A job that was so much more than following a process and pushing paper. A job working with clients to gain real efficiencies and help them expand and improve their processes.

Leaving Frivolous Living to the Obscenely Wealthy

Leaving a steady paying job is always a risk; during a recession it can seem huge. I felt comfortable because, prior to the economic downturn, I had been saving up money, had paid off all of my debt and had been contributing to investments.

Because I was living well within my means during the good times, I was agile enough to actually take a leap into the unknown when the opportunity came. I became independently employed for a larger margin of the services I already provided as an employee consultant. Through this bold step forward, I was able to determine for myself what the next best step would be and choose my own destiny, rather than wait for my turn to be crossed off of the employment list. This was my defining moment of the recession.

The Payoff

Even with my pay cut, lost benefits and the increase in expenses, I was able to maintain my quality of life during the worst of the recession and did not feel a severe negative impact.

I was driven more by my principles than economic pressures when I fought for a particular job or better compensation. Because I had banked money and new skills, invested in myself and in the market and created a sound foundation, both in terms of my finances and my network, I was able to take the risks necessary to go after my dreams.

The Deeper Lesson

I believe that sometimes things have to happen outside of your control to push you into a decision you need to make but won't. Catastrophe causes change. Without the resulting discomfort, I would have stayed in my state of complacency for far too long. You may resist at first, you may even fight for the status quo of mediocrity without even realising it. It is only when you take the step to really pursuing your dreams that you can reap real benefits. The greater the risk, the greater the possibility of reward.

The biggest lesson I learned was don't wait until someone makes the decision for you. Determine what you want to do and do it now. Look at where you are; identify where you want to be and set incremental goals to get there. Find new learning opportunities, new skill-sets and take the risk. If you do, you'll find yourself more capable than you ever imagined. I know I did.

Sally Franz

The Recession Means Re-Tooling

Current Position:	Owner of Geronto Communication since 1975
Qualifications:	Undergraduate degree was in Human Resources
Email:	Sallydianefranz@Gmail.com
LinkedIn:	www.linkedin.com/pub/sally-franz/3/99a/7b1
Twitter:	www.twitter.com/#!/Sallyfranz
Facebook:	www.facebook.com/pages/Sally-Franz-Uncorked/366432754046
Website:	www.Sallyfranz.com
Links to Other Works:	Amazon: *Monster Lies*, Beagle Bay Books www.beaglebay.com/categories_detail.html?cid=11
Contact Number:	+1 252-343-9183

Sally Franz was the Advertising Director for Revelations Shoes, the Director of AdNet Advertising Agency in New York City, and she worked at the national offices Save The Children and UNICEF managing volunteer fundraising before starting her own training company, Geronto Communications. She is certified in Myers-Briggs, trained in Marshal Rosenberg's Non-violent Communication and certified in Bob Pike's Train the Trainer program. In the 1990s, Sally was a regular on the New York stand-up comedy circuit.

Ms. Franz's client list includes: Cheveron-Texaco, Intel, SONY, Yahoo! and McCann Erickson (the largest Advertising agency in the world).

Chapter 42: The Recession Means Re-Tooling

My business is other people's business. No, I am not a gossip columnist. I am a consultant; I own Geronto Communications. As a business-to-business service during a recession I am watching two bottom lines, my clients' and my own. My firm offers training for Fortune 100 Company executives in productivity, team building and communications. Ongoing staff training is a must as corporations battle tough times.

All that said, HR budgets are notoriously hit the hardest during a recession. Many of my ongoing clients severely cut back on their training budgets or just closed shop altogether. "Should the economy worsen," Bill Pelster of Deloitte's training and development says, "...it usually takes two years from the time a recession hits for training budgets to return to previous levels."

Less money for training means people are not growing and being challenged. Efficiency in the work place slows down.

"The biggest effect of training is a reduction in turnover," Rich Thompson of Adecco says. "If 55 percent of your employees are not engaged, and 15 percent are actively disengaged, they're destroying your brand. They're telling customers and colleagues how bad the company is."

What caused this recession? Yes, our government has a huge debt problem, but the trigger seemed to be terrorism. It created a lack of confidence in investing. Add to that the fact more unskilled jobs have moved offshore, the trade imbalance increased (The United States reported a trade deficit equivalent to 38.3 Billion USD in November of 2010), 70 million baby boomers are moving out of their discretionary buying income phase (to fixed incomes, social security and Medicare) and robots are replacing jobs at an alarming rate (Samuel Circton, manufacturing author, says that in the automotive industry robots are used at a 10-1 ratio to humans).

Back at the ranch, I had to re-tool to get ahead of the technology curve. I took several courses to learn about social networking, online selling, and G-Cred. G-Cred is a term coined by John Follis, marketing guru. This is a process of getting your name to the top of search engines; thus far I have a solid 10 Google pages under 'Sally Franz'. I created a Facebook account, a Twitter page and joined LinkedIn. I learned how to upload my YouTube videos, set up Skype for face-to-face meetings and I conquered PowerPoint.

Go to your strengths. As I re-evaluated my strengths I realised that edutainment was on the rise and social media ruled (if Facebook was a country it would be the third most populated). And while content for most state-of-the art training is similar, it is in the delivery that the herd thins out.

In this area I had a huge advantage; I had been a stand-up comedian in New York City. I had to let people know that not only would solid content be delivered but it would be immensely enjoyable. The good news is that the younger generation was already sold on entertainment as a training tool. As boomers leave their posts, new blood is arriving. All I had to do is be fluent in their new language of technology.

I took as many online live classes as I could to participate in the emerging e-marketplace. I learned how to use search engines and entered the world of e-zines, blogging and interest groups. I learned to live chat, comment and comprehend text language (thanks to Michelle Cimino's book, *Cell Phone Etiquette*).

New attack

As I re-tooled my personal skills it was clear that technology was on my side. It was time to get hi-tech in my marketing plan as well. The good news? It is free to implement.

1. I increased my visibility. Prospective clients can Google my name to see the depth of my work and expertise. They can go to my webpage for monthly blogs and there they can find my training bio, rate page and client list. I extended my Facebook site to include a homepage, fan page and several niche interest groups.

2. I targeted key groups. I host several sites and guest blog on 20 different business e-zines. I respond to media calls weekly thus extending my expertise credibility to e-articles, blog talk radio and streaming radio interviews. This regular exposure also increases my Google rating.

3. I make it easy to get to know me. If a client wants to see me in action I can send them a video. If they want to meet me and they live on the 'other' coast, we can Skype. If they want to watch me perform, they can upload 12 or more YouTube videos.

4. I look for the opening. While HR departments are shrinking, smart companies are still investing in their sales force. I offer affordable effective sales-based content.

5. I use technology to enhance the training. Attendees can contact me online, ask questions and post areas they want to cover before the class begins. It means that I can tailor the class before we get in the room, saving time. And workbooks and resources are now downloads.

The Result

I increased my business flow by 20% after re-tooling. I repaid 100% of my upgraded hardware and training costs within the first quarter. My G-Cred increased by 25% and I have 1,820,000 hits/exposure credited to my name.

Bottom-line.

What we are learning in this recession is that no matter how bad the economy is people are still buying. In fact, William Strauss , Senior Analyst for the Federal Reserve of Chicago notes, "Manufacturing jobs are steady at 1% growth and production is up 3.7% and rising."

My advice?

Reach clients where they interact: smack dab in the middle of social media.

Help customers make money, save money and solve problems.

Finally, I will close with these words from my grandfather who was a successful manufacturer during the depression...

"It is as easy to make money being honest with a good product as it is being a crook; the difference is honesty equals return customers."

Jeffrey S Shattuck

Dissolution of the Middle Management Layer:
The Reason why we are Stronger than Ever

Current Position:	Cieio, creative intelligence, inc.
Qualifications:	BS Engineering, 2yrs Post Graduate AAMS, LUTCF, Registered Principal and Securities Licences, Coursework in Graduate Masters Program in Conscious Evolution
Email:	info@dreamtodesign.com
LinkedIn:	www.linkedin.com/in/creativeintelligence
Links to Other Works:	www.twitter.com/creativeintel www.facebook.com/creativeintelligence
Website:	www.dreamtodesign.com
Contact Number:	+1 0118438440775

Jeff has worked in the technology field for over 27 years. As a technologist with engineering training from Georgia Institute of Technology, USA, he invented seeding felt, wrote blogs before they were named as such, built an information technology services company, even postulating that at some point the virtual and physical worlds would eventually merge on a psychological plane more than a decade prior to the occurrence.

With numerous design awards, he has enjoyed creating advertisements, from billboards to broadcast commercials to corporate identities, formed four corporations, three of which (Creative Intelligence, Inc., Shattuck Marine, Inc., Ocean Tiger, Inc.), he manages or takes a seat on the board of directors. An author (A Kept Man Can(c) series) and media outlet contributor, Jeff is pleased to be able to voice, create and contribute to the body of knowledge that belongs to every person now and in the future.

He continues to divide his time between ocean and land, as a marine captain and rescue scuba diver.

Chapter 43: Dissolution of the Middle Management Layer: The Reason why we are Stronger than Ever

One of the reasons for starting my own company was the frustration I experienced soon after entering the corporate world. Immediately obvious to me were the useless layers of management which led to inefficiencies and were ultimately a threat to my sanity.

A business can be compared to a ship. For the ship's captain, the ship represents an entire subsistence ecosystem the same as a company does for its MD. It is through captaining that I found clarity for leading my company, allowing us to not only withstand this recession but grow 8.2% in 2009 and 9.7% in 2010. However, we did experience some net reduction from employee churn.

Continuing the 'your business is a ship' analogy, let's assimilate it in this way:

It is the product or service which moves the ship. Producers are the engines and driving force. Tucked away out of sight they produce the thing that makes our companies unique and valuable. Commonly, producers prefer this non-limelight where they are free to create, repair, service and build.

A ship's sails provide assistance to propulsion and are the most visible part of the ship. They represent the salespeople. True, salespeople are accused of being full of air anyway. Respectfully, they are always out in front, a constant effort to reach out, striving ahead. They are seen by the public first, and quite possibly the only representative of a company a client will see. Being expressive, they invigorate an entire company with their positive 'can-do' attitude, adding extra propulsion.

Responsible for cleaning and cooking, the steward and cook provide a structure of health and welfare. Likewise, assistants provide a similar service for us. We are stronger and healthier having a structured and productive life. As C-level thinkers, we often accelerate at gaining knowledge, wisdom and having a wide range vision. We identify gaps in markets and the products needed. We need people to act on the ideas and projects we started or have in mind, carrying the ideas to success. We are always in need of more capable C-team assistants.

The captain, first officer and navigator all make up the C-level. They provide the necessary long and short-range vision, decision making, guidance, enforcement and refinement. For example, with a chart plotter, an essential instrument of the helm, a captain can plot and adhere to that course, despite the undercurrent forces or surface winds that may push a company off-course. Likewise, the C-team can make decisions based on their ability to see both the great and small chart views.

Finally there's cargo and ballast. Both are at times necessary. On most vessels, ballast management is critical and since cargo is calculated into ballast, we look at them both as a load. Over-weighting a ship can exponentially increase the resistance of the hull to forward movement due to increased displacement area and friction coefficients. A weighted ship is slow to plane, requires more power and thus is more costly to operate.

Identifying ballast and cargo in the corporate environment isn't difficult. It is obviously middle management. Granted, some companies are at a size that they find middle management necessary. However, in most companies it can be either dissolved, or reduced to a mere fraction of current existence.

Upon starting my first company, I vowed with determination to minimise this middle management layer. We watch as many companies dump their middle management as a quick way to lighten the load during tough times, only to let middle management grow again in fat seasons. This happened in the early 80's in the USA and re-occurred during this era. It isn't fair to the employee, nor to the rest of the work force.

Why does middle management exist? The answer lies in two categories, both are negative factors.

Category 1- A C-level, will sometimes lose focus. Rather than moderating our schedules to match conditions, or change abilities and temperament, we hire someone as a buffer; perhaps someone who can look after the interests of the company while we step away for holiday.

Category 2- Failure to help people who do not have the capacity to be producers, or C-level. Sometimes we simply do not know what to do with some ill-fitted employees. Often people in middle management should not have been tasked with the position. The position itself breeds frustration, distrust, and ultimately a rottenness that causes volatile cargo. C-levels are frustrated knowing middle managers are a profit-vacuum-luxury; producers are frustrated that middle managers have authority and pay that they may not deserve; salespeople get frustrated as they are often held to the thinking of person who has never stepped foot in the field.

How is it possible to eliminate middle management?

1. C-levels must stick to their roles and fulfil their responsibilities, requiring balance, focus, and dedication. If their sphere starts disintegrating, identify the root cause and act quickly. The tendency to hire someone to fill a mid-management position must be eliminated. Hiring capable assistants to formulate teams works far better. When C-levels start to drift from course, other C-levels need to be there to help as the C-teams resolve to stay intact. Share assistants if necessary. Avoid dropping into creating, or expanding, middle management.

2. Strength. It takes strong determination to dissolve or minimize middle management and ensure it doesn't resurge. Positively, you are helping these people to get out of a rut and find their true calling; possibly you are even encouraging an under-performing person to re-educate and reach greater goals. If they are honestly not capable, the world still needs people to swab the deck. A noble and respectable thing to do for a living as we all cherish a clean ship.

3. Utilise technology tools. This is the key to minimising middle management, which was partially necessary in the early and mid parts of the last century, where it was born. British-American corporate structure was working well, adopted by many a company, planet-wide. Some cultures embraced and perfected the concept, creating a very well-defined corporate ladder. By making good use of the technology tools of today, C-levels can utilise multiple capable administrative assistants to produce huge amounts of work creating a more distributed C-team environment.

Middle management was doomed even before the recession hit in the USA. Technology forced the dissolution of the middle management layer. Technology tools allow C-levels to communicate rapidly, creating effective teams at a higher level than where we were accustomed. This started back as early as the late 80s and has accelerated since. Arguably, a factor that has made this recession so resilient is that the middle management layer was dissolved by many companies who are wisely not replacing them. In epiphany, they realise they have technology tools instead. Though I and others had been sharing the message to reduce middle management, it simply did not happen.

As producers communicate directly to C-level and sales, productivity and efficiency soar. Middle managers often manipulate information as job protection, at a great cost to the company. As the communication barriers and break-points are eliminated, C-teams give a company rock solid resilience from hostile competition and economic turmoil.

The first wave of technology in the 1980s affected the producers, boosting productivity and leading to declining demand of producers, in some cases eliminating their positions. A good example is robot-assisted assembly. Then in 2000, big database powerhouses became available over the internet (cloud applications), permitting software companies to produce applications of high efficiency and broad girth with powerful reporting tools - the mainstay middle management.

Currently, many people who are complaining they cannot find a job are these mid-tier people. There are plenty of jobs out there being advertised for producers, sales and C-levels. We are suffering from a middle-management 'bubble' of sorts and until these people are absorbed into the workforce, we will struggle with high unemployment. Notably, many are landing in the service sectors as producers. Others are going back to school in search of degrees which they feel might help them to reach the C-team. Indeed, we have become very leery of hiring such disguised ex-middle managers. A recent issue for us: new hires that ultimately turn out to be ex-middle managers restarting careers without the needed change of mindset. After the first painfully quick firings, we are cautious and take more time vetting.

How did this permit us growth margins in a declining economy?
In sailing optimally without the middle managers, our producers use technology tools to communicate directly to sales and C-level. They utilise tools of customer relationship management and software products to track and analyse chart trends, supply chain

management, resource planning etc. The work fodder of what was previously middle management.

Having no transition to suffer or recover from, we never really veered from our growth pattern. Meanwhile our competitors struggled, making painful cuts and subsequent difficult transitions.

As we move into 2011, I remain confident that we will not see the return of middle management in the same percentages as previous to this recession. As companies return to profitability, the C-teams that have formed now (a C-team consisting of only the C level with several assistants) will be the forward model that will take hold.

Addressing the future, my prediction is that the next wave of technology tools will deliver thinking speed applications and an efficiency that will redefine even the C-levels.

As we anticipate this, my effort is to make sure a C-level bubble doesn't exist in my company, in preparation of the next inevitable downturn. At which time, we will take even more from our competitors.

Davida Shensky

Changes to Employment due to Time and the Recession

Current Position:	CEO-Career Performance Institute, CEO-- International Disabled Entrepreneurs, Inc. NPO
Qualifications:	AAS Mental Health, BS--Psychology, credits towards a Masters in Rehabilitation Counselling, Am. Seminar Leaders Assoc. U.--CSL, Toastmasters--CTM & ATM, Stores Online--Internet Marketing, radio show Live Without Limits—BTR
Experience:	30 years in Business and HR
Email:	succoach@yahoo.com
LinkedIn:	www.linkedin.com/in/davidashensky
Twitter:	www.twitter.com/succoach
Facebook:	www.facebook.com/careerperformanceinstitute
Website:	www.1personalcareercoach.com,
Links to Other Works:	www.ideinc.bbnow.org, www.blogtalkradio.com/careerperformanceinstitute
Contact Number:	+1 678 462 0005

Davida Shensky runs Career Performance Institute. As a Career Coach she works with clients to help them find their passion and build it into a high-paying income. As a Life Coach, she helps clients find their 'limiting beliefs' and re-script them so they set and reach their personal goals in life both professionally and personally. She is publishing her book *No One Stands in Line to Become Disabled*. She is establishing a NPO, International Disabled Entrepreneurs, Inc. Davida has a weekly radio show on Blog Talk Radio called Live Without Limits.

Chapter 44: Changes to Employment due to Time and the Recession

During the early part of the 20th century there was a large influx of Europeans into the United States. Many of them brought their work ethic with them. In the home villages, they often put their wares on pushcarts and walked the streets selling them. In America, they would take their wares and put it on pushcarts and sell it on street corners.

For those who went to work for companies, they wanted loyal employers because they wanted to work. The employees would often work for free until the owner was able to pay them a salary. For their loyalty, they were rewarded by having a job for life and so they were usually willing to work for that company until they decided to retire. Often these small companies grew to become large companies and in some cases, corporations.

The first generation born in this country fought during World War II, when their country asked them to fight for freedom. After the war, this generation went to work for the corporations. They started at the bottom and worked their way up into management. After 25 years they were given a retirement party and a gold watch for their loyalty. Their children were known as the baby boomer generation.

When they were in school getting an education, schools and parents encouraged the students to go to work for the Corporation, which many did. But after 15 or 20 years, during the 1990s, many corporations had merged and had multiple people performing similar jobs so they needed to cut the workforce.

Some offered buyout packages, because until then when you went to work for the Corporation, it was an unwritten rule that an individual had a contract for life. Today if you go to work for 'The Corporation', your job expectancy may be five years or less.

Working for a corporation is a great way to learn a job ethic and then take the skills and apply it to building your own business. Not only has the job market changed with the new century, but the work ethic has changed as well. Employees are no longer loyal to a company; therefore the company is no longer loyal to the employee.

Generation X, generation Nexter and the millennial generation need to consider alternative methods of finding gainful employment. The typical job, where you work for the same corporation all your life, no longer exists.

During the current economic downturn, I have noted many more cultural changes taking place. Many companies, in order to cut expenses, are renting a smaller office space and hiring people to work from home. This allows the individual more flexi time and reduces operating costs for the company.

Another major cultural change that has taken place in the last century is in regards to the way that much business is done today. When the Europeans first came to the US, they took their wares and sold them on street corners but today business owners have websites (or e-commerce store fronts) that they load pictures of their wares on and sell internationally as well as locally.

These cultural changes have brought about changes to job titles. A secretary who would have worked in an office as an executive assistant, now works from home as a virtual assistant. A graphic designer today is also a web designer, a sales executive and a freelance consultant.

When I am working with clients, I often encourage them to think about their passions and personal interests and how they can build them into a high-paying income for themselves.

I have asked clients, "If you could do anything you love to do and earn an income doing it, what would it be?" Many have an immediate answer but they just don't know how to put together a strategic plan and build it into a business.

The future promises further cultural change, with the strong possibility of more people consciously choosing to work from home instead of working for in an office for just one company; why not choose to work for multiple companies?

Just because a company may not be willing to pay you the salary you want, they may be willing to pay you more money for fewer hours under this type of arrangement and working for multiple companies can subsequently provide you with better quality of life and a higher income.

I believe, that as children, we are good at coming up with many ideas but that education often teaches us to conform and listen to authority. Therefore as adults we lose our creativity and we lose the ability to think outside the box when it comes to being creative about employment.

To summarise, these are my lessons learned during the recession:

- Be more creative when it comes to employment and learn to think outside the box
- Do not be frightened to incorporate technology into your business
- Think about having multiple streams of income
- Think about alternative methods of financing your business
- Use the need to change as an opportunity to think about what you have a passion for and how you can build it into a high-paying income
- Build a mentor group around you so that you can bounce ideas off them when growing your business
- Since so many people are solo-preneurs today, why not use each other as a resource to outsource your business needs so that you are not wearing all the hats at the same time?

To tie all of this together, one needs to learn to become adapted to their environment because it is always changing, just like the workplace is constantly changing.

I came across an article that talked about how the job market has changed and how many jobs have gone overseas and these jobs have gone from America forever. Part of the reason is because the unions out-price the job market but it is also because third world countries are becoming more educated and technology savvy so they are able to fill positions that home-grown employees are unable to do.

Lynn Pierce

How to Attract Clients who Adore you – Even in a Recession

Current Position:	Founder
Experience:	Over 30 years of experience in sales and as a trainer. 10 years experience in product creation and marketing of information products for authors and experts.
Email:	Lynn@LynnPierce.com
LinkedIn:	www.linkedin.com/in/lynnpierce
Twitter:	www.twitter.com/lynnpierce
Facebook:	www.facebook.com/LynnPierceOfficial
Website:	www.LynnPierce.com
Links to Other Works:	www.AuthorExpertMedia.com/testimonials www.SuccessBlueprintRadio.com www.YourBreakthroughToSuccess.com www.TurningPassionIntoCash.com

Lynn Pierce, author of, *Breakthrough to Success; 19 Keys to Mastering Every Area of Your Life* and host of Success Blueprint Radio, brings you over 30 years of successfully teaching how to combine business, personal development and spirituality to reach the pinnacle of success and live the life of your dreams.

Lynn has taught thousands of sales teams and independent professionals how to tremendously increase their income (by as much as 500%) while reducing the stress of the sales and negotiation process...and having more free time to have a great lifestyle with that additional income!

Chapter 45: How to Attract Clients who Adore you – Even in a Recession

The dream of every businessperson is to create a business full of clients who happily pay what you ask, sing your praises and bring in tons of referrals, right?

When the money was flowing this was easy; then with the onset of the recession my clients, as well as their clients, started to tighten their belts and cut spending.

As the recession loomed, I realised I had to look back at what worked when I was building my business. It was time to get back to basics to be able to continue to grow.

Here's a little secret....

What I found, and really have always known, as I did this in my own business, was that it came down to sharpening my sales and communication skills to have an even deeper conversation with my past, present and potential clients. Since this is what I teach, I thought I was already doing a great job of this; the recession brought to my attention that I could be even more transparent than I had been in the past.

The issue that was made more glaring by the recession is that my prospective clients were feeling the pressure. Therefore they were being much more careful in studying their options before making a buying decision on what it is they need, what it is they can afford and who it is they should give their money to.

Just doing a Google search showed me how many people considered themselves my competition.

So the question was, 'how could I take my uniqueness to a level that created a specific niche?' This was imperative, as I knew that all my prospective clients would have to do to go from my website to someone else's is click a mouse! They don't even have to take the time to have a phone conversation with me; much less meet me in person.

This recession has taught me that in my own business and when helping my clients, we need to distinguish ourselves from the crowd. I needed to make it clear in the mind of my ideal client that I have no real competition. I realised that what makes me different, that uniqueness, is exactly what clients who will adore working with me are looking for.

By strengthening my sales and communication skills I was able to quickly eliminate my so-called competition. All I had to do, and all you have to do now, is to simply step out of the box you had voluntarily put yourself into.

I jumped out of the sales trainer box. I never really felt like that was an accurate portrayal of what I did anyway.

In order to help make the shift, I asked myself a few questions. You'll want ask yourself these too in order to become immune to the effects of the recession.

- How did I attract the adoring clients I've had for years and how can I increase that factor to approach prospective clients now?
- What did I do that was different from what they had experienced with other sales trainers?
- How can I deliver those things at an even higher level today to attract the client who is a little reluctant to spend money?

I remembered that even before I had any products, while I was still going to seminars and learning how to be an author, speaker and information marketer, I had developed relationships with fellow students and gurus who raised their hands as potential clients and literally told me what they wanted me to teach. That was quite a gift.

So I asked myself, what was it about me that created that situation when it clearly wasn't the norm?

The answer was that I had real conversations with people; I didn't look at them as walking dollar signs. I treated them as friends that I cared about and sincerely wanted to help. In turn, that made them want to do business with me before I was even in business.

I shared openly. I was helpful. And that didn't cost me any marketing dollars to do.

In this recession we can all do the things that don't cost anything to benefit our business. It is the little things such as adding a little kindness and listening to see what our market really wants that really make the difference. So that's where I started to increase my efforts. I went back to basics.

It paid off again just like it did in the beginning. I had discussions with potential clients who said they couldn't pay my rates. I asked them sincerely what they needed to take their business to the next level and what would they be able to pay for it. Because I was having an honest conversation they felt comfortable telling me. Then I created that programme for them.

To give you an example, when things started to become tight, clients who had gladly been paying me $2000 a month for private mentoring found that they no longer had that money available as their business slowed. The alternative we came up with was to do a group mentoring programme at $247 a month. This had 50% of the time together that the other programme had (two hours instead of four); meant being part of a small group (with nine new clients for me) and was at a greatly reduced price point, meaning that my clients could still benefit from my time.

Meanwhile I have increased my income by $247, freed up two hours of time and gained nine additional clients who will buy more as the years go by as well as refer additional clients. It's a win-win.

That worked for the people who needed a less costly alternative for right now and by increasing the number of participants, I was still keeping my income, staying connected to clients and actually working less hours mentoring. By having that real honest conversation and letting my clients know I was there to serve them and that together we would find a solution that worked for them, they helped me create a new programme.

Freeing up those extra hours allowed me the time to re-invent my 'Getting to Yes Without Selling' product line and has created new joint venture opportunities I wouldn't have had otherwise. So this new process is still generating benefits.

One client looked at his coaching business and realised that by writing a book he could increase his exposure better than one-on-one. I also conducted a virtual book tour for him. That connected him with current clients and potential clients while they all bonded over their love of his book.

He also started using social media to continue the conversation after the virtual book tour which greatly increased his reach. At the same time it allowed him to have those real conversations and deepen the relationships with people online. That led to more coaching clients, joint ventures and a huge increase in being booked for speaking engagements.

The uniqueness that people loved about me was how I came from a place of caring about how they wanted to live and their personal growth. I put their life first and then we worked from that standpoint to build their business.

On the other hand, I had never before come right out and said that I combine spirituality in my business training, even though I always had. When I looked at my clients, I saw that the clients who adored me the most were spiritually based.

So in my process of doing more of what had worked, I put it out there, right up front. I was a little apprehensive, thinking that it may turn off some potential clients. But then I remembered that the more I open up, the more I attract clients who adore me and the more prosperous my business is. My clients would be happier and that in turn brings in more referrals of like-minded people. And isn't that what we all want?

It's a new day and the need for having a real conversation and developing a long-term caring relationship is here to stay. The great news is that this is an easy skill to cultivate. So go ahead and create a business full of clients who adore you.

The Business Leaders Book Club
Series One: Lessons Learned From The Recession

AUTHOR
TBLBC

David Breslow
Recession Busting Lessons

Current Position:	Founder of The Personal Best Academy
Experience:	25 years as a Performance Coach, Speaker, Author Leadership Assessment Director, Executive Coach, Director of Mental Toughness at the USTA National Tennis Centre
Email:	dave@davebreslow.com
LinkedIn:	www.linkedin.com/profile/view?trk=tab_pro&id=1358632
Twitter:	www.twitter.com/#!/imsoaring2
Facebook:	www.facebook.com/pages/David-Breslow-Fan-Page/196671243680364
Website:	www.davebreslow.com
Links to Other Works:	Author, *Wired to Win* and *7 Laws of Human Performance*, Ezine Articles.com (expert author) Golf Channel Weekly Mental Game Contributor, Contributor to Active.com, Now Casting (Monthly contributor)
Contact Number:	+1 847-681-0247

David Breslow is Founder of The Personal Best Academy, Success Strategies, Speaker and author of *Wired to Win* and *7 Laws of Human Performance—21 days to Change the Way you Live, Work or Play*. He is known as The Rapid Transformation Coach and helps people reach their Personal Best with speed and consistency. His focus is on Leaders, Managers, Entrepreneurs, Salespeople and Athletes—in addition to anyone who seeks to tap into their Personal Best more consistently.

Chapter 46: Recession Busting Lessons

In his book, *The Prophet*, Kahlil Gibran writes, "Much of your pain is self-chosen. It is the bitter potion by which the physician within you heals your sick self." Tough words to heed during this time of global recession, aren't they? Even so, this global experience is yet another opportunity to put these words into action. When we look, are we really looking?

I have learned, through trial and error, that the most important thing I can do when any problem arises is this: ***look at myself first.*** I've noticed that my tendency in the past and the tendency of many well-intentioned clients, is to look at the circumstance or situation as the real 'issue' and then try to figure out how to make it better or even more tolerable. This would seem to make sense, yet I've discovered that when I change from within first, I can see more opportunities, take control of my environment and achieve real RESULTS.

The recession is yet another opportunity to learn very valuable and forward-moving lessons—if I truly look at it from this perspective. The truth is there are golden lessons showing up all the time; my clients and I now realise that they are there for us to become stronger and more inspired than before, regardless of the outer situation. We also learned that just the appearance of a lesson does not guarantee a change; it's merely a signal, like the warning light on the dashboard of my car. The warning light lets me know that something needs my attention and it is up to me to act on it.

We discovered that when any lesson in our professional or personal life shows up, we have three choices. We can:

1. Deny it
2. See it and do nothing
3. See it and take action

Using step three from the model above, I would like to share with you the three Recession Buster strategies that my clients and I have benefited from.

1. Focus on what you can 100% control

Recession news is often negative and this tends to influence a lot of what people think, believe and talk about what is going on in the world. However, this can only negatively affect us if we buy into it. My top performing clients have learned to apply this highly important principle: *only focus on what you have 100% control over.*

When we discovered that when we focus on things like the past or the future, what others say, others' fear and negativity (all things we cannot control 100% in the moment) it weakens us. In choosing to strengthen ourselves, we've learned to identify what we DO have control over in this immediate moment. We find that when we focus on what we can control 100%, we are clearer, more confident, optimistic, get more done and find ourselves experiencing the present moment more often.

We discovered that we do have 100% control over, things like the choices we make, what we choose to pay attention to, breathing properly, making that important phone call we've been putting off, preparing a proposal, locating and attending a networking function, feeling optimistic, smiling and so on.

When we focused on what we didn't have control over it weakened us by causing more stress and anxiety—exactly what we didn't need!

2. Focus on building relationships

Now, more than ever, doing great business is about building relationships that are based on trust and integrity. While everyone has something to 'sell', we discovered that we could build better relationships with potential customers by asking more questions rather than talking about our services upon meeting them. This made a tremendous difference in the comfort level and receptivity of the other person and opened the door to uncovering their real needs and obstacles. Focusing on building the relationship first is a philosophy, a mindset that built trust; since most of us prefer to work with people we like and trust, building relationships first strengthened that bridge.

3. Add Value Immediately

One of the choices we all have 100% control over, is to add value for the people we meet and do business with. During this time of recession, many of my clients thought that lowering rates was the best strategy to employ. They discovered that adding value could also get people's interest without lowering fees. Value can be measured in ways such as offering more time or content to a prospective client. I noticed that when I did this, the focus in the client's mind turned toward the added value they were going to receive for their investment. Adding value is another way to build the relationship as well and my clients found it to be an interesting exercise to discover and implement ways to add value for their clients.

Here are some ideas they came up with: write a short e-book and offer it online for free, a free whitepaper on a specific topic, give-away workbooks or guidebooks or free teleseminars on a relevant topic, all designed to provide real information to help people solve problems. Another idea is to partner with someone else who can add a product or service to theirs and create a terrific 'package' to promote.

We found that adding value deepened credibility as customers told us they thought things like, "If you have this much 'good stuff' for free, I wonder what else you have if I hire you!"

We learned that the recession can be a time of great lessons to be uncovered. When we looked at ourselves first as having the power to take action, we began to see these opportunities!

Nigel Penhearow

Continuing Improvements in Business

Current Position:	Sales Director and former Operations Director
Qualifications:	MBA – University of Liverpool
	DPIM – Institute of Operations Management
Experience:	27 years in post education experience
Email:	nigelpenhearow@gmail.com
Website:	www.operations-director.com

Nigel Penhearow has always been keen to drive improvement in business. His career started as a management trainee at a major UK bank, however, after a few years the excitement of the commercial business world beckoned. He works for one of the most prestigious names in the imaging and printing industry, having worked for the organisation for over two decades in various roles both at UK and European level. He has also acted as an independent consultant on e-commerce, social media management, business analytics and customer relationship management.

He was appointed as the Business Operations Director of a joint venture company and despite some significant business challenges in the first few years of its formation (remember most joint venture companies fail!) it was an outstanding success, with Penhearow initiating many operational and organisational improvements.

In the past few years he has held the role of Sales Director, managing a multi-million dollar region encompassing the UK, Ireland, Nordics and Baltic's indirect (distributor) businesses driving sales in hardware, software and consumables. This role too has been challenging, however, a number of changes have been made to grow the business and drive the 'costs to serve' down and to improve processes and procedures to the benefit of customers and his company alike.

Chapter 47: Continuous Improvements in Business

Leading up to the summer of 2008 everyone thought that the boom times were here to last. House prices were high and commodities were on the increase but all of a sudden, in the autumn of 2008, everything crashed.

It is at times like these when companies usually go in to 'super-panic' mode. Their fixed costs and salaries remain the same whilst margins and revenues start to feel the effect of declining activity in the market place. It is at times like these when many organisations are not prepared for what is to come!

I have seen a few recessions over the breadth of my career, of which most have been at a time when I have been working within the printing and publishing market segment. In more recent times (over the past two years) I have also been exposed to the fast-moving consumer goods industry, selling electronics.

The printing and publishing industry is usually a very good barometer as to how the economy is performing and many say that the downturn in spending is felt about three months prior to it affecting other trades and the general retail sector. This is primarily driven by the general alarm of companies to cut costs. They first look at their marketing budgets. Any collateral that is associated with the department is usually the first area where costs are slashed, thus printing declines as less brochures and other such items are no longer produced.

I drove a different view, especially when running our operations division as Business Operations Director considered ourselves the best in the industry, running on low costs but delivering superior service. As you know in all businesses there is ***ALWAYS Room for Improvement***; I will argue this case with anyone from any industry! My primary message to anyone is ***never stop looking for ways to enhance your organisation.***

Having made this statement, continuous improvement is often ignored when sales are booming and the coffers are filling with profits. There is not usually that much enthusiasm to invest or reserve cash for the bad times and let's face it, recessions are cyclical!

These were the key factors that prepared us well:

- Surround yourself with the best managers you can, especially those that you find have like-minded attitudes towards business.
- Encourage staff to think of the business as if it was their own personal business and to make the right decisions.
- The key is to give as much autonomy as possible whilst keeping an element of control using analytics, business update meetings etc. **This can save you time and in my case probably saved about *10% of my day. That 10% I used to make more improvements.***

I always came up with ideas that were sometimes considered outside the normal boundaries of thinking and whilst I had the ideas, I had to try and implement them; therefore I had at my disposal two excellent people both of which knew systems applications and Microsoft Access extremely well. These two people made my ideas become a reality.

Whilst I cannot disclose too much detail, we set about automating and all the time consuming costly functions that we faced on a day-to-day basis. We had people manually running reports, sending information to customers both on order status and shipping; we had planners having to run complex reporting in order to understand our stock positions and running complex macro's and 'v look ups' in excel to merge data. All of this added cost and was wasting time.

The changes we made meant a dramatic reduction in costs. ***Our total operational costs reduced by significant double digit percentage points over a period of time, with some departments showing truly exceptional cost saving performance.***

My view was that even in economic boom we had to be efficient. In the months that followed we were able to automate all of the local reporting. When staff came to their desks in the morning and switched on their PCs, the reports were in their email inbox. We no longer had to send order status reports to customers and we even automatically advised their warehouses of what products would be arriving before the goods turned up at their premises. Planners had almost hourly reports regarding the status of their products. The warehouse had superb analytics to determine efficiency.

There were staffing casualties but in reality we reduced head count in a controlled way, often by losing contract staff or employees who were leaving to embark on new careers and not filling their now vacant position.

You may be saying so what? All I can say is that due to the excellent work we had done in the boom times, ***when the economy started to slide we were already in a position of very high efficiency and lowest possible cost***. In a relatively short period of time costs had been reduced in a controlled way which meant we were truly 'lean'.

Looking at the current recession with my Sales Director's hat on is a little different to my operational days. General trading conditions are hard and continue to be tough even though economic forecasters predict an upturn in the UK's GDP this year and for the years to come. We do offer solutions to our customers though, which will help them through the bad times.

Our workflow software is considered the best in the pre-press area of printing. What we offer customers is very similar to what we were able to achieve in operations. We use what is called 'rules-based automation' which effectively takes out any manual process that is needed when a printing job is transmitted from the client to the printer and then through the printer's manufacturing processes.

In the past the printer had to manually handle files through their manufacturing cycle; this is no longer required thus the printer can reduce headcount cost by either reducing staff or redeploying them to other areas of the organisation where added value can be achieved. ***Where multiple people used to manage jobs submitted electronically by customers to be printed by their company, now only one person (or sometimes no one at all) is required.***

As we care about the success of our distribution partners during this time of recession, I have introduced what I consider to be a unique (and free) service. What we offer is a review of their operational costs, especially those centred on utility, warehousing and logistics. ***In one case we reduced a distributor's packaging costs by 40%; on another utility costs were reduced by 20%.***

We review their cost base, after they share their cost data, to see if we can make them savings. There has not been a single situation where we have not been able to assist them in saving cash within their business. We have been told that the service is fantastic and they cannot believe that a multi-national corporation, such as ours, offer such a service. It is unique in our field! ***The aim is to ensure our distribution partners survive when under economic pressure and I felt this was one way of helping them.***

I also personally advise them on Internet strategy and deployment so that they can save costs and become efficient. ***In respect of savings on consultancy, I cannot really quantify, however, if they had employed a professional consultant they (all the customers I have advised) would have collectively spent thousands of pounds in consultation fees.***

My parting advice is to always be prepared, employ the best people you can (make sure you retain them!) and always look for continuous improvement supported by quantifiable metrics.

AUTHOR
TBLBC

Nadeem Mohammed

You'd be Nuts not to: Using the Recession to Shake Off Old Acorns!

Current Position:	Managing Director & CTO
Qualifications:	MBA, BSc (Hons)
Experience:	20 years of experience in the IT industry
Email:	Nadeem.mohammed@deffinity.com
LinkedIn:	http://uk.linkedin.com/in/nazdaq
Website:	www.deffinity.com
	www.deffinitymsa.wordpress.com
Contact Number:	+44 (0) 7535683097

Nadeem has a solid track record within Service Delivery for a number of major investment banks. He became a Board Director for a leading London based Infrastructure Company and held the positions of CIO and Head of Service Delivery and Innovation, contributing to 40% growth by creating state-of-the-art solutions for service delivery.

Nadeem now spearheads Deffinity, creating a global sales channel to promote its unique SaaS Project Delivery solution. Deffinity simplifies the typically complex strands that make up project operations. Unlike conventional project and programme tools, Deffinity brings to life every component of a project from the moment it goes live, keeping all documentation and project schedules in a single accessible location wherever you are in the world, with internet access. It does not require lengthy training to use nor do you need proprietary software installed on every PC. It proactively sends out notifications when times slip or budgets are exceeded. It ensures everyone from project managers, vendors, engineers and procurement teams operate from a single platform and instant reports. As well as this, Nadeem is also working with a leading Datacentre Infrastructure and Support company to develop their solutions strategy.

Chapter 48: You'd be Nuts not to: Using the Recession to Shake Off Old Acorns!

The squirrel in the cartoon Ice Age clings to the same acorn as if it was the only nut in the world. Throughout the film he undertakes an extraordinary series of adventures, fighting off all attempts to wrest it from his control.

In business it is easy to become equally obsessive over holding on to cherished processes and procedures. Of course older doesn't mean less appropriate but the fact remains that technology, business and customers have changed over the years. Clinging on to the business practice acorn may soon begin to look a little obsessive.

Perhaps the biggest opportunity for acorn abandonment comes in the form of communication. The recession provides a perfect opportunity to evaluate communication and whether technology is being employed to the advantage of your staff and customers or whether the technology being used is still stuck in the Ice Age.

One of the failings of the IT era has been to shoehorn too many inappropriate technologies into the wrong places. Taking an out-dated process and wrapping it with email is tantamount to sticking the acorn in your pocket and pretending you have moved on.

The point about technology and communication is that, when used correctly, they allow you to achieve understanding and be innovative in a way that wasn't possible before. This isn't a one size fits all world but looking around shows what can be achieved.

Take, for example, Amazon, the online retailer. Without a single face-to-face interaction to impress a single customer, they have achieved a net promoter score of 74%, a good indicator of customer satisfaction. A combination of keeping customers up to date with what is being done on their behalf, together with well-managed service, allows them to delight their customers without relying overly on the human touch.

The point here is not that every business should strive to match Amazon's model, but it should look at the way that its products and services are delivered and question whether the appropriate use of technology can help them.

For a business to be the best it can be, it should be using technology to:

- Provide better control of internal processes in order to reduce administration to a bare minimum
- Track exactly how much they are making on any service or project at any time
- Reduce the headache surrounding timesheet management
- Show their customers that they have something unique, something with the X-Factor.

In my experience, the easiest way to use technology to wow customers and reduce cost simultaneously is by bringing service delivery under control. Whether your service is delivering a product on-time or carrying out a complex engagement, wasted time and poor communications can lead to the double whammy of increased cost and decreased customer satisfaction.

It may not feel like acorn abandonment, but the first step towards stemming the flow of money and customers can be to simply set out your promises to your customers and then to demonstrate that you are keeping to them. A good online service delivery solution will allow you to do this in a way that:

1. Shows you where every hour of effort and every penny of capital is being spent
2. Shows your customer what is being done on their behalf, by how many people and that it is happening exactly as promised and on time

Better still, such a system can allow everyone to log in themselves to see what's happening. So the number of phone calls from customers asking for an update falls too. In a similar way, progress reports are produced at the click of a button. All of this leaves your people managers to manage people and leaves your people to do what the customer is paying them to do.

The hardest part of the process to overcome is undoubtedly the necessary cultural shift to enable you to trust in technology to help deliver promises. When your name and reputation have been built on delivering great service, it can be hard to break the reliance on trusted long-term employees to deliver that promise.

The point here is that you are not throwing away old principles. A good service delivery package is just another tool. It is a powerful tool that, used well, will help keep customers loyal. It is also a tool that can free you from the drudgery of chasing everything through from phone calls to face-to-face meetings.

So, where our friend the squirrel from Ice Age desperately clings onto the whole acorn, the wise squirrel would take out the kernel and discard the encumbering shell. Good service delivery systems recognise the heart of your business is the skill and enthusiasm of the people in the business. They then free you of the burden of day-to-day task management, cost tracking and reporting. By involving your customers in your process, they help customer retention and provide an excellent tool to help win new business.

My lesson to demonstrate this strategy and how it helps companies to manage their business more effectively is best explained through a recent case study:

CASE STUDY: Excel IT Ltd.

Excel IT manage thousands of miles of cabling, connections and IT equipment for banks, insurance companies and other highly demanding customers. Taking responsibility for connecting people to decision-making tools and transactional systems in such IT dependent companies involves not only a great deal of technical know-how, but strict adherence to governance, risk and compliance standards.

After many years of successful business development, Excel IT set out to find a system that would allow them to achieve their next phase of exponential growth without becoming bogged down with an ever larger back-office team. Achieving this would allow them to focus their management team on exceeding customer expectations rather than in endless rounds of recruitment and administration.

The first focus for Excel was to find a system that would allow them to reduce their dependence on 'management by spreadsheet' that had grown up over the years. Typically, for a company of their size and shape, a lot of business processes had become modelled and then fixed in spreadsheets with a corporate email system as the backbone.

Whilst this allowed for great flexibility, it relied on every individual being skilled and dedicated enough to follow naming conventions, applying the correct formulae and being diligent in checking the logic of their spreadsheets.

As an alternative, a system was brought to the table that allowed Excel IT to define business rules and a project management office approach that allowed a core team to set up the time reporting, progress monitoring and IT governance. This in turn freed up customer-facing staff to focus on delivery of excellence in their individual fields. As a result, less time was spent training, fewer mistakes were made and customers were more informed.

The process of going live was equally important to Excel IT. Their requirement was immediate and any delay in implementation would hold back the growth plan, continue the existing cost base and delay their ability to deliver innovation to achieve their customer experience targets.

For Excel IT, using a service delivery package helped them to continue success for the following reasons:

- Due to well-managed installation times, cost savings became apparent almost immediately
- Customers were satisfied with the improvements as they saw a reduction in time to deliver their products
- They were able to show their brand to their customers, which in turn allowed them to demonstrate innovation to underpin their customer experience management programme
- In the back-office they reported additional benefit from being able to see 'live' project profitability through management dashboards. This allowed them to see unbilled time which had previously been 'lost' through lack of visibility in their head office
- They saw all their processes streamlined as all processes and policies became simpler and embedded in the system.

As a result of shaking off their old acorns and employing technology to their advantage, Excel IT were able to continue trade with cost savings, increased sales and most importantly, increased customer satisfaction.

Michael Trigg

Why you don't Need Pills or PowerPoint

Current Position:	Managing Director
Experience:	Over 25 years full time training and coaching
Email:	michaeltrigg@me.com
LinkedIn:	http://uk.linkedin.com/pub/michael-trigg/7/660/453
Twitter:	www.twitter.com/greatpresenting
Website:	www.presentationskillscoaching.co.uk
Links to Other Works:	Book: *Stand Out From The Crowd – 99 Tips for Successful & Powerful Presenting*
Contact Number:	+44 (0) 208 237 5600

Michael Trigg is a top-level Presentation Coach, working mostly at board and executive level. After five years in the Army, two years in merchant banking and six years with Procter & Gamble he has been training and coaching full-time for over 20 years. His speciality and passion lie in showing clients how to talk without notes or PowerPoint and transform their confidence and ability to engage and influence a client or audience.

The author of *Stand Out from the Crowd* of which Jay Conrad Levinson (The Father of Guerrilla Marketing) wrote "When it comes to speaking in public, few people know as much as Michael Trigg about the topic and fewer still have the ability to put it into words with the accuracy and grace of the man. I applaud him and highly recommend reading every word he writes and listening to every word he says."

He lives in the Cotswolds and is passionate about the arts in general and music in particular. He is a keen cook and photographer, dabbles in water colour painting, embraces almost every Apple product and is also a Reiki Master.

Chapter 49: Why you don't Need Pills or PowerPoint

I am a presentation coach specialising in the development of outstanding presentation skills at board level.

At the time of writing, we are facing 'interesting times' as the Chinese curse has it. Many highly-qualified heads are being scratched as to whether we are in a deep or mild recession and whether it will be a double dip or square root shaped; few economists agree with each other anyway. In the bigger scheme of things, we are in this place for a reason. I have found that it is how one responds to the current climate and deals with it that is the opportunity.

Firstly, the lessons I would like to share with you are drawn from a few of my clients' experiences. Secondly, I will share with you a few tips and suggestions to retain and win more business in these interesting times.

Whenever times become tough, it is an almost Pavlovian reaction of many businesses to cut back in two vital areas – marketing and training their people. Both are too often seen as an expense and not an investment. Yet if the ability to win new business in tough times (and retain the business you have) is not a priority, then what is?

Recently, I started to work for the first time with a major FTSE 500 company, a household name. They have been able to retain most of their existing business but have almost completely failed to win new clients for over a year. And after meeting with them, I can see why.

I found their pitches were mind-numbingly dull, uninspiring and PowerPoint heavy. It is too early to see the results, but after two days together we are all confident that those days are behind them.

At the beginning of the recession, I worked with some of the brightest up-and-coming young stars in one of the world's biggest PR agencies. Traditionally, this genre does not invest much time or money in developing their people, so it was a welcome surprise and privilege to be invited to work with them, even if it was only for a day. A few weeks later one of the participants phoned me to thank me and tell me his story:

"I flew to Europe to visit a major client and experienced one of the worst scenarios of my career. My plane was delayed, so not only was I horribly late but found myself pitching in front of 50 people, rather than the six I had expected. Using what I had learned from our day together, I was amazed to find that I wasn't thrown at all. I had both the confidence and a new found flexibility to adapt my approach and engage everyone. As a result, the client wants our agency to do ALL their major presentations from now on."

The lessons learned: continue to invest in training, especially marketing-related initiatives. Empower your people with the tools that they will need to win business in tough times.

Let us move on to the second point I'd like to share with you. When times are good, people like doing business with people they like. When times are tough, people still like doing business with people they like.

I think it is true to say that very few businesses are THAT unique. Your competition is probably offering a similar service or product at a similar price, with a similar track record and client list. So what's going to make them choose you?

Many things...the colour of your tie... your accent...you support the same team or love the same sport...you're from the same state or county. But probably the biggest *difference that makes the difference* is the way you engage with them, build rapport and talk their language. Complete common sense I know, but are you doing it?

One of my friends was once a few minutes into his pitch when his potential client said:

"Stop, stop, stop! I know you can do the job. So can the other three agencies I'll be seeing this week. Otherwise you wouldn't be here in front of me. What I'm here to decide is whether I want to work with you for the next couple of years!"

So how do you encourage a potential client to feel that they DO want to work and deal with you for some time to come?

I advise my clients that there are three duties or obligations of any presenter or business development professional. The first is to be interesting and engaging. This is largely to do with enthusiasm, fluency and talking their language, not yours. The second is to get your message across. To do this you first need a message and in 90% of cases it isn't clear. You also need a clear structure so the client can follow you. Thirdly, be authentic. Be you. Let your real personality come across - the upbeat and engaging side of you, rather than the manic depressive!

The work that I have been doing with my client base throughout this recession has been impactful, with real tangible results. So to present my second lesson, I would like to share with you, my top tips for creating an engaging and business winning presentation strategy.

Make the start of your business presentations engaging:

- Take the first 30-60 seconds and practice it at least a couple of times; not so that you have it memorised and word perfect, but so that you look and sound as if you know what you're about.
- Look at your client 95% of the time, and ESPECIALLY during the whole introduction. There are few things more un-engaging than a person looking at the screen or their notes for the first 30 seconds of a talk or pitch.
- Build rapport; sound and be human as if talking to a friend.
- Leave all your management speak/jargon outside the room. Every profession has its jargon but it is becoming increasingly like a disease. People seem to compete with each other as to who can use the latest buzz words. Review the sort of habits, phrases and words you are using. Here is a real example of an email sent to me six weeks ago: "...we need programmes that focus on advanced facilitation skills for new business pitches, multiple prioritisation techniques and strategic and lean thinking...programmes need to be highly-tailored and take an interactive blended learning approach..."

  Apart from the danger of management speak, do also think about words and phrases like framework, best practice, strategic, key metrics, optimal business processes, management methodology...and their ilk. Are you still awake?!

- Talk plain English, as if talking to a friend, your mother or spouse. The acid test is this:
  Imagine your audience is 16 years old, very bright, with a very low boredom threshold and knows little about what you do. If you can keep the attention of an audience of 16 year olds for twenty minutes, then you are doing well.
- If you can, do it without PowerPoint. We have all seen every single effect that it's possible to see and we are all bored senseless by them. And lines of bullet points or figures are almost guaranteed to numb the mind after the fourth slide. If you have to use slides to make your points, then make them as VISUAL as possible. Then know your subject well enough to talk around them.
- Have a clear structure, so that your client knows exactly where you are taking him and where he is at any time. And finish on your message, not the questions. So take your questions at the end if you wish and ensure you summarise AFTER them so that your message is ringing in their ears and brains.

The lesson learned: to win business during difficult times requires us to adapt our presentation style, so that we become more engaging, more relevant and more personality focused, in order to win the business.

A final thought

We are living in challenging times. So did our parents and before them our grandparents. It's how you respond to the challenges – how you think – that is the crucial factor.

Shakespeare wrote, "Nothing is but thinking makes it so."

Stand out from your competition and tip the scales in your favour. People need what you have - just ensure you make it a pleasure to do business with you rather than your competition!

And the pills?

Well, there are 130 million Americans on prescription medication for some stress-related ailment. But people and events are not intrinsically stressful. It's our response to the events that creates the condition we label stress. So in most cases we have a choice on how to respond. The same applies to how we respond to the recession and all its challenges and opportunities. And there are customers out there who want and need what you have. Nothing is but thinking makes it so.

So is it going to be the pills...or a shift in thinking and presenting your message? Be the difference that 'makes the difference'.

Paul Roebuck and Shirley Parsons

30 years of Operating and Consulting: A Reflection

Current Position:	CEO Identify Group, MD Shirley Parsons Associates
Experience:	Recruitment, health and safety, OH, telecoms, ICT
Email:	paul.roebuck@identifygroup.com Shirley.parsons@shirleyparsons.com
LinkedIn:	http://uk.linkedin.com/in/paulrobertroebuck
Twitter:	www.twitter.com/paulroebuck
Website:	www.identifygroup.com www.shirleyparsons.com

Paul Roebuck is a Computer Systems Engineering Graduate who moved from designing advanced military and communications networks into recruitment via three years as a freelance contractor. He has over 30 years in the recruitment sector as a business owner and investor. He was an early pioneer of onsite recruitment solutions in the late 80s and early 90s and is presently co-founder and CEO of Identify Group and co-founder and director of Kineticom Inc.

Shirley Parsons is a science graduate who moved from local government through consultancy into recruitment. She ran parallel careers throughout the 80s and 90s as a technical expert in the HSEQ sector as well as pioneering recruitment solutions in the Telecom and Health and Safety sectors. As the co-founder of S-Com and Sypol she is presently CEO of Shirley Parsons Associates and co-founder and director of Identify Group.

Chapter 50: 30 years of Operating and Consulting: A Reflection

The current recession marks our third experience of operating in a recession in the UK. Back in 1979 we started our first two businesses going into a recession although we were very naive then. We didn't actually realise we'd been in a recession until much later on, we just thought the trading climate was what it was.

It wasn't until the 89-92 recession that we began to understand what going through a recession was really like. At that stage we had two businesses – Sypol, the environmental and safety consultancy, and S-Com, the technical agency and computer systems and products house. August 1989 marked the end of the property bubble of that era and prices were about to fall off a cliff. I remember addressing everyone in the group and announcing that we were about to go into recession, but we still didn't really know what to expect other than things would get tough.

However new business dried up substantially, we had to release people and we all had to go back to developing as much business as we could – everyone became hands on. At the same time we were able to strengthen Sypol by merging with another small specialist consultancy and we decided to focus on the recruitment side of our ICT business and set about selling our systems house and communications products businesses.

The end of recession came as rapidly as the start. In March 1992 the tap came back on and having disposed of our systems house and products businesses and with Sypol operating autonomously with a new management team, we were well geared to expand rapidly. Both Sypol and S-Com grew rapidly throughout the 1990s and towards the end of the decade we sold both businesses.

This was followed by working earn outs and latterly, by a period as investors in a range of diverse entrepreneurial businesses. Then in 2005 we decided to start again on our own by forming The Identify Group. Our first group start up was a Health and Safety recruitment business, named after Shirley as by that time she'd become a brand in her own right. This was followed in 2008 by the addition of Kineticom Ltd, acquired from sister company Kineticom Inc. along with Malik Shaw – a small public sector agency.

We all heard Alistair Darling's warning at the end of August 2008 about the worst conditions for 60 years, but at that time we weren't seeing any effects feeding through. Even at the end of 2008 at our annual planning sessions we were asking "what recession?". Indeed it was not until mid 2009 that trading conditions began to deteriorate rapidly and we felt the effects in both our health and safety and our ICT and Telecoms sectors. The Public Sector still continued to perform well though.

It's fair to say that with the exception of those in the public sector, all of our staff began to understand what being in a recession was actually like. Then having planned for a flat year, 2010 has turned out to be good for all of our businesses. ICT/Telecoms was a little slower to get going, but Health and Safety hit the ground running and the first three quarters of 2010 were the best we've had.

So is it all over? We don't think so. We've taken to engaging with the economic forecasters at the banks and we're strongly influenced by the way they see things. We also meet regularly with our relationship mangers just to exchange views on how we all see things shaping up. The best view we have is that opportunities will still be there in 2011 and growth is possible, but expect a rocky road.

The main lessons we've learned from the previous and the current recessions concern the behaviour of finance providers. In 1987 our bankers had persuaded us to drop our invoice discounting arrangements in favour of a new offering direct from themselves. But by mid 1989 they were already getting nervous, bringing in new restrictions and generally making life difficult before finally announcing that they wanted out.

What had been a cordial relationship became one of mistrust. With the help of a former banker, we bought some time and managed to find a much better deal with a specialist invoice discounter. That relationship was also tested when one of our major clients - Ferranti - went bust, creating a £250K hole in our cash flows. The response of our new partners was to impose an overall reduction in our facility, leaving us to find more funding from private means, which we duly did and the relationship then got back on an even keel.

Similar behaviours came to the fore again in 2009. Our invoice discounting partner became very nervous and pernickety and was looking for holes in everything we did. They tried to unilaterally change the terms of our loan facilities in a really underhand way. We caught that one, but they won in the end because they invoked a change clause by claiming a breach on our part after a small error in one of our reports. Over the period, we went from being their biggest fan (and best reference site) to being their most vociferous detractor. We managed to terminate the relationship by mutual consent in 2010 and strangely our facilities are now with our High St bank (RBS) who we've been with ever since 1990 and who have been supportive through all of the ups and downs we've had over the years.

So the lessons learned are: -

- Recruitment businesses are usually first in and first out of a recession
- Property bubbles frequently precede a recession
- Banks and finance providers see the recession coming before we do
- When a recession comes many bankers show another side – not always an honest one
- If and when you do hit problems, expect the finance providers to give you a further stress test
- Long term relationships do seem to matter – but don't bank on it
- It's hard to call the start or the end of a recession in advance - just be ready to act
- Staff loyalty helps enormously

To mitigate the effects of a recession: -

- Create an operating cost base that is as flexible as possible
- Aim to create balance sheet strength that will enable you to withstand a 'sizeable' bad debt or trading losses
- Gear your business to have sufficient 'headroom' – avoid always being at the limit
- Try to spread the client base so that you are not overly dependent on a few large ones
- Be extra diligent with credit control and debt collection
- Be open internally - involve your staff more and keep them onside – you're all in it together
- Help your staff to make sensible financial plans and not to over-commit when the times are really good, unless they

have a strong personal balance sheet with good sources of liquidity.

- Know your sector cycles – some are cyclic with a recession, some are anti-cyclic and others depend more on sector investment cycles that are independent of recessions

Finally where are we now? Our figures are slightly better than they were in 2008, and we've moved our 5 year plan out by a couple of years. We're cautiously optimistic about 2011 but we still have a higher degree of uncertainty than we would like. Our balance sheets are stronger now than they were last year and we have an excellent team. Let's see what the markets do.

Addendum

Supplementary facts and figures: -

- In August 1989 we had approximately 120 contract staff working through S-Com.
- By March 1992 The number of contractors working through S-Com had declined to around 75
- In July 1997 when we sold S-Com, we had approximately 550 contractors on fees.

Throughout our time at S-Com we always supported the defence and telecoms industries and grew rapidly in the 90s in both of these sectors. The award of new mobile operator licences helped fuel the rapid growth during that period, as did the award of List-X for military work.

AU✢HOR
TB✢LBC

Pino Tedesco

Struggling Through the Recession? Try Starting a New Company…

Current Position:	Director of Ironstone Group and Group of Companies
Qualifications:	University of Western Sydney – Commerce Qualified Valuer / Appraiser Licensed Real Estate Agent Licensed Buyers Advocate
Email:	pino@capital360.com.au
LinkedIn:	http://au.linkedin.com/in/sydneybuyersagent
Twitter:	www.twitter.com/pinotedesco
Website:	www.ironstonegroup.com.au , www.capital360.com.au, www.ironstonefunds.com.au
Contact Number:	+61 8922 9666

Pino Tedesco brings 10 years of comprehensive real estate experience and a solid background in property investment acquisition, due diligence as well as property valuation and project management. From property funds management with Deutsche Bank, he subsequently built a successful property valuation firm and then most recently built one of Australia's largest buying agency offices. **Capital 360** clients regularly take comfort in Pino's valuation, buyer's advocacy and portfolio management as well as project management expertise.

Pino is frequently asked to be a property commentator and has been quoted in most major Australian property/financial magazines and regularly shares his views on wealth creation and the property markets. He is a regular speaker at property conferences in Australia and Asia and is soon to release a book that will assist property investors grow their property portfolios. Most recently Pino won the YIP Property Investment Advisor of the Year award.

Chapter 51: Struggling Through the Recession? Try Starting a New Company...

During World War II a young Italian man named Francesco Vincenzo Tedesco decided to leave an impoverished town in southern Italy, leaving his parents and four siblings behind in search of a better life. After saving up 300,000 lira (a couple of years earnings) to buy a boat ticket and 47 days travel, he landed in the land of new opportunity – Australia. He was seventeen years of age and he is my father.

Imagine landing in a new country with no education and unable to speak the language? With nothing but pure determination and an incredible work ethic my father spent the next four years saving up to pay for all his relatives to join him. Vincenzo then focused on setting up a good life for himself and his family. My father's journey has led not only to my fulfilling life but to that of many relatives – including doctors, accountants, global executives and multi-national company owners. All of this came from one man's desire for a better life.

Vincenzo's story continues to inspire me today to strive for achievement against all odds. I know that my father has transfused his ideals and work ethics into me and every day I aim to inject the same into our business and the individuals that make it up.

What I will share with you is how we successfully created the Ironstone Group during the recession. One subsidiary, Capital 360, has become the largest buyers' agency in Australia in less than two years from a standing start and is now expanding internationally. In the same period, we witnessed consolidation and downsizing of our competitors. People now question why we were able to grow exponentially during the recession while others struggled.

I put this down to 5 key principles:

1. Client – is the focus of everything we do, we revolve around them
2. Creativity – from within and not being afraid to think differently
3. Action – be progressive rather than a perfectionist, don't delay action!
4. Passion – love what you do; this becomes infectious for all

5. Rent a Hero – when times are hard seek advice by asking "what would my hero do?"

However, before we even considered our key principles, we fostered a culture of empowerment and self-belief within our team. This culture is vibrant and remains the glue in our business today.

1. **Client – is the focus of everything we do, we revolve around them**

Imagine launching a primarily service-driven company during the height of the recession (GFC)? The fight for market share was greater than ever. The wealth of many investors was under threat or had been decimated in some cases and confidence was at historic lows. Do you remember how you felt during this period? The recession scared people. We were vying for a piece of a contracting pie.

Trust in 'advisers' was at an all-time low so we made a commitment to each other and to our clients: to provide higher levels of professional advice, expertise and service.

Through this we gained respect and trust from our clients as they re-entered the property market while others were exiting in panic. Our educated clients who held their nerve have been well rewarded and are repeat clients for life. Our advice and cutting edge research has justified us as market experts and leaders in our industry.

To build a successful business we had to think of such things as:

- What do our clients want?
- How would they like to experience our service?
- How do they want to be communicated with?
- What would they expect from us before, during and after our service?

We started by researching what investors look for in buying, building and managing property. Historically, the majority of people would research, source and negotiate on a property for themselves or rely on a real estate agent (who actually represents the vendor/owner, not the buyer). In a few cases, some were aware of our cottage industry and had employed a buyer's agent to represent them.

Our research found investors were concerned with the steps before and after purchasing an asset. Who would advise on the right ownership structure and a suitable finance strategy? Who would coordinate the renovation and manage the property? Who would review their property portfolio and if they needed to sell an asset, who would manage the sales advisory?

We decided to build a business encompassing all of these steps and developed a proprietary 8 Step Process. We built eight divisions in our business to service all of the needs of a transaction rather than focus on one or two parts. Our company is one that challenges the traditional paradigms of the residential property industry, an industry which historically was based on product, not bespoke service. We brought to market truly start to finish, bespoke residential property advisory. We are unique in having a full turn-key solution and a national footprint, and this has supported our PR and media strategies well and more importantly, provided our clients with proven market beating performance

2. **Creativity – be brave enough to think differently!**

I genuinely believe that your internal team can be more creative than an outsourced solution. Get all of your different business divisions to collaborate. Try posing a question like "what shall our service offering be?" without putting ANY limitations on the brainstorming process. Seek solutions and smash through 'problems.' Without limitations you will find your staff/team can contribute significantly as they already 'live' the business. External parties should only be used for review and fulfilment. The heavy lifting should be internal.

It was our team that initially thought up a 5 step process; after much brainstorming we added three more steps and together we refined it to be what it is our proprietary 8 Step Process to property investment. This is the core of our business. The answers were within our own team. We then outsourced to experts, an external media agency, to review and refine the 'look and feel' of our proposition.

3. **Action – be progressive rather than a perfectionist. Don't delay action!**

Don't get me wrong. We are always striving for perfection but perfection doesn't happen overnight. Without progression there will be no perfection and most businesses strive for perfection at the expense of progress and ultimately their survival.

We have embraced progress and creativity at all levels of our business. We are continually improving ourselves and our systems to create mass momentum. Interestingly, I believe that our business will never be perfect as we are always aiming to improve for the benefit of our clients.

4. **Passion – our team have to love what they do; this becomes infectious for all.**

Passionate team members will lead and inspire others and through osmosis this transfers to the rest of the team. By hiring the right staff we can become the smartest and most passionate (and most creative!) property advisory firm in Australia. Our clients *feel* this when they deal with us. We look for passion, creativity and commitment.

Skills can be taught but you can't teach enthusiasm. An employee with enthusiasm will outperform every time, all else being equal. Our people have shaped our business and without them and their undying passion to create the best property portfolios for our clients, our group of companies would not be what it is today.

5. **'Rent a Hero' – when times are hard, seek advice - "what would my hero do?"**

I thought I would end with what may be a new concept and an interesting 'take away'.

The key to this concept is to use it consistently! Make it part of your culture. If you are successful in implementing this one concept, then through good and bad times, you will have an invaluable tool.

The 'Rent a Hero' concept is used in times when you need inspiration, need to solve a problem, need to resolve a conflict or need to cause action amongst others. All of these are important in running a business, inspiring yourself or simply aiming higher. I even use the 'Rent a Hero' concept in my non-business relationships.
Here it is: when you are faced with a problem, why not use the experience and wisdom of great people around you? Even if they are no longer alive! You don't even need their permission! Mark Twain once said that "the best kind of experience is other people's." He

was right! Imagine facing a situation and thinking "What would Steve Jobs do?" or "What would Nelson Mandela do?"

Problems or challenges will often seem insurmountable but by removing myself, I can look at the problem objectively and vicariously through great people. What would 'Rent a Hero' do? I have been able to look outside my 'small' world for solutions and inspiration from those that have travelled the path of life and been successful before me.

Upon reflection, I have simply followed in my father's path – he has been my hero and inspires me daily. From what he has taught me, the five key principles of our business are really his values that I have embraced and now pass onto our team. I hope that you too can take these principles and develop your life to the fullest.

Bear in mind that my parents have achieved far more than they ever thought possible. Ironically, without an education neither can even read this page. Imagine what you can achieve?

AUTHOR
TBLBC

Tom Poland

The One Idea that took me from Cleaning Toilets to Earning Multiple Six and Seven Figures in my Own Business

Current Position:	Managing Director of 8020 Centre
Experience:	31 years experience in building businesses
Email:	Tom@8020Center.com
LinkedIn:	http://au.linkedin.com/pub/tom-poland/7/479/931
Twitter:	www.Twitter.com/TomPoland/
Facebook:	www.facebook.com/tompoland8020
Website:	www.8020Center.com

Tom Poland is a serial entrepreneur who has started and sold multiple businesses and has worked with 1,796 business owners (at last count) across 193 different industries and four countries and continents. His specialty is marketing strategy – positioning products so that business owners can get more clients, make more money and have more fun.

Chapter 52: The One Idea that took me from Cleaning Toilets to Earning Multiple Six and Seven Figures in my Own Business

This is my story of how I survived the GFC (Global Financial Crisis).

I thrived before and during the GFC predominately because of the PFC (Personal Financial Crisis) that I created 29 years ago and the one idea that helped me to not only escape from near bankruptcy but to thrive in my own business ever since.

This idea is as simple as it is powerful. If you persist in implementing it then you will be empowered to create a business that not only gives you great fulfilment, but also affords you and your family both the free time and the money to create the life of your dreams.

History has shown us time and again that moments of great triumph and fulfilment are often birthed in moments of great defeat and despair.

Such is my experience.

At age 26 at around two in the morning on a dark, cold and wet winter's night, I found myself walking into a men's public toilet block. Even though this incident was 29 years ago, I can still remember the brightly lit blue linoleum floor and the shiny, new white tiled walls.

The reason I remember that scene so vividly is that as I walked into the toilet block my senses were assaulted by the sight and smell of excrement smeared all over the walls.

Normally I simply would have turned around and walked out again. But I couldn't do that because it was my job to clean that toilet block.

And so, as I took my spray bottle of multi-clean to spray the walls and I began to wipe the tiles clean with my blue Kleenex cloths, gagging somewhat as I did so, I made a vow to myself...

I promised myself that I would learn whatever I had to learn, spend whatever I had to spend and do whatever I had to do to ensure that I would never, ever have to do that again.

Briefly, here's how I got to that point.

Two years earlier, at age 24, I was an over-confident young man who had quit a well-paid job that came with a company car, generous pension scheme, yearly paid holidays, sick leave, monthly bonuses and frankly very little stress.

I'd had an entrepreneurial seizure and decided I wanted to make more money, have more free time and be master of my own destiny.

So I started my own business and naturally I wanted to do it well so I borrowed money to launch it properly. Shortly thereafter we also bought our first home complete with three mortgages; I even borrowed the legal fees.

This was all just prior to my first wife becoming pregnant.

My wife's pregnancy added to the intensity of financial pain that was to follow; eight months later her salary stopped and after one further month, our beautiful first daughter was born, bringing into my world both joy and considerably more expense.

In short, I had eliminated two generous sources of relatively stress-free income replacing them with multiple large outgoings and thus had created a financial nightmare for myself.

It was at this point that I started moonlighting for a security firm and for the cleaning job that had me in that rather sticky situation mentioned above.

So now for the important stuff...how I got out of the financial doo-doo, so to speak.

Long story short: I invested in virtually every personal and business development book, seminar, course, workshop and audio-cassette tape set that looked even half-decent.

I don't recall the name of the speaker but at one seminar I was taught that if I really wanted to experience my ideal life, complete with more than enough free time and money, then I'd better first figure out what my ideal business looked like. This one idea was to become my first step on the road to recovery and eventual business success.

As the speaker displayed a bullet point list of what he called his 'Ideal Business Criteria' I learned about the power of beginning with the end in mind.

When the speaker had finished and while everyone was filing past me to go to lunch, I remained in my seat and began to write down the first draft of my own 'Ideal Business Criteria'. I've been refining it ever since, but here's what it now looks like:

<u>General Criteria</u>

1. Enjoyable, satisfying work
2. A lot of free time

<u>Criteria for Security of Earnings</u>

3. Multiple streams of income
4. Earning from multiple market niches
5. Free from government control
6. Low start up costs
7. Low overheads and high product margins

<u>Criteria for Scalability of Earnings</u>

8. Renewals: make one sale and generate monthly earnings for years
9. Cross sell one product to another
10. Deliver value beyond time limitations
11. Motivated distribution network
12. Multiple value delivery semi/automated
13. Multiple lead sources semi/automated
14. Multiple conversion systems semi/automated

<u>Criteria for what I don't want</u>

15. No large team to manage
16. No dependency on large bank loans

<u>Criteria added since the advent of broadband</u>

17. Work from anywhere in the world
18. Deliver value to anywhere in the world
19. Earnings from multiple countries

Here is a before and after snapshot of earnings and the following is indicative of the power of shifting from a mind set of doing whatever was in front of me to building a business based on my pre-set criteria:

	BEFORE	AFTER
New Clients	5/mth	34/mth
New Sales ($)	13,509/mth	53,557/mth
Ongoing Cash Flow	0/mth	19,555/mth
Weeks Holiday	4	12

The lesson that I learned and wish to share with you is for people intent on transforming their life or business from what it is now to what they want it to be. I believe that there are really only three steps to take:

<u>Step One:</u> Get very clear about your own 'Ideal Business Criteria'. When implemented, this will create the life you truly want (feel free to 'swipe and deploy' from my list and adapt it if that is helpful to you).

<u>Step Two:</u> Find someone who has already built such a business and pay them to walk you through the process, step by step. The money part is important because it motivates both parties to persist. Without financial commitment or incentive, one or the other of the parties is likely to give up.

<u>Step Three:</u> Persist in implementing, testing and refining for as long as you own the business. The hard yards are in the first two or three years. After that you have your base built and whilst you will still need to work hard, it gets easier and you don't have to 'work long'.

AUTHOR
TBLBC

Michelle Demers
Interns to the Rescue!

Current Position:	½ of the Dynamic Duo of Super Interns
Qualifications:	MBA
Experience:	13 years of business development and marketing experience; three years specifically in internship programme development
Email:	michelle@superinterns.com
LinkedIn:	www.linkedin.com/pub/michelle-demers/23/121/916
Twitter:	www.twitter.com/#!/SuperInterns
Facebook:	www.facebook.com/pages/Super-Interns/107335392670550
Website:	www.SuperInterns.com www.GrowYourBusinessWithInterns.com
Contact Number:	+1 203-623-1564

Michelle Demers is a business development and marketing consultant, internet entrepreneur, as well as half of the Dynamic Duo of www.SuperInterns.com, a company dedicated to building super internship programmes that create win-win relationships between employers and interns.

Chapter 53: Interns to the Rescue!

Right before the world financial crisis hit, I was going through a personal crisis of my own. I had recently ramped up my part-time, fledgling consulting business to full-time. I was still in start-up phase, investing and growing and I had not yet created an income stream capable of supporting myself and the business.

As a one person business, you are all you have; in a time of so much personal turmoil as well as the shockwaves ravaging the business and financial world, it was hard to get out of bed, let alone to run a business and serve clients in the face of uncertainty. Would I get enough clients? Would they fulfil our contracts or bail? Could I deliver?

Literally some days my choices were to pay the electric bill or to get toner for my printer. I needed both but could only afford one. Those are the hard choices that force ingenuity – the things that in the moment provide the obstacle but down the road create the opportunity. When you learn how to adapt quickly to change and how to do more with less, you can handle almost anything. More importantly, you learn how to see the next hurdle coming from a distance and how to prevent it in the first place.

I could have folded and gone for a job with a steady pay cheque that paid the bills. But I would have traded my dream for a theoretical safety net. After all, we all know that no job is really safe, so if I lost that, what would I have?

At least with my business, I had something that was mine – an asset – that had the potential to grow, to create wealth for me and others and to do good things in the world. While I couldn't control the economy, I could control where I put my energy, creativity and focus.

The launch of Super Interns has created a whole new purpose and direction for my career and my life as well as opened doors of great opportunity. The potential is limitless and we plan to break the seven figure mark in 2011-2012.

Never could I imagine creating a business that could positively impact the lives of so many. This business has demonstrated that out of the ashes rises greatness; it never would have been conceived or birthed without the downturn in the economic climate.

So I thank the recession for teaching me these eight most valuable lessons:

1. **Partner up.** It's really hard to go it alone. I knew I needed someone else to collaborate with, to help bring in new business and to lend mutual, personal and professional support. Partnering can be tricky as there are many factors that contribute to fit and success. When partnering, don't jump in too soon and choose wisely as it is a marriage of sorts. Unshakable trust and shared values are extremely important. Luckily, I found the best partner in the world.

2. **Join forces with the competition.** My partner, Julie Braun and the other half of the Dynamic Duo, was another marketing consultant (www.JulieBraunDesign.com) who offered similar services and could have taken business away from me. But when we met and compared our strengths and weaknesses we realised that, by joining together, we could be stronger across the board and create a 1+1 = 10 equation.

3. **Don't buy into the fear.** You shouldn't hide your head in the sand because you do need to be informed and realistic. But you don't have to buy into the hype and hysteria that is created by the masses. Everyone from the news media to Uncle Charlie who has just been laid off will tell you it's hopeless out there. Why even try if the world is about to go up in flames? You may as well light the campfire, ready to toast your marshmallows in the coals. Instead, you have to believe in yourself, your business, and your success.

4. **Solve the NEW problems.** Businesses make money by solving problems. In a recession, the problems have changed or increased in magnitude. Therefore new, different and more robust solutions are needed. In any economy, the people, businesses and industries that are solving problems will make money, grow and create new opportunities. So we thought, "What problems could we

solve?" As companies were laying off employees, small businesses stopped hiring and non-profits were closing their doors, we realised that there was a growing need for talented but affordable labour. And, if done right, that this could actually jump-start the economy and create more jobs down the road for everyone.

5. **Monetise your intellectual property.** Intellectual property consists of ideas, insights, experience, expertise, designs, systems and methodologies. While our primary business was marketing, we realised that one of our internal systems that we had created to advance our own business could help others and be our new 'big idea'. We had learned how to utilise interns to produce high level work while providing skills and experience that increased the interns' earning and hiring potential -- a true win-win situation.

6. **Productise your services.** There were only two of us; we knew there were only so many hours in the day and so many clients we could service. In addition, most of our clients were also solo and small businesses just like us, which did not have the resources to hire us to create their internship programs for them. So we took our 'system' and turned it into an affordable product – *The Super Interns System™* – a step-by-step self-study course, complete with CDs and text materials that provided all of the knowledge and tools necessary for any business or organisation to build their own internship program. We turned our service into a tangible product at a lower price point that businesses and organisations of any size could now invest in. With the world as our marketplace, there was no limit to the number of programmes we could sell.

7. **Build it on a shoestring.** We didn't have much money to put into this 'big idea', especially if it didn't fly. Luckily, the evolution of the Internet and technology had made it affordable and easy for us non-techies to use. There are now so many do-it-yourself software programmes and outsourcing options, such as print-on-demand fulfilment, that makes it very inexpensive to produce information products. We were able to create and publish a product,

to build a website and to utilise internet marketing strategies to drive traffic and sales, mostly with the skills, knowledge and resources we already had. And with such a small investment, if the idea tanked, then we didn't have much to lose.

8. **Leverage the talents of others (and give back).** We walked our talk and used the very same 'system' that we created. Essentially, we have utilised interns to build a new brand, product and company out of nothing. Many of those interns are now in satisfying careers thanks, in part, to the opportunities they received with us. While we still are just a two-woman business working solely with interns on staff, we plan on hiring for full-time positions soon. This business and these jobs never would have been created without the help of interns in the first place.

Recessions test your faith and your resourcefulness. While challenging and downright painful in the moment, ultimately, recessions serve a greater purpose. They push us to the edge of who we are and what we know; they force us, personally and professionally, to dig deeper, reach higher and to expand into the cracks and hollows of our untapped potential. They also remind us to be humble and grateful for what we have in times of abundance, even simple pleasures like just having the lights on.

And the day came when the risk to remain tight in a bud was more painful than the risk it took to blossom. Anais Nin

Suzette Flemming

The Three Big Lessons we Learned from the Recession

Current Position:	President + Senior Accountant
Qualifications:	B.S. Ed. – Accounting, Speech Communication
Experience:	16 years working with Small Businesses
Email:	suzette@flemmingbusinessservices.com
LinkedIn:	www.linkedin.com/in/suzetteflemming
Website:	www.flemmingbusinessservices.com
Contact Number:	+1 406-788-5227

Suzette Flemming has been assisting service corporations, e-commerce, construction, start-ups and non-profits in untangling their finances and providing clear financial direction since 1994.

Suzette's passion is helping businesses thrive and prosper and educating business owners about how to best manage their finances. She keeps all of her clients informed about the latest tax laws, financial strategies and new technology to ensure her clients benefit from the latest developments.

Contact FBS today for a free, one-hour consultation. They will review your company's financial goals and unique accounting needs and provide a detailed proposal of solutions tailored specifically for you.

Chapter 54: The Three Big Lessons we Learned from the Recession

We are a two person, family-owned, micro business in North Central Montana. We started the business in 1994 while living in Seattle to help small businesses that couldn't afford an in-house accounting department but wanted one-on-one attention, guidance and service. Thirty percent of our clients were local at the time. We built a virtual business so that if the opportunity to move back to Montana ever presented itself, the business would be fairly easy to move and would still be successful. By divine guidance and destiny we sold our home in Washington in February of 2007 and moved right before the real estate market crashed.

Our clients experienced very little disruption from the move. We were delighted that all of our clients stayed with us. Then the recession really took hold and lessons were learned.

Relationships can't always be number one

We pride ourselves on the relationships we build with our clients. We are trusted advisors and, in many cases, almost become part of the family. We learned that being this close to our clients can have an adverse affect on our bottom line.

We bill our clients a flat fee based upon the services requested. Our normal style of operating is to bill clients on the 25th of the month for the next month's services. Payments are required by the first of the month. Until the recession started to cause issues, we would stop work until the invoice was paid. However, our clients started to suffer so we gave them a grace period and continued to perform services. For some, a short grace period of a week grew into a month or longer.

As we extended services to our clients without payment, our cash flow was reduced, as was our ability to pay our vendors and meet our obligations. We continued to work for these clients because we could feel their pain; they promised to pay and deadlines had to be met.

That was until we realised that we were really giving away our services, that paying clients should be getting more of our time and that, realistically, three clients were not going to survive the recession. Those three went on to declare bankruptcy and we had to discharge the debt. We wrote off five percent of our 2008 billing and three percent of our 2009 billing to bad debt. For a micro business like us, this was huge.

While relationships remain a very big deal to us, we no longer let it completely cloud our judgement. We allow payment plans and credit card payments but we do not let our clients get so far behind in paying us. Our vendors and our bottom line are thankful for that.

Find the best avenues for marketing and brand placement

Accounting and tax preparation is a somewhat recession-proof business. Businesses still need to have their books kept and tax returns prepared and filed. The supply of providers and the demand for services shifted but the need is still there. We have used forums, article placement and referrals as our front line marketing and branding activities for many years. As the recession grew, we found that we started to question our methods.

We decided to try radio spot ads, a large marketing firm specialising in finding clients for accountants, advertising in the yellow pages and local networking events. We doubled our 2006 marketing budget for each of the next three years so we could try these marketing avenues. We spent $5,500 to find out what we already knew; these avenues do not work for us. The $800 yellow page advertisement was the only one of the four new avenues that has yielded a positive ROI. It paid for itself by the end of the year we ran it.

Since we provide virtual services, having our brand visible in forums and on blogs is the best marketing avenue for us. We have expanded into other avenues of social media in the past year. If we had used Facebook, LinkedIn and other social media sooner, we would have more brand recognition today.

Use resources efficiently

When our cash flow started to decline due to late payments, we decided it was time to look at how our cash was being used. We discovered it wasn't being used efficiently. We were spending money that we really didn't need to spend to keep our business running smoothly or to provide top notch services to our clients.

We started to reduce our spending. First, we eliminated our landline. We both have cell phones so a landline was redundant. We stopped printing non-essential reference materials and started using split screens for data entry. This drastically reduced paper and ink consumption as well as the overall cost of office supplies.

We also started using Logmein for several clients as well as our own computers. The free version allows us access to a variety of computers, reduces the cost of software and streamlines some of our activities.

We cancelled several monthly publications. The information we were getting from these publications is available online from several sources without cost. We also cancelled our weekly online backup. We purchased two external hard drives and backup weekly. During 2007, 2008 and 2009, we reduced our dues and subscriptions by 92 percent, office supplies by 42 percent and our telephone expense by 57 percent.

Unfortunately, there is one expenditure that has caused us much grief. In late 2006, we entered into a five year lease of a postage machine. The machine saved a great deal of time and energy initially. However, six months later we moved and no longer had need of the machine. We were unable to sublet the lease and have been paying for a machine we have no use for. We will never enter into a long term lease again.

We remember and apply our lessons every day

We had three big lessons to learn. Relationships are very important to every business but can also be detrimental. Continual marketing and brand placement are important but are effective only if used correctly for our business. Cash is a valuable resource and should be spent carefully. The tangible result of these lessons is an increased net profit of 70 percent flowing through to the employees and shareholders by the end of 2010.

Bill Hartman

A Communication Style that Improves Business: Even in a Recession

Current Position:	Founder and President of Hartman Business Services®
Experience:	40 years in Business
Email:	hartman.businesses@cox.net
LinkedIn:	www.linkedin.com/in/billhartmanawarenesscoach
Twitter:	www.twitter.com/b2bawareness
Website:	www.b2bawareness.com
Other Works:	www.successfulbusinessawareness.com
Contact Number:	+1 877 851 9131

Bill Hartman is an experienced business professional specialising in improving profits, employee morale and productivity; he also assists with the career development of business executives and managers at all levels. Bill has more than forty years of progressive experience in managerial accounting, human resources management and business improvement coaching.

He is founder and president at Hartman Business Services® offering a significant benefit to businesses online. They provide a total business improvement process called *Successful Business Awareness*©, available as an executive tutorial, downloaded in PDF format, and including full coaching support. This concept is saving many companies from hundreds of thousands, to millions of dollars annually. This is being accomplished through the implementation of an enlightening new technique of interacting with staff and employees, called 'panorizontal communication', in the workplace. This process is helping many companies improve their profits, raise employee morale and increase productivity...it also helps advance business careers...all at the same time! It can be applied in any business, any industry and in any country.

Chapter 55: A Communication Style that Improves Business: Even in a Recession

I have been coaching 'Successful Business Awareness'© for over a quarter of a century now. But what happened to this concept, me and the client whose story I will tell between 2007 and 2010 in my home state, during one of the worst downturns in world history, is nothing less than amazing.

This particular story is about a company that actually improved dramatically, in almost every way, during a three year period, in one of the hardest hit areas in America (Phoenix, Arizona) right in the middle of its building boom bust! In late 2007 this company, a case goods furniture plant, had just over 400 employees with several, worrisome, internal problems to cope with. For the previous five years they had averaged about 3-5% profit before taxes.

I was invited to come in and do whatever I could to help them to improve. At this point I want to make something very clear. This story is not about me, my process of 'Successful Business Awareness' or the executives of this furniture factory. It is about the rank-and-file employees and the unique and innovative ideas they came up with during those three years...simply to keep their jobs. 'Panorizontal communication' is the catalyst that brought these people together and made 'awareness' work.

This story begins in early December of 2007. I was hired at a time when corporate officials were planning layoffs right after the first of the year. The economy was already in a tailspin, with growing signs of it becoming even worse. The client who hired me was chairman of the board and CEO of this multi-plant case goods operation. From here forward let's call him Norm. He was headquartered at this plant - their largest of four.

Following a few meetings with Norm, several of his staff and many managers, supervisors and factory workers, I came up with a written proposal. My most significant suggestion was that they postpone laying anyone off for at least six weeks thus allowing awareness and its panorizontal communication a chance to work.

WHAT IS SUCCESSFUL BUSINESS AWARENESS?

The basic concept of 'successful business awareness' is to put into place a system of communication that is so 'panorizontal' in nature that it allows executives, middle management and rank-and-file to all know exactly what is happening in their workplace simultaneously. An excellent way to do this is to meet on a regular basis, with each department represented, to discuss what is happening each day in their departments. The meeting process should lean towards voluntary contributions with a focus on doing things better, more efficiently and at lower costs.

The basic premise of these meetings is for project leaders to ask the participants,

"How can we help you to do your jobs to the best of your ability?"

Responses can range from the predictable to the startling, from employees not having the right tools to work with, to reasons why they are not able to do what we expect of them. The leader of these meetings should be a neutral party with no authority over any attendant, nor a subordinate of a common superior. This purpose is to eliminate any possible intimidation and free up communication; no names are to be mentioned at the meeting or in the minutes to allow people to open up more.

If anyone is struggling to do their job properly it is important to know what they need to do it better. Why are they not able to do them right? What if you hear some of the following responses to that question:

I have not been trained properly.
I am not capable of doing this job.
I do not have the right and necessary tools to do this job.
Enough time is not being allotted to do my job.
I am not paid a fair amount.
I am not being treated fairly.
I am being discriminated against.
I am being harassed.
There is favouritism in this department.

Each one of these responses, if true, is a legitimate reason for your people to have some difficulty to do the best they can. You may not like what you hear but that is how the concept goes to work for you. It is essential to record and post 'minutes' from each meeting in a conspicuous place in each department; the purpose of these is so all employees have an opportunity to know what was discussed. Your primary focus should be to arrive at the root cause of problems and fix them. The focus should never be to offend anyone, get anyone in trouble, make anyone feel uncomfortable or to create negative feelings. The frequency of these meetings will depend upon department size as well prominent issues and needs of colleagues.

As this process progresses and improvements become obvious, people become more comfortable with the concept and open up more making this an improved communication tool. Everyone's aware of what is going on in the business and what problems are being encountered.

The results should be more positivity across the workforce board and happier employees displaying more noticeable smiles.

WHAT IS PANORIZONTAL COMMUNICATION?

If horizontal communication is considered to be 'among peers in other divisions', then 'panorizontal communication' is my metaphor for communicating across a level plane; 'Pan' as a prefix means all, every, universal. But now, everyone is actually on a level and even keel in which to communicate.

Everyone is asking, listening and understanding each other. I believe any form of vertical communication is poor at best. Too much is lost between the top and bottom of the ladder. Everyone has seen or participated in the game Chinese Whispers where a message is passed around a group in a whisper; the end result is normally a much misinterpreted and unrecognisable version of the original.

My form of panorizontal communication goes a long way to help eliminate this. I was confident my plan would prove to be beneficial for Norm and his company.

It is at this point in the story I describe the epiphany I experienced and how it has changed my approach to coaching 'Awareness', and how this company made an 'about face'. In early January we began our 'awareness' meetings, by department, with myself (at Norm's insistence) as the project leader. They got off to a slow start (based on my previous experience) and I noticed the people were not as open as they should have been or normally were. After deep urging on my part, the epiphany finally manifested itself.

During one of the meetings (when a supervisor was not in attendance) one of the girls asked why their boss had to be included when he was the one responsible for most of the problems. Bingo! When they finally opened up and began to describe the intimidation, harassment, favouritism et al that was going on, they asked me, "How are we expected to do our jobs right under these conditions?" As a result of this disclosure, and its importance, a new edict was added to my 'awareness' regiment ...

No departmental supervision should ever be present at these meetings, unless invited by the department representatives or the project leader with the permission of the representatives.

The reason for this should be obvious. If there is any form of previously unknown bullying, harassment of any kind, anti-company policy direction or favouritism taking place in a particular department, under the control of a supervisor or manager in that department, how will executives ever know if their only source of communication is coming from that department's supervisor or manager?

What happened next is the crux of the story. During the next three years many positive things happened to this company. These 'awareness' meetings created suggestions and made discoveries that surpassed all of my previous successes. People in the main work force were the primary focus to getting to the root cause of problems, and coming up with corrective actions to fix them.
See chart below:

	2007	2008	2009	2010
% Net Profit Before Taxes	3.4%	7.2%	8.7%	11.2%
% Indirect Labour to Net Sales	33.5%	29.8%	28.6%	26.9%
% Waste Factor	55.3%	51.2%	49.8%	47.6%

Following my experience with this firm, I began to exclude supervision in all subsequent 'awareness' meetings and with greater success. The approach I now take with supervision is...if you are doing the right things, you should not have to worry about what is happening behind your back. If your people are complaining, then you are doing something wrong and you have to fix it.

The primary objective of 'awareness' is to establish an ongoing and panorizontal, two-way dialogue to discuss what is actually happening in every corner and every 'nook and cranny' of your place of business.

In closing, good things happen to companies that treat their people fairly and honestly. Over those three years I learned more than I thought I knew as did Norm, his management and their rank and file. Profits improved, employee morale soared, productivity and efficiency increased and these people actually received pay raises each year - while enterprises around them were declining and failing.

There were never any layoffs, the bad managers and supervisors were replaced and the camaraderie continues on. Norm actually helped me write 'Successful Business Awareness'© in 2008. He has told me many times since, "Business leaders must open their office doors more often and go out and see what their people are doing, talk with them, listen and respond to their needs in a more positive way."

The lesson to be learned...

Senior executives and managers DO NOT KNOW all they should know and need to know about what is actually going on in their workplace ...especially during a recession.

Anna Allen

A Networking Approach to New Business

Current Position:	PR and Marketing Consultant
Qualifications:	Degree in Languages from UCL CIM Advanced Certificate in Marketing
Experience:	14 years in PR, Marketing and Events
Email:	anna@laanassociates.co.uk
LinkedIn:	www.linkedin.com/in/annalaanassociates
Website:	www.laanassociates.co.uk
Contact Number:	+44 (0)1908 502626

Anna Allen has spent over 14 years working alongside clients to understand their key objectives and then develop and deliver sustainable and impactful PR and Marketing campaigns across a number of industry sectors.

Working primarily in Manufacturing, Engineering and IT, Laan Associates was founded in 2003 and aims to provide a refreshing approach to PR and Marketing campaigns, using a variety of communication channels. Website creation/reviews, corporate collateral, internal communications, design, print and fulfilment, eMarketing, online PR and social media all provide avenues for relevant, targeted and insightful brand awareness and promotional activities.

From start-up businesses to larger SMEs, Laan Associates provides a dedicated and professional service, offered on either an ad hoc or longer term project basis to suit each client's needs.

Our business is understanding and promoting *your* business.

Chapter 56: A Networking Approach to New Business

For nearly eight years, I have been running my own PR & Marketing consultancy with clients primarily in the Manufacturing, Engineering & IT sectors, although a number of Consumer clients also make up my portfolio. I'm possibly not going to compete with the big agencies out there but I like to think my company offers a knowledgeable, professional and refreshing approach.
With clients in two of the sectors outlined above taking the brunt of the recession, the first negative sign came as no surprise. Budgets. As with most businesses, advertising, marketing & PR spend is usually top of the list for the chop. All too quickly, it became clear that clients were becoming more hesitant, more controlling and more sceptical, even though positive results were still being achieved.

'Batten down the hatches' was the common cry and a large proportion of planned spend was withdrawn. This equated to a downturn of approximately 20-30% in revenue.

So, what next? Offering a service, rather than a product, comes with its own set of challenges. It's not easy or even possible sometimes to quickly offer something else, at a lower price or in different market sectors. I'm all for progressive diversification, but wary of moving into unchartered territory without undertaking comprehensive research into markets, pricing and competition.

So, believing in my own offering and that good will prevail, I decided to focus my efforts on a different route to market by reviewing the way I marketed myself, as well as the approach and perception of PR which may be creating barriers to new clients.

However, changing perceptions is not always easy. Especially as PR has often been considered a little 'fluffy' or maybe only relevant for large corporate companies either with shareholders to update or embarrassing product recalls to tone down. But PR can be so much more than that and certainly over the past two years, has increasingly become all about you: your business, values, beliefs, messages, brand and personality. And the channel which is opening up the most effective way to market 'you' is social media.

Step 1 – New Direction

Talking to peers, customers, prospects and those met via online forums, it was clear that things were already fast moving away from traditional PR and marketing activities to attract new clients. Significantly they were turning more towards networking, connections and relationships, as well as being seen as a trustworthy and open industry expert.

From all the feedback and research results, it was time to approach companies differently, so they too could believe in the value of PR via online and social media and appreciate that it is not just an avenue for companies selling consumer focused products and services (although they may claim a large stake).

Step 2 – Branching Out

So, with my new direction agreed and despite being a less than confident individual, I joined two local business networking groups and soon forged some long-term, mutual partnerships. As well as building business relationships, receiving introductions and helping others to find new clients, one of the most surprising yet rewarding aspects has been collaboration, even with a direct competitor.

There will often be times when you are not able to take on a particular client or part of a project due to manpower or experience, yet having collaboration options available can be extremely beneficial. And on a personal note, networking has also offered some peace of mind knowing that there are many others in the same position.

Step 3 – Focused Approach and Strategy

Due to the nature of networking, i.e. you only have a few minutes to describe your business, what you do and in which sectors, it ensures that you are able to define yourself and the business in a simple and concise way. The more others understand what you do and who you are targeting, the more they can help with referrals, new contacts etc.

This really helped to focus my service offerings and ensure they continued to be communicated in the most efficient and relevant fashion. In contrast to strong sales and marketing strategies, networking offers different opportunities to build connections through trust and mutual respect, all of which can be further enhanced via PR activities.

Even with small budgets, a little PR is better than no PR and some effective activities that anyone can do include:

- Offer to talk at a business seminar or networking group
- Set up a free webinar to demonstrate the benefits of a product/service
- Start a blog
- Send a regular, targeted and informative eNewsletter to customers/prospects (with limited or no sales messages)
- Join online business groups and forums and offer your industry expertise

I have found that many of these small steps have helped to get me noticed and have subsequently generated opportunities.

Outcome

Adaption has been key for me. Understanding the evolving market place and customers' concerns and objectives has changed the way I market myself and my service offerings. Through a targeted and concise strategy which included regular networking, relationship building and collaboration projects, there has been an upturn of 40% growth in the past six months. No sales or marketing activity, just PR.

A contributing factor to this revival figure has been a new manufacturing client who I happened to meet under an entirely different third party project. Sometime later they contacted me directly and asked for a proposal as they liked my approach and valued my industry knowledge. A few months later, I was taken on as PR Manager and we have bravely launched a technology product suitable for several key industry sectors.

With no advertising budget and very limited marketing/PR spend, we have worked together to focus on the most cost-effective priorities including a website, online opportunities and collateral, yet only where relevant and necessary. Just one month after a small PR launch campaign, enquiries are flowing in, interest is snowballing and a well-known global company has just become their first customer. Very satisfactory all round and it proved that building trust and connections, even indirectly, would be a vital part of my ongoing business development strategy.

Lessons Learned

The past two years have been challenging. But at the same time, it's been an insightful and inspirational time and I feel I've emerged as a much stronger, more knowledgeable and confident person as a result. A definite silver lining.

In an age of transparency, my advice would always be to remain honest, giving and above all, human. Your customers and peers will respect, admire and remember you for it. And it certainly worked for me.

On a final note, as many companies venture back from the darkness I would urge that whatever you decide - regardless of budgets, industry sector, product or service offering – you should do something. Because doing nothing won't get you anywhere.

Betty Murray

Surfing the Storm: How I Rode Out the Recession Wave

Current Position:	President and CEO of Living Well Dallas, Inc
Qualifications:	17 years as a business development professional
Experience:	Six years in Medicine pursuing passion in nutrition
Email:	betty@livingwelldallas.com
LinkedIn:	www.linkedin.com/in/bettymurray
Twitter:	www.twitter.com/BettyMurray
Website:	www.livingwelldallas.com www.bettymurray.com www.metabolicblueprint.com
Links to Other Works:	www.cleansethebook.com www.truthaboutthin.com
Contact Number:	+1 972 930 0260

Betty Murray, CN, HHC, RYT is a Certified Nutritionist & Health Counsellor, founder of the Dallas-based integrative medical center, Living Well Dallas, Inc. and creator of the Metabolic Blueprint™ wellness program. Leading the charge to change health care in America, Ms. Murray created an integrative clinic specialising in cutting-edge medicine combined with nutrition, mind-body and lifestyle services to address the whole person. An accomplished author and speaker, Ms. Murray has an impressive client list from corporations to non-profit organisations. She is a member of the Institute for Functional Medicine and the National Association of Nutrition Professionals.

Chapter 57: Surfing the Storm - How I Rode Out The Recession Wave

'What separates the winners from the losers is how a person reacts to each new twist of fate.'
Donald Trump

Bad times can sink an entrepreneur or make them strong.

In early October 2008 we were three months into a growth initiative with an angel investor to develop three locations in 18 months. Our investor was heavily leveraged in real estate. When the market crashed, our angel panicked fearing total loss of their real estate portfolio.

More concerning was our recent commitment to several initiatives based on the support of our investor. When the future funding was withdrawn, I was left with a liquidity issue, a pending buy out of an angel investor and an overwhelming message of gloom and doom from everyone.

As an integrative medical centre on the bleeding-edge of health care, we have a very high fixed cost; a small reduction in income could affect the level and quality of service that often has lives at stake and will impact overall service delivery. Secondly, we are often a discretionary spend for our clientele. As a cash-pay for health care service provider, we provide cutting-edge medical and complementary services such as nutrition, counselling, energy medicine, acupuncture, massage and life coaching.

I was told by everyone that restorative medicine is one of the costs our clients could do without. As I strategized, worried and waited, an unexpected result appeared. The end of October came with a bang. We had taken a 30% leap in total revenue for the month of October alone.

From that moment forward we saw a steady increase in revenue that ended 2008 with an outstanding growth of 46% from 2007 with over 30% of that growth happening in the period of October through December. The recession has not stopped our trajectory; quite the contrary, our business was growing in spite of the economy. Over the next two years, revenues grew 23% in 2009 and over 28% in

2010.

The standard rule of thumb in a recession is you should cut costs to the bare minimum and hope to ride out the storm. We chose to look instead at the opportunity the market showed us in late 2008. We decided to grow the business and innovate to ensure the business is stronger at the end of the recession than we were at the start.

The down economy had given us a clear opportunity to sharpen our business processes and solidify our core competency. At Living Well Dallas, Inc. the result of taking this attitude has given us the strength to build our core business and develop a strong growth plan for the next five years.

Here is what I learned over the past two years:

<u>You can't get emotional</u>

Emotions often enter into everyone's business decisions. Many people start a business to make a difference, do what you love or create something that pulled your heartstrings. It's only natural and often wrapped in emotion. We often fail to realise that emotions can be the determining factor in winning or losing in business or not being as profitable as you could be. I was no exception. I wanted and still want to change the definition and the practice of health care in America. I am still committed to this.

Because emotions drive our behaviour, we cannot ignore them but we can use them as a gauge. I used emotions as a tool rather than the rationale to approach each situation. Honour the feelings but bounce them against facts. Every new idea or strategy was questioned against, "will this be good or bad for the business?" Then every emotional concern was gauged against statistical fact.

For example, we often ask our clients to gauge their readiness to change based on a one to ten scale. Using this same technique I would question my emotions against cold, hard facts such as revenues, expenses, personnel and future planning. Emotionally-driven discussions such as increasing revenues by bringing a lab in-house (seen as a great money maker in medicine) would feel like a good idea. But bouncing this idea against cold hard revenue comparisons and costs helped us see that it was a deviation from our core competency.

Never make decisions out of fear

This one seems easy but our angel investor made a fear-based decision and did not benefit from the growth the business has since enjoyed. Fear can be irrational and your business decisions must remain rational, calculated and focused.

Innovate

Innovation is a must during a recession, but not just any old innovation; solution focused innovations that are customer-centric not business revenue-centric. Many businesses focus on what will bring in more revenues and the customer is left out of the decision until how to monetise the idea comes into the picture. Solution-customer-driven innovations are led by first identifying what the customers are trying to do and how to help them achieve their goals.

Revenues are secondary to the customer

We approached innovation by reaching out through social media, survey and feedback to the customer to have them tell us what they wanted from our business; our customers rewarded us with increased traffic. Customer-driven innovation enabled us to capture revenue from a wider economic base by creating more affordable programmes that were group-focused and virtual delivery rather than expanding cost-heavy one-on-one services.

Learn to say no

You don't have to take every opportunity that comes your way. Remember your core business and do not stray because someone has a 'great opportunity' for you. We entered into a strategic partnership to develop a new programme with a non-profit which would expand our brand. We had the skills to do it but the program was not our core business or what we got into the business to do. Our emotions led us down the road to potential stardom when the project was not our core business.

Two years later, we have ceased working on it after having wasted hours in planning, meetings and deliberation only to realise this.

Treat the customer like they are everything

The idea that the doctor is always right and it is your privilege to be seen is, in my eyes, a travesty and an expectation the public should never accept. You should expect service in a service industry and medicine is no exception. At Living Well Dallas, Inc. we pride ourselves on no wait times and a personalised, in-depth service in a warm and inviting atmosphere. Our revenue growth during the downturn shows that our customers expect and appreciate the effort.

Research long-term investments carefully

Use the trends in the market to your advantage. In 2010, at the height of the economic real estate collapse in Texas, we were outgrowing the space we moved into in 2007. With a massive inventory of commercial real estate available, we were in the driver's seat to make rewarding real estate decisions that we would not have been able to had the market not declined.

The result was that in autumn of 2010 we were able to relocate our offices to a prime location with double the square footage at the same monthly fixed cost. As we put the pieces in place to grow our initial location to three locations in the next 18 months, we have the potential opportunity to acquire low cost prime real estate reducing our overall risk.

Hoard your cash

The one downside to the recession for our business was and still is access to capital. Even with our outstanding growth, lines of credit and cash were hard to come by. Money literally dried up for small businesses over-night. We turned frugal. We reduced inventory levels, focusing on top moving products and started providing a personalised shipping service to our customers. These two adjustments allowed us to not tie up valuable cash on inventory.

Revaluate your marketing strategy

In my estimation, the old guard media of print, direct mail and TV are expensive and best left for the big boys with deep pockets. Guerrilla marketing and social marketing wins the business when you are on a tight budget. We stand apart with community-based outreach approach marketing mostly by word of mouth. But you cannot be just self-promoting. Your marketing must be content rich and have a genuine connection to use the power of the new social media.

Understand the power of free

We offer free, monthly one-hour events at local strategic partner companies such as Whole Foods, Central Market, yoga centres and hospitals. These educational events let us share our knowledge and give service in a soft-sell way. Since the event welcomes the public, it's the perfect opportunity for potential long-term customers to get exposed to our message, services and brand before they decide to buy with a competitor.

I know in the last two years I have had a crash course in business development, sustainability, marketing and finance that would put the best MBA programme to shame.

The lessons learned have been at some times painful. Losing the angel was actually a blessing even though at the time it felt like the end of the world. Having to innovate with no access to capital to fund growth made me look at different opportunities and operational changes that made us profitable and more responsive to our customers. In the end I hope we never have to go through another financial crisis and recession of this magnitude again. But much like everything in life, we grow and improve from our experience and response to adversity not ease. For me, I would not change the last few years. My life is richer from the experience.

Freddi Donner

Look at What you Don't See!

Current Position:	Owner of Business Stamina VP of Marketing and Communications
Experience:	20 + years for B2B service firms, entrepreneur
Email:	freddi@businessstamina.com
LinkedIn:	www.linkedin.com/pub/freddi-donner/0/618/338
Twitter:	www.twitter.com/freddidonner
Website:	www.busnessstamina.com www.forhealthandbalance.com
Contact Number:	+1 **571.266.7600**

Freddi had a very successful career (about 20 years) as a corporate marketing professional and business owner and then, starting in 2004, as an executive coach that specialises in communication coaching. Communication styles can create and *diminish* relationships and effectiveness in the workplace.

She teaches clients how to improve connections and decrease misunderstanding by the way they talk. Through her coaching, Freddi addresses beliefs, habits and language patterns that impact a person's success. Using her education in health and wellness she also helps clients discover the resources they have in themselves to develop their personal presence and energy.

Her interest in serving leaders and managers in pivotal positions is no accident. Freddi herself had this responsibility and began to experience symptoms (tiredness, irritability, headaches, back pain) that interfered with her performance. Through her own personal journey and education she got certified to coach individuals in how to become better at dealing with the multiple demands on their time. Hence the name: Business Stamina.

Chapter 58: Look at What you Don't See!

Woven through my five businesses and three jobs is a mountain of lessons about what works, what doesn't, what and who to trust/avoid and how to make the most of your time and energy. In an effort to shorten the path for others, I share My Big Three Words: Focus, Fear and Finesse.

In 2004, after leaving my last corporate job (that was destroying me) and getting a certification, I started my third business in communication coaching. I joined a business owner's roundtable to develop my business further, only to discover that I want to do something BIGGER than just be a solopreneur working for myself. So I began my investigation on businesses to buy and build...and shifted my FOCUS.

First lesson in hindsight: my focus shifted from using my current platform to get 'bigger' to opening a whole new adventure. Although I have no regrets, find out how you can get what you want from what you already have...it is faster and cheaper!

The story unfolds:
I took a close look at four businesses and came to the conclusion that the best one for me was 'For Health and Balance', a small 'mom and pop' massage therapy practice which I had been visiting for several years and knew the owners well. They wanted to sell and move to the Midwest. My estimates were that this small business could generate $50,000 in profit the first year without a lot of work.

My vision was crystal clear: I could make this a wonderful wellness destination (adding nutrition, coaching and personal training) without falling into the 'spa' category. That's focus...right?

I huddled with my accountant to review the historical information, did the due diligence and numerical possibilities. I surveyed the existing customers and created a marketing plan. I checked out the competition which was scarce in our niche (serving athletes).

I was so excited and saw all the reasons why this would work. BUT....I did not use the benefits of FEAR: I did not do 'Worst Case Scenario' like all the business books tell you to do! Looking back, all the evidence was there that this was NOT an intelligent move...starting with the exceptionally high price I paid for the business.

But, I was on a roll! I did not want to see (FOCUS) on what could go wrong.

So in April of 2006 I became the proud owner of For Health and Balance and began the most important part of my entrepreneurial education. On day one, I had cash flow which is both novel and wonderful. I quickly learned the ropes on the client record keeping and scheduling (all in paper form): client names, the therapists' preferences, schedules and the varying pay rates. The revenue goal was about $16k per month. This was doable with just eight to nine appointments per day. That can't be that hard!

Within the first week, I felt it for real: The FEAR. My gut told me that this whole idea was a big mistake! But as egos go, I did not want to drop back and fold.

Warning:
Your ego can be really stupid sometimes!
Hindsight lesson:
Use the fear and use it wisely; I could have finessed my way out before I got too far in.

But I persisted. I put the scheduling online so that appointments, room scheduling and payroll could be managed automatically - my first paper-based payroll took me six hours to complete! OK, I thought, improvement number one done!

I found the nutritionists and personal trainers and developed a programme, where a client receives coaching, nutrition, massage and training under one agreement. I then took another huge leap and added space so that we could offer all these services in one location. This of course came with the added overhead costs. All before I had sold the first customer on the programme...another no no.

Again, if I had used FEAR as a friend, I would have tested the programme before committing to it. But I was so FOCUSED on the programme that I did not see the obstacle that I had just created.

Next step:
Get the word out there more. After the logo redesign, I plunged into direct mail, mail box flyers, sponsorships in the local chamber, online advertising, search engine optimisation, brochure and signage updates and even private label bottled water! Wow, we were rocking now!

I then added laundry services, housekeeping and a receptionist. That year I won Pioneer of the Year Award from the local chamber. But this was all before the original owners actually moved on: they were the largest producer of sales. Why did I not see that in the forecast? I was so FOCUSED on what I thought was possible, that I overlooked what was probable!

At the end of 2006 I missed the revenue target by 30%. But the real loss came from the high expenses incurred in professional fees, marketing and advertising which I highly underestimated. I was spending all that was coming in and then some. My thought: OK...well it's just the first year...I can live with this, next year will be better.

I start 2007 by hiring a sales planning guy to help me set the goals, targets, etc. All by the numbers! My new revenue target was $50K per month. All optimism. All possible.

I am still paying all my bills, all my contractors, but not myself. Hmmm...I remember being here before with a previous business. Does it occur to you that making the same mistake twice is just dumb? Why won't I listen to that FEAR and let that lesson from the past be my friend?

Persevere! Let's do some health fairs, fun runs, 'girls' night out' and other events to get the word out. Then, I raise the prices and change the compensation of the contractors so that I get to KEEP more of the money that was coming in. After the first quarter I see that, on average, I am missing the mark by 50% of my goal. Lesson in hindsight: Optimism is NOT a strategy!

I keep that 'fake happiness' going so no one really knows that I am dying on the vine and swallowed up by a new FEAR - I am going to screw this up too! I have not learned how to FINESSE this business of running a business. I am working six or seven days a week and come to the incredible reality that I am also not practising what I preach! For Health and Balance.

I have no balance! I have become consumed with this business and it has consumed me. I have compromised my values so that I can keep my ego intact! That is called FINESSE but my reality is suffocating me.

By Autumn 2007 news of the slowing economy is creeping into the headlines. Hmm, here I am offering what most people consider a luxury, not an essential and the economy is working against me. I toss and turn restlessly every night and ponder new ways to make this work. I investigate buying another practice and expanding, I research franchising and licensing the brand/package. This all takes more money, of which I have run out of (along with my retirement fund).

I finally hire a business coach to help me. The beauty of a coach is that their ego, reputation, and emotions are not all wrapped up in your business. They have FOCUS, they have experienced their own FEAR and can help you FINESSE your way to success. He basically shoved my face into my accounting records; he made me look at my realisation rates, the profit margins and the cost of doing business. I was shocked to figure out that I my realisation rate on each appointment was $3.50!

THEN...January 2008, I went on a cruise. Nothing like a break to help you FOCUS, step away from the FEARS and FINESSE a new plan. The headlines in the news are now consistent with 'bad' news and as I return to 'work' I feel sick and angry. My subconscious takes over and I hear myself say to my coach:

I am getting out of this mess. I am selling and going back home to recover from my 'education'.

With the help of the good Lord, my first call to my competitor results in a journey to selling the assets to him. We FINESSED the 'buy-out' to look like a merger so that clients felt solid and my ego was not demolished.

It was humiliating. I thought I had actually added to the value of the company but the final negotiated price simply helped me pay off the line of credit/debt. I still had the original note to pay.

Lessons learned:

- Use FEAR to your advantage...don't let it stop you, but don't ignore it.
- Stay FOCUSED on what you know you are good at; you only get better with FOCUS!
- And use your experience (good and bad) to FINESSE how you do business now. I am back to being a solo-preneur, keeping my overheads low and my dreams high.

I now use all my experience to help others get what they want, get organised, track numbers, take effective action and get to their goal faster with more energy and support.

Rob Parker

Lessons I should have Learned Before but Took a Recession to Hammer Home

Current Position:	Consultant
Experience:	30+ years sales and marketing experience
Email:	rob@momentumconsultinguk.com
LinkedIn:	http://uk.linkedin.com/in/robjparker
Twitter:	www.twitter.com/RobMomentum
Website:	www.momentumconsultinguk.com/
Link To Other Works:	www.momentumconsultinguk.com/content2/sales-bytes-54.htm
Contact Number:	+44 (0) 845 224 2294

Rob is a hands-on sales and marketing professional with a sales pedigree stretching back nearly 35 years.

Having left school at 18 and worked for the old British Rail for six years he felt it was time to get a 'proper job' – and was lucky enough to get one with Procter & Gamble. Never one to do it by the book, Rob developed much of his early success through a combination of listening to what others said, and working out what worked best for him. At the time he felt that he was taking a maverick approach, but these techniques are now well documented as sales best practice.

Since these early years Rob's career has flourished and he has held the Sales and Marketing Director position with some major Corporates. Rob now applies his expertise to help small and medium sized businesses grow, and finds that he is being increasingly approached to help businesses successfully negotiate the process of formally tendering for contracts.

Chapter 59: Lessons I should have Learned Before but Took a Recession to Hammer Home

The corporate world and I parted company in August 2007. Perfect timing! The recession had not quite appeared over the horizon and I was just far enough ahead of the rest of the pack leaving corporate life to be able to get myself established as a consultant before the rush.

That meant that, as the recession broke, I was able to find my way ahead, making a few mistakes along the way and yes, I made some mistakes but was able to learn from them. The recession served to bring into sharp focus a lot of the lessons I had learned in the past and which would prove to be critical as I moved forward.

Mistake Number One – Selling the Wrong Service

Having been in sales and marketing for a little over thirty years I thought I would turn my hand to sales and marketing consultancy. Of course, that led me into the trap of thinking that as a sales and marketing professional I could do many things related to sales and marketing, therefore I should market myself as a consultant who could provide a range of services. This was a big mistake and I should have known better!

I knew in my heart of hearts that I should concentrate on a focused service and sell this to a defined market. In fact not only did I know this but I also had a friend and former colleague telling me the same – and also telling me what that focused service should be! I tried many things, created a lot of general interest, undertook some interesting assignments, but didn't really generate a consistent stream of business. So, having gone down a few blind alleys, I now sell a defined service: I support people who need to submit formal tenders. Lesson number one learned. It doesn't mean that I only provide this service, but I certainly have a well-defined message that hits the spot.

Mistake Number Two – Addressing the Wrong Need

A really important point, emphasised by the recession, is that if people are going to invest money in growing their business (or retaining market share) they need to see something tangible in return.

One of the messages that I was promoting through my regular marketing activity went as follows...

Do you sometimes feel frustrated that your prospect just won't make the decision to buy? This could be particularly when you are trying to sell something that is obviously good for them. If so, are you trying to close the sale by emphasising the:

*Opportunity to be gained by buying?
*Or fear of the consequences of not buying?

Well, research shows that the strongest motivator for people to make the decision to buy is not opportunity or fear but pain! This often applies even if pain is only a secondary issue!

In order to close the deal, even if the primary element in the sale is opportunity or fear, look for the way in which your proposition will remove pain.

Given this, the most tangible kind of benefit is one that eliminates pain. Providing general sales and marketing support does not necessarily address pain (in fact it might even create pain, particularly if it requires the client to engage in sales activities that take them out of their comfort zone).

This was another big mistake, particularly in a recessionary climate when people are reluctant to part with cash, unless there is a pressing need. However, supporting people who need to submit formal tenders does address pain! Trying to submit an Invitation To Tender or a Pre-Qualification Questionnaire when you don't have the time, expertise or resource can be extremely painful. Lesson number two learned.

Mistake Number Three – Using the Wrong Route to Market
As a local businessman, as I now saw myself, I was keen to develop my business locally. What better way to do this than to join local business networking groups? This was great, I enjoyed it and I got to meet lots of people - and this was mistake number three. It took up a huge amount of time and didn't really provide a meaningful return for me.

I was beginning to realise that when people needed my service they were looking for it urgently. They weren't looking for it through networking but rather through Google. I have now cut back on networking and invested in my website and on search engine optimisation. Lesson number three learned. I now stay put and the business comes to me.

So these were the key messages for me:
1. Define your message and stick to it
2. Don't be vague
3. Don't be all things to all people
4. Define your market and stick to it
5. Sell to those with a tangible need
6. Define your route to market and stick to it
7. Don't be seduced into sales and marketing activities which are costly in terms of time and money and don't produce a worthwhile return.

One final lesson I have learned from the recession, or at least the final one for this chapter, is that things constantly change. It would be dangerous to assume that lessons learned in the past will always apply in the same way in the future.

Communication is changing daily, for example, email marketing has replaced direct mailing to a large extent in recent years and there will undoubtedly be many changes in the next few years.

However, the underlying principles will always apply. Keeping up with the pace of change and applying the timeless principles will be increasingly essential.

So, in essence, I guess my message is this. It is always important to develop a focused business model that fits with your business and your market. Sometimes things can get a little blurred, and in a healthy economic climate it is possible to get away with it. Not so in a recession - you have to get it right!

Chrissie Lightfoot
Recession? Eat My Dictaphone – Says The Naked Lawyer

Current Position:	CEO & Solicitor (non-practising) EntrepreneurLawyer Limited
Qualifications:	Qualified Solicitor; Masters in Law degree; BA (Hons) First Class Leisure Studies degree; Certified Social Media Strategist;
Experience:	20 years business experience and seven years in the legal industry
Email:	Chrissie@entrepreneurlawyer.co.uk
LinkedIn:	www.linkedin.com/in/chrissielightfoot
Twitter:	www.twitter.com/thenakedlawyer www.twitter.com/entrepreneurlaw www.twitter.com/fullonliving
Website:	www.entrepreneurlawyer.co.uk
Contact Number:	+44 (0) 113 2444228

Chrissie Lightfoot is a 'prominent legal figure' and a Top Ten Legal Tweeter (*The Times*). She is an entrepreneur turned solicitor (non-practicing) turned entrepreneur. Her company helps lawyers and entrepreneurs come together in a positive way. She is a published author (*The Naked Lawyer: RIP to XXX – How to Market, Brand and Sell YOU!)*, a national award and prize winning researcher, a women's enterprise ambassador, a mentor on behalf of The Prince's Trust Million Makers Corporate Challenge and ultimately a sales educator helping professionals and entrepreneurs of today become professionals and entrepreneurs of tomorrow, today.

Chrissie has a formidable track-record in strategising and innovating and achieving quality sales lead generation, quality referrals and increasing sales value in a short period of time. In her capacity as business consultant she has helped many UK, USA and International organisations and their people grow.

Chapter 60: Recession? Eat My Dictaphone Says The Naked Lawyer

It was autumn 2008. I was a trainee solicitor in a mid-tier law firm in Leeds, UK. I remember distinctly my head of department (Partner), looking rather grey, calling me and my fellow colleagues into a private office to explain (not ad verbatim) that "the global recession is having and will continue to have an effect on the firm but we're going to do everything possible to ensure we keep as many of you as possible. We're just going to have to work really hard and get more business in."

Stating the obvious, I thought.

I was also thinking that this is going to be a real challenge ahead for any lawyer who hasn't got a clue how to market, brand and sell themselves in this economy where the real goal is to win new business (of value) and achieve more business from existing clients through building value referrals and relationships.

Fortunately, I'd already been preparing and planning for this day, regardless of whether the recession hit or not.

Why?

Choice, change and control

I believe the global recession had simply accelerated (by five years or so) the inevitable chop chop of the sword of Damocles that was about to strike the privileged legal world...

The self-reliance human economy, combined with the Legal Services Act 2007 and alternative business structures, would mean that increased competition from client-centric major players, 'DIY free legal documents providers' via the internet, virtual law firms and virtual lawyering, would all challenge the legal profession's established engagement model.

Throw into the mix, the enlightened consumer – who is more demanding and discerning with increased levels of expectation, responsible for setting new higher standards in customer service – together with the disruptive technologies of the past few years along with future anticipated technological advances, and what have we got? The traditional way of lawyering under threat, juxtaposed with an opportunity to mould a brighter future, if we dare to choose, change and take control.

Major lesson number one: I realised I had to embrace change, make the inevitable, difficult decisions and choices necessary and ultimately, take control and action... fast...

Entrepreneurial and naked

The legal world ('law law land' as I refer to it) inevitably was (and is) experiencing an unprecedented transitional period, the likes of which it has never so far experienced.

For me, it was no great shock to be told to "work hard," that's a given. Nor to be told "we'll all have to try and get more business," that's a necessity.

I admit though, this was a wee shock coming from a Partner where the culture (rightly or wrongly) within the firm (and most traditional established law firms with traditional partner structures, systems and policies for that matter) is very much, 'it's our job to get the work in, it's your job to do it'.

Furthermore, let's be frank, from what I'd witnessed and experienced within the firm and within the profession by and large - as an employee and as a buyer of legal services as an entrepreneur prior to entering the profession - the majority of lawyers are not hot on marketing, branding and selling themselves; take a look around any networking event, offline or online.

Plus, the lawyers who are expected and/or tasked to do it are not always comfortable with marketing and selling themselves, let alone skilled-up to do it.

It's because of the present and future trend, in which the buyers of legal advice, services and provision (entrepreneurs/business people) can choose who, where, what, why, when and how they wish to purchase legal products and services, that we lawyers need to arm ourselves with 'soft skills' in order to prepare and position ourselves for the evolution and arguably, revolution of an outdated profession; whether we are entering a recession, living and working through a recession or exiting a recession, or not.

To survive and thrive in the years to come, a paradigm shift is required in our mindset (thinking), behaviour, actions, focus and expectations by the law firm (partners/owners/directors), existing practising lawyers and next generation lawyers.

I reckoned we lawyers need(ed) to become more entrepreneurial and to 'get naked'.

So, what did I do?

C-C-C-Courage

I took action. I defied gravity. I challenged the 'old guard' and status-quo. I decided to take control because I wasn't going to wait for the day when the Partners would invest in training/up-skilling their lawyers with the 'soft-skills' they would desperately need in order to help 'the firm' and each and every one of us lawyers through this difficult period.

I had to draw on my own experience, strengths, knowledge and talent to date. More importantly, I had to be bold, courageous and confident in my abilities...

I also wanted to be master of my own destiny (or mutiny) as I could see where the path ahead lay for the firm, my colleagues and myself...

Before entering the legal profession I knew that to survive and thrive, simply being a technically excellent lawyer was not going to be good enough (at any stage of my legal career) to deliver extraordinary client service and be successful in the digital age.

When the global recession hit in Q3 2008, it was patently obvious to me that technical expertise alone was not going to guarantee that I would distinguish myself and those in the firm whom I served from our peers in the legal world, be able to bring in new clients, achieve sales and even perhaps secure my and/or our future.

I knew deep down that I needed to be *present and available* for our potential clients (and existing clients) where they were then and would be in the future... and that meant venturing into social media, social networking and the 'trending' platforms. We are, after all, each blessed with the greatest gift of all... choice.

In my role as a trainee solicitor back in 2008-09 I had a choice.

Positive mindset, paradigm shift

For me, stepping into the legal profession after experiencing the leisure industry, new media industry and management consulting industry in my capacity as an employee, entrepreneur (business owner) and consultant – with their new world cultures, innovative business approaches and models, and in some cases, horizontal structures – was like stepping back to the land that time forgot.

Dealing with the mindset of the lawyers (colleagues and superiors) was a whole new ball game for me. I'd never experienced such parochialism and resistance to change before.

I remember vividly a discussion with a colleague in which she said, 'I hear the same complaint about you Chrissie. You're so focused on marketing and sales. Why can't you just sit there and do as you're told like the other trainees, Mary-Ellen, John-Boy and Jim-Bob?' (pseudonyms), meaning sit there and do the legal work; which I was doing in addition to the marketing and sales 'fluffy stuff' above and beyond the call of daily duty.

We were at the start of the global recession. Go figure? You don't have to be an Einstein to work out why I saw the need to use some marketing and sales initiative.

Put up, don't shut up

I could either 'put up and shut up' – be another trainee clone in the old way and learn the old outdated 20th century ways of the forefathers – NOT – since they were already five to ten years behind the rest of the business world – or I could do something positive and innovative; cut a new way with a 21st century approach and add some value wherever possible.

I chose the latter.

The colleagues who 'got it' were grateful. Who wouldn't be in the middle of a recession if a trainee took the initiative to help bring in more work? I couldn't just sit there. Could you? If your future and your colleagues' futures were at stake and a gaping opportunity to serve new clients was apparent?

I made the right choice... in spite of resistance and 'cold shouldering' from the old guard.

The majority of fellow trainees, qualified lawyers and partners couldn't understand where I was coming from.

But clients did.

Personal brand faith

Throughout my final year as a trainee solicitor and since founding EntrepreneurLawyer Limited (a period of a little over a year during the 2008-09 recession), I managed to build a global business network in excess of 1500 key contacts (from a standing start) utilising a joined up relationship marketing approach culminating in my generating and referring £562,000 of new client legal work enquiries.

How did I achieve this?

It was a combination of things, all of which I cannot possibly cover in this limited space but is documented in *The Naked Lawyer: RIP to XXX – How to Market, Brand and Sell YOU!*

Briefly, I was entrepreneurial. I created a personal brand together with devising a refreshingly unique relationship building, relationship sales and relationship marketing approach. It was achieved using soft-skills and social media which appealed to prospective clients and referrers. It involved mixing traditional and conventional marketing and sales methods, techniques and systems with new, unconventional and innovative techniques – the ROAR model.

I was privileged with the opportunity to 'legally serve' entrepreneurs for a while alongside one or two lawyers who did 'get it'... until a greater calling beckoned whereby I could utilise my true talent for the benefit of many, rather than a few. Toward the end of my traineeship in 2009 I was offered the role of a corporate solicitor at the firm but I chose a different path.

I founded EntrepreneurLawyer Limited at the height of the recession (September 2009) in a bid to help lawyers and entrepreneurs come together in a positive way by helping 'both camps' understand real value and to relate better.

Dare to be different

The recession instilled in me further the need to be true to myself, to be authentic, entrepreneurial, innovative, pro-active and of a positive mindset, relationship-focused, client-focused and 'soft skilled up' to attract the clients/customers of the past, present and future.

I believe the lessons I learned from the recession are applicable to all business people, not just lawyers. Accordingly, whether you are an individual or an entity entering or exiting a recession, my advice is simple...

If you want a successful career and/or business you will need to defy your comfort zone and dare to be different.

You will be vulnerable - naked - but the transition into the new way could possibly be what saves you and/or provides you with the fulfilling career and life that you dream of.

It is fair to say that the legal profession, per se, is very conservative and traditional in many respects, particularly in relation to extraordinary client service - and building from the foundation blocks and concept that each and every lawyer should embrace personal marketing, positioning/creating a niche, branding and selling. But I am confident that those who 'get it', albeit they are the minority, will be the change that they (and the buyers of legal service – entrepreneurs, business people and even lay people) want to see in the legal world for the better for us all.

Today, I help lawyers and entrepreneurs of tomorrow become the lawyers and entrepreneurs of tomorrow, today. I feel truly blessed to be offered key-note speaking engagements around the globe to share my experience and thoughts, particularly on the subject of personal marketing, branding and selling - including the use of social media - using the lessons, template and ROAR model.

I truly hope that the very small part in which I am privileged to be offered a role to help make a difference for a wee while will touch and improve the lives of many... perhaps yours included?

Book Sponsor

Book Sponsor

Sponsors Message: Reading about how other businesses and industries have coped with the recession is very useful and the REC looks forward to future books in the Business Leaders Book Club series.

The Recruitment & Employment Confederation (REC) is the professional body dedicated to representing the interests of the recruitment industry.

The REC is:

- Recruitment's biggest lobbying voice
- The source of recruitment knowledge
- Raising recruitment standards
- Developing successful careers in recruitment
- Exceeding member's expectations through business support.

The REC represents over 3,600 Corporate Members, with more than 8,000 branches. In addition the REC represents over 5,500 individual members within the Institute of Recruitment Professionals (IRP).

The REC is committed to raising standards and highlighting excellence throughout the recruitment industry.

Contact REC:

www.rec.uk.com
info@rec.uk.com
020 7009 2144

Book Sponsor

Milton Keynes
& North Bucks
Chamber of Commerce

Sponsors Message: The pursuit of relevant success for business leaders is to provide a sense of purpose, steer direction and instil confidence, and to achieve this a support network of sharing advice and best practice with confidants, colleagues and experts is a must. This book is a fantastic initiative which we consider as part of that vital support.

The Milton Keynes & North Bucks Chamber of Commerce supports its members by encouraging the development of an economic environment where all businesses and their employees can prosper.

We represent business interests in the county to local and central government, MPs, and all other relevant bodies and contribute to the development of Chamber policy nationally.

The Chamber boasts a great number of successful networking opportunities which attract a diverse range of business people and are delivered across the county.

We exist to ensure that business receives the support it needs, **JOIN US TODAY.**

Contact Milton Keynes & North Bucks Chamber of Commerce:

www.mk-chamber.co.uk
information@mk-chamber.co.uk
+44 (0)1908 259000
www.twitter.com/MKChamber